History,
Culture,
and Society:
Chicano Studies
in the 1980s

Bilingual Press/Editorial Bilingüe

General Editor
Gary D. Keller

Managing Editor
Karen S. Van Hooft

Senior Editor
Mary M. Keller

Address
Bilingual Press
Department of Foreign Languages
and Bilingual Studies
EASTERN MICHIGAN UNIVERSITY
Ypsilanti, Michigan 48197
313-487-0042

History, Culture, and Society: Chicano Studies in the 1980s

National Association for Chicano Studies

Editorial Committee
Mario T. García, *Co-Chair*
Francisco Lomelí, *Co-Chair*
Mario Barrera
Edward Escobar
John García

Bilingual Press/Editorial Bilingüe
YPSILANTI, MICHIGAN

ISBN: 0-916950-36-0

Library of Congress Catalog Card Number: 83-70277

PRINTED IN THE UNITED STATES OF AMERICA

Cover design by Larry Scheffler

TABLE OF CONTENTS

To
Carey McWilliams
Ernesto Galarza
and
Américo Paredes

INTRODUCTION: CHICANO STUDIES
IN THE 1980s

Mario T. García

Beginning in 1967 in the first issues of *El Grito*, Octavio Romano called for a new approach to the study of Mexicans in the United States. Harshly criticizing Anglo scholars for treating Chicanos as a passive and ahistorical people, Romano challenged Chicanos to produce their own scholarship, one that would recognize Mexican Americans as agents in the making of history and as a people with some control over their own destiny. Romano's fiery assault on traditional scholarship and his zeal for Chicano studies ranks as a major intellectual contribution.

Since the publication of Romano's now classic essays in *El Grito*, younger Chicano scholars have heeded his call. We have witnessed not only the unprecedented growth of a generation of Chicano intellectuals, but an increased production of scholarly books and articles on Chicanos written by Chicanos. This by no means downgrades the contributions of sympathetic Anglo scholars— writing in the tradition of Paul Taylor and Carey McWilliams—such as David Weber, Abraham Hoffman, Mark Reisler, and Lawrence Cardoso. However, the most significant changes in studies pertaining to Mexicans in the United States has been that for the first time, on a relatively large scale, Chicanos themselves are writing about their own people.

There has always been, of course, an intelletual stratum of Mexicans north of the border. During the post-Mexican War period in the nineteenth century, as the United States extended its control over the Southwest, writers of Mexican descent published essays and poetry in predominantly Spanish-language newspapers from Texas to California. This tradition of intellectual-journalist was augmented during the early twentieth century when over a million Mexicans entered the United States. Numerous Spanish-language newspapers circulated on the American side of the frontier; these contained the thoughts of writers and editors such as Ricardo Flores Magón, Silvestre Terrazas, Julio Arce, and Ignacio Lozano. By the 1930s, as a generation of bilingual and more Americanized Mexican Americans came of age, a small handful of university-trained intellectuals also appeared. Here, the early contributions of George Sánchez, Arthur Campa, Carlos E. Castañeda, Ernesto Galarza, and the young Américo Paredes can be cited.

Yet this early intellectual presence was either limited due to its transmission in Spanish only, as in the case of those who wrote in barrio newspapers, or curtailed by the small number of Mexican-American university professors. These intellectual boundaries, to a large extent, are now being transcended by the new generation of Chicano intellectuals.

Writing predominantly in English, Chicano scholars are reaching larger audiences not only among second- and third-generation Mexican Americans, but among Anglo-American students and in Anglo intellectual circles. Chicanos are not only speaking to one another, but are beginning to influence the type of traditional Anglo scholarship that Romano lambasted. By no means has Chicano scholarship been fully integrated into the mainstream of academia, but it has grown to the extent that the various disciplines in the social sciences, humanities, and arts must in one way or another take Chicano studies into account. With the addition of more Chicano scholars in the 1980s and beyond, the integration of Chicano studies will be close at hand.

There are, unfortunately, some perils concerning this integration. As it proceeds, it is possible that the spirit which gave rise to Chicano studies may be in some jeopardy. This discipline arose out of the renewed struggles by a generation of Chicanos during the late 1960s and early 1970s which challenged the American system in a most militant fashion. Heavily influenced by the rebellious climate of the period, including the civil rights movement, the Black Power movement, the anti-Vietnam War crusade, the youth rebellion, the struggles of Third World people for self-determination, among others, Chicanos also reacted to the contradictions facing them in the United States. While Mexican Americans had experienced some degree of mobility, they still represented a relatively poor people subject to racial and cultural discrimination. At the same time, the prosperity of Lyndon Johnson's "Great Society" surrounded them, fueled by a war economy. Moreover, Americanization and insensitive treatment by schools and other institutions that impinged on

Chicano life had resulted in a great deal of Mexican cultural erosion, accompanied by the loss of identity and self-esteem among Chicanos.

To overcome these contradictions, young Chicano activists appealed for a new movement among Mexican Americans. They called not only for an acceleration of the historic struggle for civil rights waged by older organizations such as the League of United Latin American Citizens (LULAC), but for a cultural renaissance to deal with the issues of identity and cultural alienation. As cultural nationalists, this activist generation appealed for the birth—or re-birth—of a "new Chicano." Whereas older Mexican Americans had held to a belief that they should stress their similarities with other Americans as a way of combating prejudice and discrimination, the Chicanos of the 1960s boldly and defiantly called attention to the differences between themselves and other Americans. They were proud of these differences, whether of a racial or cultural nature. It was not for Chicanos to change and acculturate, it was for the American system to accommodate to Chicanos, and if not, to bear the possible tragic consequences.

Out of the Chicano Movement came the demands that educational institutions at all levels address themselves to the Chicano experience and recognize the validity of Chicano history, culture, language, literature, art, music, theater, and the like. At the college and university level, departments and research centers in Chicano studies were fought for and established. This was complemented by the growth in the number of Chicanos admitted to graduate schools and receiving doctorates.

Hence, Chicano studies as an institutional movement and as a field of study was rooted in political struggle. Its vitality and direction was initially geared to issues and questions emanating from political movements in the Mexican-American communities. Chicano studies, in turn, was to add to those struggles by providing new intellectual and cultural alternatives. Chicano scholarship, in fact, has displayed much of the questioning spirit that gave rise to it. What is not clear, however, is whether that scholarship has had much effect on community political struggles. Hence, as Chicano scholarship becomes more integrated in academic life, a real question exists about whether it can at the same time maintain its contact at the community level. This is the question posed by activist and teacher Bert Corona in his lead essay.

If the relationship between Chicano studies and the community remains unclear, what is certain is the maturation of Chicano studies as an intellectual discipline. This volume—the proceedings of the

National Association of Chicano Studies (NACS)—is evidence of that growth. It includes papers, revised from their original forms, delivered at the Houston (1980), Riverside (1981), and Tempe (1982) meetings. The essays cover such disciplines as history, political science, sociology, and anthropology and include a variety of subject matter. Displaying a recognition of the interrelationship between Chicanos in the United States and *mexicanos* across the border, several of these essays make that crucial link. This publication also combines the work of younger Chicano scholars and that of more established ones.

Chicano studies in the 1980s is coming of age, and this decade will witness continued growth, together with new and challenging issues and questions posed by Chicano intellectuals.

The Editorial Committee of NACS would like to thank all those associated with the publication of these proceedings. Since the date of the first NACS conference in Las Vegas, New Mexico (1973), it has not been easy to publish the proceedings of each conference due to financial and other factors. Hence, we are particularly pleased with our relationship with the Bilingual Review/Press and would like to give special thanks to Gary D. Keller and his staff for the final editing and publication of this volume. We likewise are grateful to Professor Miguel Carranza for initiating the link between NACS and the Bilingual Review/Press and for his leadership of NACS during the last two years. Finally, we would like to thank the authors who have so patiently stayed with us as we struggled to publish these proceedings and who have graciously permitted us to publish their fine work.

HISTORY AND CHICANO STUDIES
UNIV. OF CALIFORNIA, SANTA BARBARA

CHICANO SCHOLARS AND PUBLIC ISSUES IN THE UNITED STATES IN THE EIGHTIES

Bert N. Corona

In these times of extensive crises, scholars, academics, and intellectuals are very deeply affected by the convulsions and contradictions that society and humanity in general suffer. No more true is this than for the scholars and intellectuals of the Mexican communities of the United States.

The present crisis through which the Mexican people are passing in the United States is a deeply based crisis with broad international proportions and characteristics. As it unfolds, what is becoming more and more relevant to the Mexican people in the United States are the struggles of the peoples of Central America. It is ironic that those forces and representatives of the policies favoring the preservation of military regimes and the status quo and the destruction of the forces for change and for liberation of the peoples of Central America are now telling the world that the very reason for their resistance to change is to insulate Mexico and the Mexican people from the effects of the struggles of the people of Guatemala, Nicaragua, El Salvador, and Honduras—from the contagion of revolution.

Domestically our communities are living through the sharpest and deepest manifestations of the national crisis affecting all of North American society and all of the peoples in our country. Unemployment, the closings of mines, mills, smelters, refineries and factories, inflation, high interest rates, cutbacks in educational and public services, foreclosures on home purchases, evictions, high taxes, and growing militarism are felt especially hard by the common folks of our land and most especially by Mexicans and other nonwhite peoples within the United States.

Chicano educators, scholars, and intellectuals are also caught up in all of these manifestations of crisis. They are becoming increasingly subject to dismissals or threats of dismissal. Tenure or permanent rank are more and more difficult to secure. The cutbacks in education funds are bringing huge and sharp drops in the numbers of Chicano university students, staff, and programs. Racism and discrimination against Chicano scholars, students and intellectuals are still pervasive and rob Mexican scholars of the right to fulfill their just aspirations within the colleges and universities.

Chicano scholars and intellectuals are not only being victimized in the areas of obtaining appointments, the type of appintments, and the fullest opportunities to work, but we are also being victimized in not being able to retain our independence and right to our own philosophies, concepts, and ideology. Under the pressures of "conform-or-else" many of our scholars have succumbed to the demand to accept the establishment's philosophies and ideology. Many have accepted the roles prescribed for them by deans, committees, and administrators out of pragmatism and practical considerations.

The results in most of these cases have been a pulling back from real community involvement and most especially from the really burning issues and from the segments of our people who are suffering them. Our poor and working poor are still too great a proportion of our total population. Those who are in unions are being forced to resort to strikes or to accept wage freezes and cutbacks in benefits or to renew contracts without improvements. Unfortunately, many of our scholars, teachers, and intellectuals have been so engaged in their own personal struggles to obtain tenure, permanent status, and career advancement that they have become insulated and isolated from the new active forces in our communities. In fact, many of the individuals involved in their own career advancement have too often turned against not only their own departments but have sought refuge and support in college committees, deans, and administrators who have traditionally fought the establishment and growth of Chicano Studies departments. The results have been disastrous for the departments, the students, and all Chicano scholars in those universities. We also see here the turning away from identifying our own career and role with that of the fate of our people and its needs within our country.

The struggle from within is made in close relationship with the struggle from without. The abandonment of the community and its daily life-needs under the rationale and excuse that one has to make it according to the man's rules and on his turf in order to survive, or the excuse that once we have made it and are secure enough within the university we'll go back to the community.... once we have gotten ourselves and our personal lives "all straightened out" we will go back to work in the House of the Lord, reminds me of a story told to a group of us who came from grassroots communities by Dr. Martin Luther King in Atlanta just before he went to Memphis, Tennessee to help the garbage and sanitation workers establish their union.

> A preacher in a poor church had noticed that one of the bright and promising members of his congregation had absented himself for some months from the work in the little church and in the ghetto. Upon encountering him one day he asked: "Deacon Jones, we have missed you. Where have you been? We need your great talents." The young man replied: "Pastor Smith, I have decided to get myself all straightened out financially and have enrolled in real estate school. As soon as I pass my broker's exam and receive my license, I will be back all straightened out to work in the House of the Lord, but here is $5.00 towards that cause." A year passed and Deacon Jones had not returned to work in the Church, and again he encountered Preacher Smith downtown, who again asked him when he was going to return to the work of the Lord. Again Deacon Jones replied: "Preacher Smith, I am just about ready to get myself all straightened out by getting into commercial real estate where I can really make some big money, but rest assured, as soon as I get myself all straightened out, I will be back to help with the work of the Lord, but in the meantime here is $50.00 for the cause." Another year passed and Deacon Jones had not returned and soon thereafter Preacher Smith ran into him coming out of the stock exchange and again posed the question: "Deacon Jones, when are you coming back to help your people in the work of the Lord?" Deacon Jones replied: "Preacher Smith, I am now getting into real estate development and am closing six-figure deals, but as soon as I get myself all straightened out and established as a big-time developer I will be back to do the work of the Lord. In the meantime here is $500.00 for the cause." A few years thereafter Deacon Jones died, and the family had Preacher Smith officiate at the funeral. As the casket was brought up the aisle before the altar, Preacher Smith raised his eyes upward and began the funeral oration: "Dearly beloved, we are gathered here today to pay our final respects to an honest man." And he proceeded to recount the story of his encounters with Deacon Jones, concluding as follows: "Yes, he always said, 'as soon as I get myself all straightened out I will be back in the House of the Lord' and indeed here he lies... ALL STRAIGHTENED OUT."

Our scholars are told that what is safe, proper, and acceptable academically is the past—not the present nor the future. While it is inescapable to learn from the past, its study must take place from the imperatives of the present. Glorification and focus on the past for its sake alone, as is the case with research, documentation, and the accumulation of data, are in effect escapism and self-indulgence. Scholarly research, documentation, data gathering, their interpretation, and evaluation are truly meaningful only when they are intimately and inseparably tied to the present struggles of the Mexican people for defense of their working and living conditions, for their struggles to accomplish gains and breakthroughs towards higher and fuller levels of living. It is entirely possible to combine two elements: the past and the present, study and thought with action, the university and the community. It is a thorny and tortuous path, but the only one to follow.

We have some worthy examples of the past in the lives and works of persons like Paul Taylor, his wife, Dorothea Lange and his collaborator Dr. Stanley Gulick, who researched and advocated fiercely for farmworkers in the 1920s. Dr. Manuel Gamio's original research was coupled with very strong advocacy and involvement on his part, especially during the administration of president Lázaro Cárdenas, which accepted Dr. Gamio's recommendations and implemented a new policy on behalf of the rights of Mexicans living then in the United States. His research led to the implementing of practices ordered for all Mexican consulates in the United States for the creating of Juntas Patrióticas and Comisiones Honoríficas in each Mexican barrio and colonia in the United States. These peoples' committees were an official part of the consulates and had authority to represent the rights of Mexicans until the consuls themselves could bring their offices into the picture. This broad and extensive network of committees and organizations served the Mexican people well during the difficult times of the mid- and late thirties. Gamio's research and writings influenced the Cárdenas administration policies on behalf of the daily life-needs of El México de Afuera. From 1941 onward, the Mexican governments of Avila Camacho, Alemán, Ruiz Cortínez, López Mateos, Díaz-Ordaz, Echeverría, and López Portillo have maintained and deepened a policy of disdain, rejection, and even exploitation of Mexicans who come to this country. Dr. Jorge Bustamante's fine research and documentation has not prevailed against the PRI-Gobierno-Oligarquía policies of accommodating United States users of cheap labor from Mexico, be it undocumented or braceros.

In the late thirties and early forties we have the work of Luisa Moreno, a graduate of the College of the Holy Name of Oakland, California, who through her investigation of the conditions of field and farm workers in the United States contributed to the formation of the first truly modern mass union of a national scope of agricultural workers, the United Cannery, Agricultural, and Packinghouse Workers of America, C.I.O., which at its peak had over 400,000 workers, and Luisa was its international vice president. Almost single-handedly, Luisa Moreno was the founding organizer of tobacco, cotton, and other picking and packing unions throughout the United States. The principal canners of California, such as Del Monte, CAL-PAK, Rosenberg, Hunts, Campbell, Heinz, Libby, S&W and many other giants were organized into the C.I.O. under her direct leadership. In the state of California alone, some 90,000 workers were unionized into industrial unions. Her genius as a trade union strategist and tactician is recognized by friend and foe alike. Her skills as a writer and conceptual thinker are demonstrated in her editorials, articles, leaflets and speeches or presentations at the union national and state conventions. She was the first woman to become a state vice president of the California State Industrial Union Council (C.I.O.). Finally, during the year of 1937, she traveled at her own expense throughout the United States visiting every barrio, colonia, and parroquia, inviting people, priests, pastors, activists, educators, writers, trade unionists, youths, mutualists, workers, campesinos, women, Mexicans, Puerto Ricans, Spaniards, Cubanos, Centro y Sud Americanos to come to the First National Congress of the Spanish Speaking People in the United States, convened for early spring of 1938 in Albuquerque, New Mexico. The two co-hosts were Doctors Campa and Sánchez who were professors at the University of New Mexico. Immediately after the announcement that this First National Congress of grassroots people from the Spanish-speaking communities was to be held, the House Un-American Activities Committee descended upon Albuquerque, and using its congressional powers and immunities, proceeded to vilify and accuse the congress' sponsors as Communists, Radicals, and unpatriotic elements. Both good doctors were forced to give up their roles as co-hosts and sponsors by the university authorities and the congress was tranferred to Los Angeles, where it took place very succesfully and enjoyed almost twenty years of active political life.

Luisa Moreno suffered along with the migrant workers and shared their conditions of life as she traveled from field to field, from packing shed to packing shed, from cannery to cannery, sharing her meager organizer's pay with the most often unemployed field and shed workers that she loved. She was jailed in Texas and other southern states, beaten and driven out of town by vigilantes and sheriffs' deputies many times. In the early 1950s during the McCarthyist hysteria she was deported to Mexico, where she now resides.

In the founding convention of the Congreso Nacional de los Pueblos de Habla Española, Luisa Moreno was joined by another young college graduate sociologist named Josefina Fierro Bright, who was married to John Bright, a Hollywood screenwriter who became later a victim of the Hollywood witch hunt in which our present President Ronald Reagan participated. Josefina became secretary of the National Congress of the Spanish-Speaking People and together with Luisa Moreno forged a powerful alliance of trade unions, churches, community groups, and youth organizations within the congress. The Congreso rallied broad support for strikes waged by both industrial and field Mexican workers. It mobilized broad coalitions to defeat antiworker and repressive legislation and punitive immigration measures that were enacted by both Washington and Sacramento legislators.

In 1942, Josefina Fierro, as national secretary of the Congreso Nacional de los Pueblos de Habla Española, carried out two very significant actions. One was the formation of the Sleepy Lagoon Defense Committee (contrary to the distorted version in Luis Valdez' play *Zoot Suit*) which conducted the public defense of the twenty-two Mexicans who were tried for the death of one. Josefina traveled all over the nation, assisted by Luisa Moreno, to develop the broad national campaign against the racist and divisive indictments and yellow journalistic press descriptions of the Hearst Press, and to bring the message to every town and village in America that only Hitler and the Nazis stood to gain from the extreme racist statements of the authorities, the jingoistic journalists, and those who were instigating the riots upon the Mexican youths by members of the armed forces. It is to be deplored that Luis Valdez could find insufficient drama in the true facts about the Defense of the Sleepy Lagoon and Zoot Suit victims that he had to rely upon Hollywood gimmicks of a fictitious melodrama between two persons that never took place in order to tell his story.

The other significant action that she organized was the massive survey of 50,000 Mexican persons who were registered as available for work in the war industries in the Los Angeles area. It was the largest ready-for-work survey ever taken in the nation. It took place as follows: when the U.S. War Manpower Commission announced in mid-year 1942 that the production of planes, ships, tanks and other war-related items needed by our troops fighting in the Pacific and against the Nazi armies in Europe were not being produced in Southern California due to a very severe shortage of labor, the Congress of Spanish-Speaking People, the Sleepy Lagoon Defense

Committee, the Congress of Industrial Organizations (C.I.O.), Catholic and Protestant churches, and the few Mexican community groups in the barrios carried out a door-to-door survey and work registration campaign in the Mexican communities that produced the very significant number of persons who were available to work in the war production industries, thus answering the charge made by the racists and others who were opposed to the entry of Mexicans in large numbers into industrial and production jobs that Mexicans were not available for such jobs. As a result of this scientific, broadly-based, and mass-supported survey, the giant airplane, shipyard, tank, and other war-producing industries were forced to employ tens of thousands of Mexican workers—men and women for the first time in history. Josefina too became a deportee.

In the present period we have seen other examples of the uniting of our intellectuals, thinkers, and teachers with the people or our barrios in their struggles to change the conditions of denial, stereotyping, and oppressiveness. One such very outstanding example is that of Dr. Ernesto Galarza. Ernie not only did research work, wrote articles, books, produced films, lectured, and conceived mass national campaigns about the need to end the powerlessness of migrant farm workers as a prerequisite to ending the "harvest of shame," misery, and exploitation of these workers by unscrupulous growers, farm labor associations, and labor contractors, but he became an organizing director of the National Farmworkers Union, AFL-CIO. He became a direct participant in the struggle of Mexican farm workers to end the inhuman conditions under which they worked and lived. His book, *Merchants of Labor* provided the data, the documentation, and the soundest arguments and detailed experiences which were used to win support for an ending of the bracero programs. Dr. Galarza was very active in the national movement to end the use of bracero labor from Mexico as a solution to problems of production in agriculture. Opposing giant agri-business, banking, railroading and their powerful allies in government brought immense personal problems to Dr. Galarza and his family. He combined his great talents as conceiver, thinker and designer of strategy and tactics, and scientific researcher with his ability to identify, to live daily, walk picket lines, go to jail, and starve alongside of struggling farmworkers.

We, the Mexicans of the United States, have a great tradition and legacy of commitment to struggle in the face of great odds. Amongst the noblest examples of this tradition have been intellectuals and scholars who dedicated their lives to the emancipation and betterment of the masses of our people. From the lives of Juan Nepomuceno Cortina, Esparza, Lucy González Parson, Teresita Urrea, Ricardo Flores Magón and many of his followers, Luisa Moreno, Josefina Fierro, and Dr. Ernesto Galarza, we can draw great insight and inspiration to stand us in the face of the difficulties that we find ourselves facing when we put our thoughts, ideals, and study into action on the side of the masses of our people. These were all writers, thinkers, and conceivers who put their ideas into action, sometimes paying dearly for doing so. Our scholars today are beginning to face perilous times for all who want change for the better for the many. I believe that our intellectuals and our thinkers will produce those who will carry on the tradition and legacy of those who brought our people to this moment. *SÍ SE PUEDE.*

LOS ANGELES, CALIFORNIA

THE QUEST FOR PARADIGM: THE DEVELOPMENT OF CHICANO STUDIES AND INTELLECTUALS

Carlos Muñoz, Jr.

More than a decade has passed since the first Chicano Studies program was created in 1968, and much has been published on the experience of people of Mexican descent in the United States. As practitioners in the field of Chicano Studies, however, we have not yet made an effort to assess the state of our research in a systematic and critical manner vis-à-vis the original objectives defined during the late 1960s or at the time of the founding of this association (NACS) in 1973. For any assessment of our research to be meaningful, however, I think it imperative that it be placed in historical perspective and within the context of the development of academic intellectuals of Mexican descent in the United States and, most importantly, in relationship to the question of the role of Chicano Studies and Chicano intellectuals in both the university and in our respective communities.

We are all aware of the fact that until very recently there has not been any "critical mass" of scholars of Mexican descent in institutions of higher education in the United States. As a people we have not had the benefit of our own institutions of higher learning as has been the case with the Black experience. With all the limitations of the Negro colleges, those institutions did make a significant contribution to the development of a black bourgeoisie and, more to the point, an intelligentsia that was able to establish a black intellectual tradition long before a few of our own were able to gain access to white colleges and universities. Prior to the sixties, many of those few who gained such access did it with the direct assistance of individual clergy from primarily the Catholic and Protestant churches, although the Mormon church also played a role. Many of the few who eventually became teachers or academics were products of religious and private institutions of higher education. The G.I. Bill and the civil rights movement made it more possible for youth of Mexican descent to attend public institutions of their choice. The end result was that prior to the creation of Chicano Studies programs there were only a handful of academics of Mexican descent in institutions of higher education. Four of them gained importance in the development of Chicano Studies as a new field of study and research.

First there was the late George Sánchez who, during the 1930s, was the first to wage battle against the racism of white schooling in general and the first to issue a critique of society from the perspective of oppressed Mexican people in the United States. In his classic study of New Mexico, *The Forgotten People,* he concluded that "in the march of imperialism a people were forgotten, cast aside as the byproduct of territorial aggrandizement" and made it clear that he did not divorce his scholarship from his commitment to his people. As he put in the preface to that study:

> It has been found necessary and desirable throughout . . . to point out faults and weaknesses in various sectors of the present situation . . . The deficiencies are revealed and criticized with impersonal detachment and with all the scientific objectivity permitted to one who, at the same time, seeks emotional and mental identification with the mass of the people . . . In this nation there is no excuse for human misery and . . . good intentions cannot substitute for good deeds (Sánchez, 1940, viii).

Not only was Sánchez a distinguished academician whose research had been oriented to confronting the social inequities faced by his people, but he also directly participated in the politics of his community. Throughout his academic career at the University of Texas at Austin he was an outspoken community leader and in 1941 served as the national president of the League of United Latin American Citizens (LULAC). Prior to his death in 1972, he lent his support for the creation of the Mexican American Studies Center at the Austin campus.

Américo Paredes has also been important to the development of Chicano Studies research. His research has been aimed at capturing a history of resistance and struggle on the part of Mexican people in the United States through his study of Texas Mexican folklore and music. From his classic study, *With His Pistol in His Hand,* published in 1958, until his more recent study, *A Texas Mexican Cancionero,* his work reflects the dedication he has had for his people and a concern for critical interpretation of the Chicano experience. He was instrumental in the establishment of the Mexican American Studies Center at the University of Texas at Austin in 1970 and served as its first Director.

Julián Samora has been another whose work has been important to the development of our field. He was the first scholar of Mexican descent to focus his research on the problem of political leadership in a Chicano community. In particular his doctoral dissertation, completed in 1954, took a critical look at the process of cooptation of Chicano politicians by white power structures. He has devoted his scholarly career to researching the Chicano experience that eventually compelled him to establish the Mexican American Studies Center at the University of Notre Dame and contribute to the creation of a Mexican American Studies publication series through the University of Notre Dame Press.

We must not ignore another important scholar of Mexican descent who, although having never pursued an academic career, has through his independent research and writing made crucial contributions to our field. I refer to Ernesto Galarza. His work has resulted from many years of active participation in governmental affairs and the labor movement. His work as a farm worker organizer during the 1950s became the background for his first book *The Merchants of Labor,* a study that contributed heavily not only to our understanding of the Bracero experience but also to the termination of that exploitative program, a program he described in the following terms:

> The bracero system might have been a higher stage in American civilization as slavery was in Roman. If so, the affluent society, imperial in its own fashion, could ponder its good luck. It had only to reach out across the border down Mexico way to tap a reservoir of millions ... who longed to toil as managed migrants for a season ... (Galarza, 1964, 259).

Sánchez, Paredes, Samora, and Galarza individually or collectively not only contributed to the training of young scholars of Mexican descent but touched a chord among those of us of the 60's generation searching for a "new" activist-oriented scholarship that could result in the kind of research we envisioned as necessary and useful to the struggle for Chicano liberation. We, however, were caught up in the politics of our times, a politics of mass protest that gave rise to an ideology of "cultural nationalism," an ideology that stressed a *Mexican* identity and rejected assimilation and integrationist strategies that had been advocated by the older generation of activists. We therefore did not immediately give them the proper recognition they deserved. Instead we criticized them for their assimilationist and reformist bias and stance and we did not attempt to understand the nature of the politics of their times. Américo Paredes has offered valuable insight into the politics of his generation. As he put in his *A Texas Mexican Cancionero,*

> ... conditions in the majority culture must be taken into account in any attempt to assess the work of the activists of the post-World War II period. Mexican-Americans were ready for a change, but the United States was not. Post World War II attitudes ... resembled those of the late tens and twenties; the decade of the 1950s was a period of conformity and superpatriotism. We must keep this fact in mind to understand why the Mexican-American activists of the period surrounded their efforts with an aura of super-American- ism ... The principle of the Melting Pot was in full force during the fifties, fortified by the anti-communism fervor of the times. Under such circumstances, Mexican-Americans of this period had to cope with an aggravated problem of identity ... (p. 158).

As I have shown in a forthcoming work, the politics of assimilation and integration during the politics of their times were indeed, upon careful and critical evaluation, a progressive politics (Muñoz, forthcoming). For prior to the sixties, especially during the twenties and thirties, the nativist racist ideology that permeated the dominant white culture promoted an attitude that Mexicans were not assimilable because of their Indian blood and origins. The concern on the part of earlier generations of Mexican activists had therefore been to promote the counter ideology of the "melting pot" which held that the origins of the dominant culture were not simply rooted in English or German Protestant culture, but in fact were derived from various distinct immigrant cultures that had made United States society unique in the world. By placing Mexicans in the framework of the melting pot, they believed our people would eventually gain access to the rewards of "American democracy." Although the activists of that period emphasized the Spanish or white aspect of Mexican identity, they did not generally withhold criticism of dominant institutions for their policies of systematic exclusion and their oppression of Mexican people. Many struggled for the desegragation of schools and public facilities.

The work done by these four scholars has been important to the development of Chicano Studies as a new field of study and research and, most importantly, to the establishment of a Mexican academic intellectual tradition in the United States. We need to understand, however, that Chicano Studies was a generational phenomenon of the sixties and that it was defined in the process of the struggles of those times. The movement for Chicano Studies and the Chicano student movement were originally one and the same, as student activists of the 60's perceived the establishment of Chicano programs at institutions of higher education as a means of placing the resources of those institutions at the disposal of those engaged in the struggles for political and social change in their respective communities.

An examination of proposals for Chicano Studies in Texas, New Mexico, and California, reflects an antiassimilationist thrust and the general objective of using such programs as means to provide direct Chicano access to institutions of higher education and to legitimize the existence of Chicano culture through the creation of curricula designed to teach students about the Mexican experience in the United States, and to prepare students to become community leaders and knowledgeable activists in community struggles for social change. *El Plan de Santa Bárbara* is one of the documents that spells out the objectives of Chicano Studies in a coherent and clear manner. It has become an historic document which provides us with insight into the politics of the Chicano intellectual generation of the sixties. The Plan was prefaced with a militant manifesto that declared in part:

> For the Chicano the present is a time of renaissance, of renacimiento. Our people and our community, el barrio and la colonia, are expressing a new consciousness and a new resolve . . . We pledge our will to move . . . forward toward our destiny as a people . . . against those forces which have denied us freedom of expression and human dignity. For decades Mexican people in the United States struggled to realize the "American Dream" and some—a few—have. But the cost, the ultimate cost of assimilation, required turning away from el barrio and la colonia. In the meantime, due to the racist structure of this society, to our essentially different life style, and to the socio-economic functions assigned to our community by anglo-american society—capitalist entrepreneur—the barrio and colonia remain exploited, impoverished, and marginal . . . Culturally, the word Chicano, in the past a perjorative and class-bound adjective, has now become the root idea of a new cultural identity for our people . . . [it] signals a rebirth of pride and confidence . . . we believe that higher education must contribute to the formation of a complete man who truly values life and freedom (pp. 9-11).

Basically, *El Plan de Santa Bárbara* was a blueprint for the creation and institutionalization of various Chicano programs that could promote access to institutions of higher education. It outlined a strategy and a step by step process delineating how those programs could be implemented under the direct control of Chicanos. To some extent it was similar to other proposals for Chicano programs throughout the Southwest but it differed in that it did offer a substantial framework for Chicano Studies research and for the formation of a new kind of intellectual, one who could see research in the following terms:

> The role of knowledge in producing powerful social change, indeed revolution, cannot be underestimated... research will not only provide Chicanos with action-oriented analysis of conditions, it will also aid significantly in politically educating the Chicano community... it will help measurably in creating and giving impetus to that historical consciousness... Chicanos must possess in order successfully to struggle as a people toward a new vision of Aztlan (p. 78).

What was being called for, although not articulated as such, was the development of organic intellectuals of Mexican descent within the university, i.e. the kind of academic who would be an integral part of his community and actively participate in the Chicano Movement, do research critical of society, and simultaneously contribute to the shaping of a Chicano consciousness. The Plan went on to underscore the importance of research to Chicano liberation.

> The systematic character of the racist relationship between gabacho society and Chicanos will not be altered unless solid research becomes the basis for Chicano political strategy and action. Rigorous analysis of conditions must be undertaken, issues identified, and priorities determined as Chicanos adopt strategies and develop tactics for the purpose of realigning our community's structural relationship to gabacho society... (ibid.).

The plan was the product of a three-day statewide conference held at the University of California, Santa Barbara campus, during the month of April, 1969, and was to some extent a followup to the first annual national Chicano Youth Liberation Conference sponsored by the Crusade for Justice in Denver, Colorado, where "El Plan de Aztlán" had been proclaimed a month earlier. Aware of the crucial importance of research to the successful implementation of the goals of Chicano Studies, a group from the Santa Barbara conference, all in the disciplines of history and the social sciences, began to raise important questions as to the nature of research in the university. Specifically, some of us saw the need to critically examine the question of the role of Chicano academic intellectuals in the Chicano Movement and to question in a fundamental and critical way the various assumptions and perspectives of the dominant paradigms of our respective disciplines. Soon after the conference several of the participants founded a journal for Chicano Studies at the University of California, Los Angeles (UCLA) which was to become the vehicle for the achievement of those objectives. The Journal was named *Aztlán: Chicano Journal of the Social Sciences and the Arts.* The first issue appeared in the Spring of 1970, a year after the Santa Barbara conference, with the manifesto from "El Plan de Aztlán." The stated purpose of the journal was to "Promote an active quest for solutions to the problems of the barrios of America" and to "focus scholarly discussion and analysis on Chicano matters as they relate to the group and to the total American society" (p. vi). The articles in this first issue were prefaced by a poem about Aztlán by Alurista, one of the first poets produced by the Chicano student movement. The editors of the journal were all graduate or undergraduate students and members of "El Movimiento Estudiantil Chicano de Aztlán" (MECHA) at UCLA. The chief editor, Juan Gómez-Quiñones, in addition to being a graduate student was also an instructor in the department of history at UCLA at the time. He had been one of the prime movers of the Santa Barbara conference and a member of the editorial group that produced the Plan de Santa Bárbara. The articles in the first issue dealt with the question of culture and identity, Chicano history, the Chicano Movement, and a Chicano worker strike in 1933.

The second issue of Aztlán included a paper I had delivered as a graduate student in the 1970 annual meeting of the American Political Science Association wherein I called for a "Chicano Perspective of Political Analysis." As a member of the Santa Barbara group I was concerned with the need to go beyond the question of negative stereotypes and myths about Chicanos perpetuated by social science. It had been my feelings at the time that a primary factor for the lack of understanding about the Chicano dilemma in American society could be attributed to the fact that what had been written about Chicanos had been largely based on "a dominant Anglo perspective which has been predicated on the cultural values and norms of the dominant society (Muñoz, 1970, 21). I argued that it was imperative for those of us concerned with research on the Chicano experience to critically examine the paradigms of the various disciplines that had developed from the dominant ideological perspectives. I concluded my paper with the following words:

> The Chicano scholar must realize that it is not enough to write critiques pointing out the stereotypes and myths that social science has perpetuated about Chicanos. The crisis that confronts his people is too great and profound and it compels him to develop new paradigms of research and analysis that will adequately deal with the problem of poverty, alienation, and political powerlessness. He now,

more than ever, must commit himself to the emancipation of his people. For he does not have the luxury of remaining in the ivory tower nor to engage in "objective" analysis while his people are in the throes of crisis. The challenge before the Chicano scholar is to develop a Chicano perspective of political analyusis. A perspective that will assure that his research will be oriented toward the needs of his community (Muñoz, ibid., 24).

In the third issue of Aztlán, Juan Gómez-Quiñones carried forth the argument for the need to develop a new paradigm for Chicano history.

The paradigm should reveal, historically, the interrelations between culture and economic role, group personality configurations, mechanisms of social control, and the accumulating weight of historical experiences—all of which form the historical context. With such a paradigm one can begin to investigate the pressures, structural characteristics and events that combine to produce the Chicano community of today... Chicano history is, and must continue to be, innovative... because it calls for a reconceptualization of history and the role of history in society. This means the use of new methods of inquiry and a reconstruction and reinterpretation of available sources... a union of history as discipline and history as action on behalf of a community in its struggle for survival... It is not the listing of "important" names and contributions of "Mexican Americans" to the development of "this great country"... but must realistically reflect the historical context of the Chicano community vis-à-vis other oppressed groups in U.S. society... Chicano history involves more than the creation of a new discipline or area of study... It involves the *self definition* (his emphasis) of a people (Gómez-Quiñones, 1971, 2, 39).

Others outside the Santa Barbara group called for a new paradigm for the study of the Chicano experience. Octavio Romano, one of the founders of *El Grito: Journal of Mexican American Thought,* the first Chicano journal, founded in 1968, and the first to criticize the role of social science in the perpetuation of negative stereotypes and myths about Chicanos, called for a paradigm to be based on the following criteria:

All that is necessary at this point is an historical perspective and a paradigm by which to articulate that perspective... [T]he eight point paradigm that follows seems most useful at present... First, Chicanos do not view themselves as traditionally unchanging vegetables,... but rather as creators of systems in their own right, for they have created cooperatives, mutualist societies, political blocks... Second, Chicanos view themselves as participants in the historical process... Third,... this population... constitutes a pluralistic people. Fourth, Chicanos see in their historical existence a continuous engaging in social issues... Fifth, the concept of the illiterate Mexican-American must go... Sixth, the Chicano must be viewed as capable of his own system of rationality... Seventh, intellectual activity has been part and parcel of Chicano existence... and Eighth, as a population whose antecedents are Mexican, the bulk of Chicano existence has been oriented to a symbiotic residence within ecosystems (Romano, 1970, 13-14).

What was to be the new paradigm? Among those of the Santa Barbara group and others who generally adhered to the principles of the Plan de Santa Bárbara there was some difference of approach. The problem posed by the question was perceived differently by those who were committed to the development of Chicano Studies outside of existing academic units and those committed to doing research on the Chicano experience from within traditional disciplines. There were those few who were junior faculty members in traditional departments who believed research from a Chicano perspective could be done within the confines of such departments. Others believed it was essential to be either in the newly formed Chicano Studies departments or programs or in interdisciplinary academic programs they perceived as more fruitful to the development of an alternative paradigm. Some deemed it essential that Chicanos become faculty in traditional departments in order to maximize Chicano access to the resources of the university. Others believed that being faculty in traditional departments would compel them to do the kind of research called for by those departments in order to eventually be promoted to tenure. Furthermore, having to teach traditional courses, it was believed by some, would greatly hinder their efforts to develop Chicano Studies curricula and do meaningful Chicano Studies research.

Those committed to the development of a Chicano Studies paradigm began to conceptualize the Chicano experience in the context of Chicanos as a colonized people. We were influenced by the writings of Fanon, Memmi, Carmichael, Blauner, the analysis of the Black Panther party of blacks as a neocolony in the United States, and various Latin American scholars who had developed analyses of internal colonialism within their countries (Frank, Nun, Gonzales-Casanova, Stavenhagen). George Sánchez had been the first to write about Chicanos as a colonized people in his classic study of New Mexico published in 1940. He did not develop his analysis in the context of a theoretical framework, but did lay the foundation for its development.

The framers of the Plan de Santa Bárbara, familiar with the work of these writers, made reference to Chicanos as a colonized people. The analysis derived from the literature on colonialism and the black experience made more sense to us than did any other interpretations of Third World people in the United States offered by social scientists and historians who reflected the biases of the dominant paradigms. We launched the effort to develop a body of literature on the Chicano internal colonial experience. In a paper delivered at a symposium on the urban crisis, I challenged the work of Edward Banfield and referred to Chicano communities as internal colonies (Muñoz, 1970). In an article published in the third issue of *Aztlán*, Tomas Almaguer, then a student activist at the Univesity of California, Santa Barbara campus, argued the need to study the Chicano experience within the context of a process of colonization (Almaguer, 1971). Then three of us committed to the principles of the Plan de Santa Bárbara wrote an article wherein we developed a theoretical framework based on our interpretation of the "Barrio as Internal Colony." We presented the work as a collective effort and a preliminary step in the development of a paradigm for Chicano Studies. We defined the internal colony framework in the following terms:

> The crucial distinguishing characteristic between internal and external colonialsim does not appear to be so much the existence of separate territories corresponding to metropolis and colony, but the legal status of the colonized. According to our usage, a colony can be considered "internal" if the colonized population has the same formal legal status as any other group of citizens, and "external" if it is placed in a separate legal category . . . Chicano communities in the United States are internal colonies, since they occupy a status of formal equality, whatever the informal reality may be . . . [I]nternal colonialism means that Chicanos as a cultural/racial group exist in an exploited condition which is maintained by a number of mechanisms . . . [and] a lack of control over those institutions which affect their lives . . . It . . . results in the community finding its culture and social organization under constant attack from a racist society (Barrera, Muñoz, Ornelas, 1972, 483, 485).

Historian Rudy Acuña, one of the few faculty who participated in the Santa Barbara conference, then published what was to become the first book-length study of the Mexican experience in U.S. society from a Chicano perspective. He made internal colonialism the framework for his interpretation.

> Central to the thesis of this monograph is my contention that the conquest of the Southwest created a colonial situation in the traditional sense with the Mexican land and population being

controlled by an imperialistic United States... I contend that this colonization... is still with us today. Thus, I refer to the colony, initially, in the traditional definition of the term and later... as an internal colony (Acuña, 1973, 3).

Guillermo Flores, a former MECHA activist and a graduate student at the time at Stanford University, linked the analysis of Chicanos as an internally colonized people with a Marxist theoretical framework in his article on "Race and Culture in the Internal Colony: Keeping the Chicano in His Place":

> There is considerable overlap between monopoly capitalism and internal colonialism within the U.S.... [T]he utilization of the Chicano and other racial minorities as a carefully regulated colonial labor force contributed to the capital formation and accumulation processes necessary for the development of modern capitalism 's monopoly stage (Flores, 1973, 190).

By 1973 a significant amount of literature had been generated based on the various internal colony analyses and many in Chicano Studies programs throughout the United States used it as the key literature in their courses. Internal colonialism became the "model" for Chicano Studies research and many perceived it as the alternative to the dominant paradigm of the social sciences and history. Juan Gómez-Quiñones put it in these words:

> A modified colonial framework allows us to relate factors that heretofore have been kept separate... The status of the Chicano as a minority-territorial enclave is analogous to other colonial cases in different parts of the world. The aspects that this situation produces and the actions that it engenders, are important in the historical formation of the community and in its historical patterns. Some of these aspects are the caste-like social-economic relations, institutional hostility and neglect, and movements of resistance and assertion (Gómez-Quiñones, 1971, 5-6).

In spite of the popularity of the internal colonial concept, we perceived that the "model" was still in its embryonic stages and was far from becoming a viable paradigm. Two symposia were organized to discuss the status of the "model" in 1973 where we engaged in self-criticism and probed the further refinements we deemed necessary for it to become more meaningful and applicable to the kind of research we believed was needed by the Chicano Movement. The first of the symposia was held at the University of California, Irvine, and the second at UCLA. At the Irvine symposium, there was a general feeling that the "model" was vulnerable to becoming academically rigid thus redirecting Chicano research into a respectable and legitimate direction acceptable to the university but not necessarily conducive to the struggle for Chicano liberation. At the UCLA symposium we reached general agreement that in order to assure the internal colonial analysis remained meaningful to its original objectives it should take a Marxist approach. In this regard I argued that the "colonial model can be a transition from a cultural-racial interpretation of the problems of the Chicano to a class analysis of the Chicano experience" (García, 1974, 27).

The Formation of NACS

Both symposia raised the question of the role of the Chicano academic intellectual in the Chicano Movement in critical terms. How were those in Chicano Studies or those doing research on the Chicano experience going to prevent their work from becoming purely abstract or coopted by the dominant paradigms? What was to be done to ensure that Chicano research in general, and the internal colonial analysis in particular, was applied to the needs of the community and the Chicano Movement? Whereas the literature on Chicanos and internal colonialism had reached a certian amount of respectability within Chicano Studies circles, it was not considered good scholarship by those in traditional departments of the university, both Chicano and white. Those of us involved in Chicano caucuses in the various social science associations therefore formed the National Caucus of Chicano Social Scientists and agreed to the need to form a national association of Chicano social scientists that could become the mechanism whereby these concerns could be collectively dealt with by Movement scholars throughout the country. Such an association was perceived by some of us as the crucial foundation for the development of a Chicano Studies paradigm. We believed it could join together a community of Chicano scholar-activists—organic intellectuals—dedicated to pursuing the same basic objectives.

The National Caucus of Chicano Social Scientists held a meeting at the New Mexico Highlands University in May of 1973 for the purpose of creating a national association. The meeting was attended by approximately 50 people, most of whom were graduate students and a handful who were junior faculty, recent Ph.D.'s or at the dissertation stage. We focused our attention on the nature and direction of Chicano social science research and the structure of the proposed association. Agreement was reached that traditional social science research was to be discouraged within the proposed association in favor of more critical analysis as afforded by the internal colonial and Marxist class analysis. The question of the role of Chicano academic intellectuals was heavily discussed. We agreed that Chicano social science research should fall under the following criteria:

> (1) Social Science research by Chicanos must be more problem-oriented than traditional social science;... scholarship cannot be justified for its own sake: It must be a committed scholarship that can contribute to Chicano liberation. (2)... research projects must be *interdisciplinary* in nature... traditional disciplin(es)... serve... to fragment our research in a highly artificial manner, and obscure the interconnections among variables that operate to maintain the oppression of our people. (3)... research and action should exist in a dialectical relationship... in order to bridge the gap between theory and action, Chicano social scientists must develop close ties with community action groups. (4) Chicano social science must be highly *critical*... of American institutions... (5)... We must study the Chicano community... within the context of those dominant institutional relationships that affect Chicanos... research has to do with the relationship between class, race, and culture in determining the Chicano's historical experience (Caucus Newsletter, 1973, 2).

The proposed association would set the example and the direction for Chicano research as outlined above. Its task would be to establish communication among Chicano scholars across geographic and disciplinary lines, encourage the development of new social theories and models, struggle for the recruitment of Chicanos into all graduate levels of social science institutions, and attempt to generate funds for research by Chicanos that met the objectives of the association. Membership in the association was to be on the basis of participation in interdisciplinary, local and regional, collective research units called "focos." It was agreed the name of the association would be the National Association of Chicano Social Scientists (NACS) and that it would hold annual meetings where the work of each foco would be presented. At the 1977 annual meeting held at the University of California, Berkeley, the asociation changed its name to the National Association for Chicano Studies.

By the time of the founding of NACS, however, the concept of internal colonialism began to lose much of its original thrust. It became clear that, at least as we had applied it to the Chicano experience, there was no true concensus to make it *the* paradigm for Chicano Studies research. For if we agree with Thomas Kuhn that a paradigm defines "the entire constellation of beliefs, values, techniques, etc, shared by the members of a given community" of scholars, then we were not even close (Kuhn, 1970, 175).

The initial basis for the founding of NACS had been a general agreement about the failure of the dominant paradigms of the social sciences to meaningfully address themselves to a proper interpretation of the Chicano experience and the desire to develop an organization that could be in tune with the need to do interdisciplinary research of import to the Chicano Movement, e.g. that could contribute to Chicano liberation, specifically, to encourage the development of alternative modes of analysis that could be applied to the resolution of problems in the Chicano community. The founding of NACS, however, took place at a time when the nationalist-oriented student movement was already in decline. The politics of "Chicanismo" or "cultural nationalism" were being questioned in critical terms by those of us who saw Marxism as the alternative paradigm that needed to be applied to Chicano research and political action. The first analyses developed of Chicanos as an internally colonized people had been directly the result of our participation in the student movement, the Santa Barbara conference, or the various Chicano struggles of the late sixties addressing the quest for Chicano identity and culture as a means for liberation. Internal colonialism had been meaningful as a concept that offered an alternative interpretation of the Chicano experience that stressed racism and directly related to our task of interpreting the Chicano movement as a struggle for decolonization and antiassimilation.

By 1973, the time of the founding of NACS, most of us who had earlier applied the concept of internal colonialism had engaged in self-criticism of our own work. Mario Barrera, for example, placed the origins of the concept in critical perspective at the UCLA symposium on internal colonialism prior to the founding of NACS.

> I think there is truly no colonial model as such . . . we tend to fall into the habit of using and talking about the colonial model . . . there's rather a concept . . . that some of us have tried to use in order to try to understand the experience of the Chicano, Puerto Rican, black and native American . . . There is no one interpretation of colonialism . . . when it started to be used . . . to refer to the experience of national minorities here [it] was really used in a kind of polemic against liberal interpretations of the experience of these minority groups. I think the fact that it began in that kind of context influenced its direction, its central themes . . . [It] still represents that kind of dialogue (Proceedings, 1973).

It had become clear in most of our minds that Marxist theory and class analysis offered much in the way of potential contributions to the development of a truly alternative paradigm for Chicano Studies.

Within the NACS constituency at that time, however, there was much diversity of thought as to the validity of Marxist methodology and theory in the reinterpretation of the Chicano experience. Many remained committed to a research focused on the question of culture vis-à-vis the ideological framework of the Plan de Santa Bárbara. Others agreed that class analysis should be incorporated into the internal colonial framework, while still others became convinced that the question of paradigm was best addressed by limiting it to a classical Marxist-Leninist framework of class struggle. One of those with the latter perspective was Gilbert González, a participant in the Santa Barbara conference in 1969 who rejected internal colonialism on the following grounds:

> The theory of the internal colony model... focuses attention upon the national question... However, it is full of dangers and idealistic assumptions which are inherent in non-Marxist as well as anti-Marxist works. It does not place into proper perspective the questions of class and racial (and ignores sexual) exploitation. In the long run the contradictions of the theory are such that it would be of little use in the destruction of racism and exploitation. For one truly interested in the liberation of oppressed peoples (for example, whites in Appalachia) the internal colony model is an incorrect, ineffective, and ultimately counterrevolutionary theory (González, 1974, 160-161).

González and others holding to classical Marxist-Leninist schools of thought critiqued the concept of internal colonization as positing a "racial war" as opposed to a "correct theory" of class struggle.

Another critique of the internal colonial concept was made by Fred Cervantes in a paper delivered at the annual NACS meeting in Austin in 1975. According to him, the concept was limited because it did not truly place the "realities of contemporary Chicano history and politics" in proper context (Cervantes, 1975, 16). According to this critique, the oppression of Chicanos was due to a "legacy of colonialism rather than as an example of internal colonialism" because Chicanos in American society were in reality a "post-colonial minority" (ibid.).

The limitations of the internal colonial concept, as outlined by those of us who first applied it to the Chicano experience and our critics, made it clear that a paradigm that could result in the further definition of Chicano Studies could not be restricted to the type of analysis that concept generated. The concept was of great significance in that it was the first concrete effort to radically depart from the dominant paradigms and free Chicano research to some extent from dependence on the theories and methodologies of the traditional academic disciplines. The limitations of the concept notwithstanding, it has contributed significantly to our collective development as Chicano academic intellectuals and to Chicano Studies as a new field of study and research.

The concept of internal colonialism, however, never achieved legitimacy in the university in the context that we applied it during the early seventies. In the minds of white academics and those scholars of Mexican descent removed from the struggles for Chicano Studies who perpetuate the myth of "objective" and "value-free" research, the concept was simply a polemic or political ideology that had little to offer in the way of scholarship. Academic Marxists held a similar attitude since the concept did not neatly fit into any of their paradigms. In contrast, those of us who applied the concept to our research and interpretations of the Chicano experience viewed our quest for paradigm as inseparable from the Chicano struggle for in our minds just as the Chicano Movement had directly challenged the dominant institutions of the State for their failure to meet the needs of our people and communities, we perceived Chicano Studies as a challenge to the dominant paradigms that had either failed to properly interpret or that altogether ignored the Chicano experience. Both the Chicano struggle and Chicano Studies were movements aimed at altering the nature of the status quo, the former being concerned with changing existing power relationships and the latter with challenging the perspectives, models, and theories that had legitimized those relationships. In a very real sense we were engaged in the process that Thomas Kuhn has described as follows.

> This genetic aspect of the parallel between political and scientific development should no longer be open to doubt... political revolutions aim to change political institutions in ways those institutions themselves prohibit... Like the choice between competing institutions, that between competing paradigms proves to be a choice between incompatible modes of community life (Kuhn, 1970, 93, 94).

The consequence has been that most Chicano Studies research produced thus far reflects a scholarship rooted in the dominant paradigms of the established disciplines. Collectively speaking, we have yet to liberate ourselves from those disciplines to the extent we are free to seriously and critically ponder the theoretical and methodological questions that need to be examined in any effort to develop a new paradigm or discipline. We continue to refer to ourselves as historians, political scientists, sociologists, etc, as opposed to consciously making the effort to underscore the interdisciplinary nature of Chicano Studies research.

Why is this the case? The answer lies in the structure of the university. We remain victimized by it and are powerless to control our collective intellectual development. Our survival as faculty is dependent upon how well we meet the criteria for excellence in scholarship as defined by the dominant paradigms. We are not in the position whereby we can profoundly influence the graduate training of Chicano students since we have as yet not established a single Chicano Studies Ph.D. program anywhere in the country that is under our full control and gives us the opportunity to produce Chicano organic intellectuals. In short, Chicano Studies scholarship has not yet been legitimized although Chicano scholars as individuals have.

If we critically evaluated the research that has been produced thus far in accordance with the criteria defined by El Plan de Santa Bárbara and the founders of this association some no doubt would consider most of it as not legitimate Chicano Studies research. The development of any field of study, however, must be placed in the context of a process of intellectual development that takes place not in a vacuum but that originates from the larger societal situation that in turn influences the political consciousness of intellectuals. The quest for paradigm is therefore a continuous process and one that is never ending. The restrictions placed on our research by the structure of the university can be overcome and have been, as the fruit of our collective labor is beginning to show, and there is evidence that a critical Chicano scholarship is alive and well. Many of us are finally at the stage of producing works that have for many years been in the process of intellectual and political percolation.

The state of Chicano Studies research is a healthy one, for in spite of the pessimistic forecasts about the future of our programs that have been made since the 1970s, a small but significant number of us have survived in the university. Sánchez, Paredes, Samora, and Galarza established a Mexican intellectual tradition of critical inquiry and advocacy in this society and we of the generation of the sixties have built on it and will preserve it.

CHICANO STUDIES
UNIV. OF CALIFORNIA, BERKELEY

36   THE QUEST FOR PARADIGM

References

Acuña, Rodolfo. 1972. *Occupied America: The Chicano's Struggle Toward Liberation.* San Francisco: Canfield Press.

Almaguer, Tomás. 1971. "Toward the Study of Chicano Colonialism." *Aztlán: Chicano Journal of the Social Sciences and the Arts,* Spring, 1971, pp. 7-21.

Barrera, Mario; Carlos Muñoz, Jr.; and Charles Ornelas. 1972. "The Barrio as Internal Colony." In Harlan Hahn, ed., *People and Politics in Urban Society,* pp. 465-498. Los Angeles: Sage Publications.

Cervantes, Fred A. 1977. "Chicanos as a Post-Colonial Minority: Some Questions Concerning the Adequacy of the Paradigm of Internal Colonialism." In Reynaldo Flores Macías, ed., *Perspectivas en Chicano Studies.* Proceedings of the Third Annual Meeting of the National Association of Chicano Social Scientists. Los Angeles: NACS.

Chicano Coordinating Council on Higher Education. 1969. *El Plan de Santa Bárbara: A Chicano Plan for Higher Education.* Oakland: La Causa Publications.

Flores, Guillermo V. 1973. "Race and Culture in the Internal Colony: Keeping the Chicano in His Place." In Frank Bonilla and Robert Girling, eds., *Structures of Dependency,* pp. 189-223. Stanford: Institute of Political Studies.

Galarza, Ernesto. 1964. *The Merchants of Labor.* Santa Barbara: McNally & Loftin.

García, Mario. 1974. "A Report on the UCLA Symposium on Internal Colonialism and the Chicano." *La Luz,* April, 1974, p. 27.

Gómez-Quiñones, Juan. 1971. "Toward a Perspective on Chicano History." *Aztlán,* Fall, 1971, pp. 1-49.

González, Gilbert G. 1974. "A Critique of the Internal Colonial Model." *Latin American Perspectives,* Spring, 1974, pp. 154-161.

Kuhn, Thomas. 1970. *The Structure of Scientific Revolutions.* Chicago: University of Chicago Press.

Muñoz, Carlos, Jr. *Youth and Political Struggle: The Chicano Student Generation.* Forthcoming.

_____. 1970. "On the Nature and Cause of Tension in the Chicano Community: A Critical Analysis." Paper prepared for delivery at the Invitational Research Symposium on Urban Problems, Institute of Government and Public Affairs, UCLA, April 2, 1970.

_____. 1970. "Toward a Chicano Perspective of Political Analysis." *Aztlán,* Fall, 1970, pp. 15-26.

National Caucus of Chicano Social Scientists Newsletter. 1977. In Reynaldo Flores Macías, ed., *Perspectivas en Chicano Studies.* Proceedings of the Third Annual Meeting of the National Association of Chicano Social Scientists, pp. 215, 216. Los Angeles: NACS.

Paredes, Américo. 1976. *A Texas Mexican Cancionero.* Urbana: University of Illinois Press.

Romano, Octavio Ignacio, V. 1970. "Social Science, Objectivity, and the Chicanos." *El Grito: Journal of Contemporary Mexican-American Thought,* Fall, 1970, pp. 4-16.

Samora, Julián, and James Watson. 1954. "Subordinate Leadership in a Bicultural Community: An Analysis." *American Sociological Review,* August, 1954, pp. 413-421.

Sánchez, George. 1940. *Forgotten People.* Albuquerque: University of New Mexico Press.

Symposium on Internal Colonialism and the Chicano. 1973. Unpublished proceedings of symposium at UCLA. Author's files.

PEASANT REVOLTS DURING THE MEXICAN REVOLUTION: A SOCIAL-STRUCTURAL AND POLITICAL APPROACH*

Alma García-Marsh

Introduction

In his *Social Origins of Dictatorship and Democracy: Lord and Peasant in the Making of the Modern World,* Barrington Moore states that the "process of modernization begins with peasant revolutions that fail. It culminates during the twentieth century with peasant revolutions that succeed. No longer is it possible to take seriously the view that the peasant is an 'object of history,' a form of social life over which changes pass but which contributes nothing to the impetus of these changes" (Moore, 1966: 453). With the publication of Moore's seminal book, a body of literature began to address itself to the issue concerning the revolutionary potential of peasants "in the modern world." This literature focused on one major question: what explains the occurrence of peasant revolts? Researchers soon provided a variety of answers based on wide-ranging case studies of peasant revolts.

This essay will present the thesis that the rise of a peasant revolt during the Mexican Revolution of 1910 was produced by a combination of social-structural and political factors. At the local level, the institutional framework of surviving peasant villages provided the needed organizational capacity facilitating armed uprisings. At the national level, a severe but not total collapse of the state's political machinery, precipitated by both national and international factors, provided a social setting that further enabled

*I would like to thank Theda Skocpol for her helpful comments on earlier drafts of this paper.

agrarian uprisings to develop. The breakdown of the Díaz state will be analyzed in a world-historical context. Such a breakdown led to the emergence of specific elite group conflicts that had direct bearing on the fate of peasant revolts. This study will then assess the significance of peasant revolts on the outcome of the Mexican Revolution. It will trace the fate and limits of peasant contributions to the Revolution as a whole.

Among the various theoretical approaches developed to explain the rise of peasant revolts, the Marxist and the social-structural perspective share a common emphasis. Both deal with the social forces to which peasants are exposed and the historical setting within which these occur. A Marxist analysis examines peasants within a context of social class relations, the economic system, and the inherent conflicts within each. Land ownership among peasants becomes a critical variable for this approach in explaining the likelihood of revolts. A direct relationship is posited between the peasantry's class behavior and the type of land patterns under which they live. Types of landholdings are believed to be major determinants in the rise of the peasantry as a revolutionary threat. A debate concerning which type of peasant is most likely to engage in revolutionary activity remains open, with some viewing the "middle peasantry" (owners of small plots) as more prone to mobilization and rebellion (Alavi, 1965; Wolf, 1969). Some researchers, on the other hand, identify poor peasants (sharecroppers) as the strata ripe for insurrection (Stinchcombe, 1962). Paige (1975) argues that a peasant's revolutionary potential is also a function of the interests and capacities of their class opponents. Unlike Wolf (1969) who explicitly identifies the landholding middle peasant as the group with the greatest propensity for rebellion due to their isolation and autonomous village communities, Paige considers the propertyless wage-laborers as most prone to rebel. Such peasants, according to Paige, are the opposite of the landholding peasants, who tend to be economically competitive among themselves and strongly tied to and dependent on rich peasants as well as the landed upper class. Those peasants who work for wages and are no longer tied to the land will develop a greater capacity to participate in revolutionary movements. Paige's work, although methodologically elegant and logically argued, remains economically deterministic, reducing peasant political behavior to class relations.

Controversy over the identification of the peasantry with the most revolutionary potential continues. Many researchers, nevertheless, are in agreement on the role of a revolutionary ideology within the ranks of the peasantry and the development of revolutionary activity. The crystallization of such an ideology is viewed as a prerequisite for mass action. Migdal (1974) takes issue with such a position arguing instead that peasant mobilization is a product of trade-offs and incentives between peasant groups and an urban-based revolutionary organization. Twentieth-century peasant revolutions develop due to the organizing and mobilizing efforts of armed revolutionary forces aimed at the peasants and the organized programs offered by urban revolutionaries to provide solutions for such crises.

In an attempt to overcome the limitations of economic determinism evident in many Marxist works on peasants, Barrington Moore (1966) provides a social-structural approach that maintains a Marxist foundation but concentrates more on the overall social and political setting. Moore is critical of past theories that focused primarily on the peasantry and as such neglected the structural relationship between peasant and overlord. Such a relationship is conditioned by several variables: the degree of peasant village solidarity, the hierarchical divisions within the peasantry and, above all, the degree of peasant exploitation by the class of overlords. Exploitation, then, becomes the most significant causal factor in explaining peasant uprisings.

Building on Moore's approach of emphasizing the historical and social-structural setting of peasants and their relations with other classes, but critical of the weight ascribed to peasant exploitation, Goldfrank (1976) and Skocpol (1978) offer an alternate structural explanation. An analysis of a given peasant revolt requires an examination of the peasantry's political capacity and the strength of the repressive machinery at the disposal of the government (Goldfrank, 1976). Incidences of peasant revolts are explained by Skocpol (1978: 210-211) by three critical factors: "1) the degrees and kinds of solidarity of peasant communities; 2) the degrees of peasant autonomy from direct day to day supervision and control by landlords and their agents; and 3) the relaxation of state coercive sanctions against peasant revolts."

This paper will focus on three areas in explaining peasant revolts during the Mexican Revolution of 1910 from a social-structural and political perspective: 1) the agrarian structure of prerevolutionary Mexico; 2) the structural characteristics of the Díaz state; and 3) the role of peasant revolts during the revolutionary period. Such an analysis will thus address itself to the question raised earlier by Barrington Moore (1966: 453): "What kinds of social structures and historical situations produce peasant revolutions?"

Agrarian Structure of Prerevolutionary Mexico

A wealth of historical material exists dealing with Mexico's agrarian structure. This paper will draw on such sources to argue the position that the survival of autonomus forms of peasant communities was crucial to the development of peasant revolts during the Mexican Revolution.

The types of agrarian communities found in twentieth-century Mexico are products of the country's colonial legacy from Spain. As a colonial society, Mexico inherited from its mother country several persistent features: 1) a subordinate position in the world economic system, and 2) an agrarian system in which a small group of landowners dominated the masses of landless peasants.

An analysis of Mexico's agrarian structure that emphasizes its role in a world economy represents a departure from previous historical accounts. A common theme prevalent in such accounts depicts Mexico as well as other Latin American countries as tradition-bound societies with few outside linkages. Social structures, therefore, are explained largely in terms of intranational factors. Alternate attempts to study Latin American societies begin by asserting the need to view Mexico, for example, vis-à-vis its relations with Spain and similarly vis-à-vis Spain's relations with Western Europe (Frank, 1967; Stein and Stein, 1970; Beckford, 1972). Although Mexico functioned as a colony of Spain, both countries served as sources for exports for Western Europe. From the last part of the sixteenth century, Mexico provided Spain with such items as silver, gold, agricultural products (particularly sugar), meat, and leather. Spanish merchants occupied a peripheral location within a world economy and thus the export-oriented nature of Mexico's economy became both a colonial and, as will be pointed out, a postcolonial feature (Chevalier, 1963; Stein and Stein, 1970; Wallerstein, 1974).

A direct relationship is discernible between Mexico's export-oriented economy and the form of land ownership patterns that developed. These in turn had direct bearing on the regional variations among peasant communities. Much has been written to trace the origins, changes, and consolidations of the Mexican hacienda (McBride, 1923; Tannenbaum, 1929; Chevalier, 1967). This paper is concerned with the effect that Mexico's peripheral position in a world system as a colonial society had on its agrarian structure and, above all, what consequent effect this had on its peasantry's capacity for insurrection.

Despite the weakness of the Spanish state during the seventeenth century, the Spanish metropolis firmly dominated and shaped the internal affairs of its colony. The Conquest transformed "New Spain's" social organization; a new system of domination-subordination replaced preexisting indigenous social structures. Such systems varied by region throughout Mexico with the northern section characterized by nomadic tribes while the Central and Southern parts contained highly organized villages. Spain proceeded to impose its own social-structural patterns on the indigenous population, and nowhere is this process most clearly demonstrated than in the rise and consolidation of the great landed estates: the haciendas.

The haciendas as a system of land ownership developed in Mexico not as a product of a feudal or semifeudal heritage from Spain, but rather as a direct response to meet the needs of an export-oriented economy. Such needs led to the concentrated drive by the Spanish elite to obtain large tracts of land and consolidate them into haciendas capable of producing those items that the Western European market demanded (Tannenbaum, 1929; Stein and Stein, 1970). Two critical problems confronted the hacendados: the need for more land and a sufficient labor force to work it. Mexican sugar, for example, became a primary export item from as early as the seventeenth century, and its production demanded both fertile land and an abundant labor supply. Sugar plantations in central Mexico represent the origins of the classical Mexican hacienda (Chevalier, 1963). The means utilized by such land operations proved disastrous for the indigenous population. The conflict between a landed Spanish aristocracy and the peasantry represents a long-rooted historical process. This paper contends that the outcome of such conflicts had direct bearing on future patterns of peasant revolts.

Mexico's agrarian history can be described succinctly as a struggle between the large landed estates and the peasant communities (Whetten, 1948). According to Tannenbaum (1929: 7) the Spanish colonial system saw to it that "the best lands ... passed into large estates and the people upon them became bound serfs of the conquerors and their descendants." The process by which the institution of debt peonage developed to meet the needs of the hacendados began soon after the arrival of Cortez and had reached its highpoint on the eve of the 1910 Revolution. As previously stated, regional differences in Mexico played a significant part in the degree to which debt servitude became imposed on the peasantry. An analysis of the revolutionary potential of Mexico's peasantry during the early 1900s begins with an understanding of the relationship between peasant and hacendado as it was shaped by the process of the latter's encroachments and imposition of debt peonage on the peasantry.

In terms of geographical and regional differences, Mexico can be discussed within the context of its northern, central, or southern areas. In each section, geographical considerations stood as a background for the more significant social factor: the subordination of the Indian masses by the landed elite. Beginning with the Spanish conquest, this struggle helped to shape the agrarian structure of the country. On the one hand, a system of tightly knit freeholding peasant villages existed primarily in central Mexico. These villages sought to maintain their autonomy from the hacendados. In contrast, land encroachments by the hacendados proved victorious against the nomadic Indians of the north and the village dwelling Mayan Indians of the South. In both of these regions, debt servitude and with it peasant dependence on the landed class developed.

The hacendados' need for increased land equaled their demand for a reliable and large labor supply. The freeholding peasant village posed a serious threat. As long as the peasantry remained within the realm of their village communities, they constituted a reservoir of untapped labor. Even when village-based peasants were forced to take part-time or seasonal work on the haciendas, the regularity of their labor could not be guaranteed. For the hacendados, the profitability of their operations demanded a resident labor pool. Debt servitude developed side by side with the growth of such estates.

Tannenbaum (1950) describes the conflict between peasants and hacendados in terms of a clash between communal and individualistic ideas of land ownership. Mexico's hacienda system originated directly from the destruction of preexisting villages, a destruction triggered by an expanding export-oriented agricultural system. The nature of the agricultural requirements of such items as sugar and henequen resulted in the concentration of the hacienda system in central and southern Mexico. The arid and mountainous North assumed importance primarily as a cattle raising and mining extraction zone with few labor demands. Hacendados in southern and parts of central Mexico solved their labor demands by creating a resident labor force. Contrary to the conditions found within a freeholding village where peasants controlled their land by a system of communal rights and privileges, the indebted servant resembled a near feudal vassal of the landowners (Wolf, 1969).

By various mechanisms, peasants were systematically driven from their villages to the haciendas where they became exposed to a vicious cycle of debt. As a result of substandard wages, these peasants were forced to ask for pay advances from their overlords that were to be paid back at high interest rates. This inevitably led the peasants to obtain more advances merely to secure the necessary interest (Brinsmade, 1916; McBride, 1923). Such a system tied the peasant to the hacienda, and thus the hacendado solved his labor problems. Southern Mexico, an area of henequen production, became notorious for its imposition of debt peonage (Turner, 1911; Katz, 1974).

In addition to the system of indebtedness, repressive police measures kept the peasants living on haciendas securely under the control of the landowners. Vigilance over the peasants was constant and repression came swiftly and effectively. The use of government armed forces to protect the interests of the landed class emerges throughout Mexico's agrarian history. During the Díaz regime such an alliance was greatly strengthened. Debt servitude stripped the peasantry of their land and destroyed their network of village organization. The development of successful repressive control mechanisms kept such peasants from rebelling although exploitation was intense.

Land encroachments on peasant communities by hacendados reached their peak during the eighteenth century (Chevalier, 1963). During this period the large estates consolidated their holdings and received legal recognition from the Spanish Crown. The majority of peasants became a permanent resident labor force under the domination of the landed elite. While the Catholic Church had once rallied to protect the peasantry, the eighteenth and nineteenth centuries revealed a close alliance between Church and landed aristocracy. Despite the nineteenth century Independence movement, Mexico's land system witnessed few changes. The transition from colony to statehood did little to alter the structural relationship between hacendado and peasant except perhaps that the former was from then on predominantly of Criollo origin rather than of Spanish (Stein and Stein, 1970).

Although land seizures in Mexico intensified during the nineteenth century, pockets of freeholding village communities managed to survive. In the isolated, mountainous regions of central and some parts of southern Mexico, peasants warded off the onslaughts of the hacendados. An analysis of these village communities will illustrate why such areas proved to be potential locations for peasant insurrections during the 1900s.

Two essential characteristics distinguished those peasants residing in freeholding village communities from those reduced to debt servitude. First of all, village peasants continued to have access to plots of land which they worked and over which the community held jurisdiction. Such land could not be sold; it was held in perpetuity by the entire community. The village structure provided an organizational network with which to handle village business. As such, village peasants exhibited significant amounts of solidarity as all were interconnected by the village's decision-making process (Tannenbaum, 1929). Second, the isolated location of the majority of these peasant enclaves served to guarantee their autonomy from the landed elite. The retention of their native Indian language further illustrates the peasantry's isolation from the world of the Spanish-speaking hacendados. Peasant solidarity, therefore, continued as long as the hacendados remained outside the village organizational and territorial network. Wolf (1969) refers to such peasant village structures as providing the internal leverages that were instrumental in the development of revolts. Peasants could employ the organizational capacities that the freeholding village structure provided, and they could transform it, when land encroachments threatened them, into a basis for revolutionary action. A strong relationship has been established between areas characterized by freeholding peasant communities and revolutionary uprisings (Tannenbaum, 1929; Parkes, 1950; Katz, 1974). As Chevalier (1963: 220) states: "In the 20th century, these same communities [freeholding villages] were to supply, to a much greater extent than peons and other estate dwellers, the revolutionaries who would destroy the hacienda."

During the Díaz dictatorship, the peasant village communities experienced intense and sustained attacks. Such pressures, however, did not in themselves prove completely responsible for the peasant uprisings located primarily in central Mexico. Attention needs to be focused on the national and international factors which accentuated the structural weaknesses of the Díaz state. An immediate result of such deteriorations was the temporary relaxation of the repressive forces being used against the peasants which provided a climate conducive to the rise of peasant revolts.

Structural Characteristics of the Díaz Regime, 1876-1911

Mexico emerged from its colonial status into nationhood maintaining nearly intact its highly complex system of social stratification. The Independence period brought a change at the elite level of the social hierarchy rather than one involving the entire social system. An account of those groups which supported the Díaz regime provides an overview of the country's class structure. Such cleavages became an important part of the process that culminated in the revolutionary conflict of 1910.

The social legacy of Mexico as a postcolonial society consisted in the continuation of a social system dominated by a small elite. Factional strife and disunity within this elite group led to the development of strong regional "oligarchies." As a result, the country became characterized by a weak "national" government. During the fifty years after Mexican independence, for example, thirty different men served as president (Cumberland, 1968). Porfirio Díaz set out to forge a strong executive in an attempt to overcome such a political situation. His policies directed at the various elite factions involved appeasement measures rather than consolidation ones. Consequently, the weakness of the Mexican state persisted. With a dictator at the head of the government, a façade of political stability masked many unresolved political conflicts (Stein and Stein, 1970).

Beginning with his rise to power in 1876, Díaz attempted to form a coalition government composed of representatives from the various factional sectors within the elite class. His slogan of *pan o palo* (bread or the club) represented his political philosophy whereby various groups such as the clergy, hacendados, top military personnel and foreign capitalists were persuaded to give support to his regime. In return, the government gave concessions to these groups (Parkes, 1950). Díaz thus established a chain of patron-client relations between his regime and the dominant social classes of Mexican society. Without really integrating the various competing forces, Díaz managed to consolidate sufficient power to maintain his dictatorial position. Díaz proved to be quite effective in playing these social groups against each other and thereby preventing them from uniting to challenge his hegemony (Priestley, 1923; Callcott, 1931; Calvert, 1968). To further assure his control over the state, Díaz adopted several policies to alter the state machinery for his benefit. One measure in particular—the building of a national standing army—had direct influence on the one social group towards which Díaz made no conciliatory overtures: the peasantry.

A major drawback of previous analyses of the Mexican peasantry and their participation in the Mexican Revolution has been a failure to identify the relationship between the government's repressive capabilities and the development of such insurrections. Skocpol (1978) places strong emphasis on such a relationship. By examining the repressive power of the Díaz regime, both the possibility for and the nature of Mexican peasant revolts come into historical perspective. It will be seen that as the regime's repressive might weakened due to the development of various crises, peasants in those areas most likely to revolt took advantage of the situation and actually revolted.

Two main factors contributed to the strengthening of a national army by Díaz: his alliance with the landowning class and his own modernization policy. To begin with, the hacendados' identification with the country's conservative element dated from as far back as the Independence era. Díaz started a movement towards the centralization of state authority and renewed an alliance with the Church, an alliance that had been severed since the Reform period under Juárez. Such measures gained the support of the majority of the landed class. As the regime's conservatism increased, so did the moral, and more importantly, the financial support of the hacendados (Cumberland, 1952; Brandenburg, 1964). In return, Díaz utilized such financial resources to build a strong but not independent army. Díaz clearly wanted to avoid the rise of an army with the potential to overthrow him. Through a carefully executed system of bribes and coercion, he managed to maintain strict control of his military machine. Time after time, this repressive force represented the might behind the landowners' claims to peasant lands. The most blatant example of the swift repressive capabilities of the army can be seen in the treatment of the Yaqui Indians during the late 1800s. Their near extermination and their eventual mass deportation from their lands in northern Mexico to the plantations of the South is a testimony to the application of government force, a force repeatedly used to solidify the hacendados' domination vis-à-vis the peasants (Turner, 1911; Callcott, 1931; Parkes, 1950; Hu-Dehart, 1974).

A second impetus for the expansion of the armed forces stemmed from Díaz's views concerning the course to be set for the modernization of Mexico. The Díaz regime developed a systematic policy to deal with the Indian peasantry and their relationship to its efforts to bring "progress" to the country. Such a policy was refined by Díaz's clique of followers called the "científicos" (the scientists), a group of scientific positivists (Wolf, 1969). Bankers, industrialists, rentiers and other upper class elements combined to form this group (Herzog, 1959). According to the científicos, the Indian peasant masses were inferior and thus incapable of "progressing." Mexico's future development demanded, then, a reduction if not the complete obliteration of this population (Herzog, 1959; Chevalier, 1960; Wolf, 1969). According to White (1969: 113), the científicos "maintained that economic development would be accomplished only by Creole control and preventing political participation by the illiterate masses." By 1879, only two years after Díaz was in office, the federal army had already established its notoriety for its suppression of the peasantry (Hart, 1978). In summary, the Díaz regime used the army to stifle any outbursts that occurred among peasants and, more significantly, served as an inhibiting force against the formation of future revolts.

The Díaz State and the World Economy

The period between 1876 and 1911 represented a major shift in Mexican economic life. The world capitalist economy experienced a dynamic expansion; Mexico became a part of such an expansion as its mines, particularly those in northern Mexico, began to serve as key suppliers of gold, silver, lead and copper. Cotton, leather, henequen, and meat—all represented export items that were demanded in the capitalist centers. A review of the regime's policy of industrialization from above and abroad will show that the peasants were not the only group to be excluded from the locus of power. The native Mexican bourgeoisie whose ranks had been increasing since the latter part of the nineteenth century felt restricted, if not totally excluded, from the state's plan for national development. Díaz and his group of científicos aimed to present Mexico as an ideal environment for foreign, particularly American, business enterprises. Through the Díaz policy of "desarrollo hacia afuera" (externally-oriented development), foreign penetration of the Mexican economy proceeded at a rapid rate during the entire span of the dictatorship.

Porfirian peace represented one of the conditions for increasing the amount of foreign investments entering Mexico. The early years of the Díaz period witnessed conditions that included abundant but uncultivated arable land and large amounts of untapped mineral resources. By 1877 state activity began to promote foreign investments in such areas as mining, railroads, oil, and agriculture. The state elite set out to create the economic infrastructure that would provide a support system for foreign enterprises. The extractive industries, export crops, and manufacturing led in the expansion of the Mexican economy (Reynolds, 1970: 27). Between 1877 and 1910 the value of Mexican exports increased over 600% in real terms. In addition, Mexican exports reached such a level of diversification that in 1904 gold and silver accounted for less than 50% of all export earnings (Hansen, 1971: 14-15).

The Díaz state elite set out to create the "peace" necessary in order to make Mexico a "modern" Latin American country. Such development depended on the succesful economic expansion of key sectors to which the state aimed to attract large scale foreign capital. Such investments included mining, railroad construction, public utilities, banking, and textiles (Wright, 1971: 53). Estimates concerning total foreign investments vary, but one study indicates that it stood at $1.7 billion in American currency. Of this amount, $646 million came from the United States, $494 million came from England, and $454 million came from France. France, however, led in indirect foreign investments, sending close to $165 million into the Mexican economy (Wright, 1971: 54).

Hansen (1971: 16) further documents the predominance of American foreign investments (38 percent). Railroads and mining represent those areas in which American capital was most heavily concentrated. American investments accounted for over 47 percent of all foreign capital in railroad construction and 61 percent in mining. Some of the major mining concerns in Mexico included the American Smelting and Refining Company of the Guggenheims and the Cananea Consolidated Copper Company. When taken together, railroads and mining accounted for almost 80 percent of all American investments in Mexico, 41.3 percent and 38.6 percent respectively (Hansen, 1971: 17).

France provided Mexico with the majority of capital to begin a commercial banking system. Over 60 percent of all investments in Mexican banking came from France. Much of this capital came from French families living in Mexico since the early 1800s. Their capital provided banking services to foreign investors in export-oriented activities. Mexicans, generally speaking, were unwilling to provide the capital for this system and also were unwilling to incur the potential risks associated with such ventures. As a result, the French moved in quickly and filled such a vacuum (Hansen, 1971: 16).

England's investments concentrated primarily in the area of public services; 89 percent of the total foreign investments in Mexico were controlled by England. In addition, England expanded its interests in Mexican oil. Close to 55 percent of all foreign investments in oil remained under British control (Hansen, 1971: 16). When the total British investment in Mexico is analyzed, railroad construction emerges on top; 40.6 percent of all British investment in Mexico was tied to the railroads. As Wright (1971: 53) concludes:

> Whatever the actual figures, it appears that by the end of the Díaz era foreigners probably owned over half the total wealth of the country

and the foreign capital dominated every area of productive enterprise except agriculture and the handicraft industries.

Statistics for the major foreign investment concerns in Mexico lead, then, to two general conclusions. First, Mexican exports exceeded imports. Between 1905 and 1906, exports exceeded imports by more than $30 million. Another $24 million left the country as a result of the railroad industry. Mexico had to pay close to $4 million to pay bank dividends primarily to the Bank of London. Exports represented a flight of domestic capital to pay for the creation of an infrastructure. Díaz's financial wizard Limantour continued, however, to praise the benefits accruing to Mexico as a result of all this foreign investment (Wright, 1971: 53-59). This leads to a second major conclusion regarding foreign investment. The immediate effect of such policies whereby the Díaz state favored foreign interests produced an increasingly dissatisfied middle class. This middle class viewed themselves as a marginal class within Porfirian Mexico. The conflict between this Mexican bourgeoisie and the Díaz state increased as foreign business ventures continued to receive preferential treatment. The bourgeoisie found itself handicapped by the competition with foreign investors. It would be this group that led in the overthrow of the old regime and thus the peasants that would eventually revolt found themselves in alliance, at least temporarily, with the dissatisfied Mexican middle class. Such an alliance helped to shape the outcome of peasant revolts.

Final Collapse of the Díaz State

The Díaz regime experienced a variety of conflicts throughout its rule, but prior to the turn of the century such disturbances had been checked. From about 1900 to the dictatorship's overthrow in 1911 the Mexican state proved incapable of dealing with its problems. Outward appearances of national development spearheaded by the aging dictator began to give way revealing unresolved conflicts (Quirk, 1960). With the intensification of such crises, the state's repressive machinery weakened, allowing various dissenting sectors within Mexican society to crystallize. Before analyzing the agrarian sector's response to such a situation, several other main factors contributing to the near total collapse of the state will be reviewed. Emphasis will be placed on the world-historical conditions leading to the demise of the Díaz political apparatus. This paper asserts that many national crises were a consequence of developments of the international world scene. A need exists to examine political development by "placing the experience of specific areas squarely within the larger international processes which help to create that experience. [In this way] they avoid the characteristic weakness of the 'political development' literature: the treatment of each country as a separate, self-contained, more or less autonomous case" (Tilly, 1975: 627).

In analyzing the sources of conflict within Latin American societies, Wolf (1969) emphasizes both the colonial legacy and the effects produced by the extension of American capitalism. Wolf argues that a causal relationship exists between the spread of capitalism and agrarian revolutions. The spread and intensification of capitalism in Mexico did in fact precede the peasant movement but it did not directly cause its development. Rather than adopt a deterministic approach as Wolf does, this paper will argue that Mexico, as a country occupying a subordinate position in a world economy, experienced internal problems attributable to this very position. The financial problems plaguing the Díaz regime, therefore, were not primarily produced by its widespread corruption and inefficient operations. These contributed but did not cause its demise in and of themselves. The economic difficulties crippling the state resulted from developments taking place at the international economic level. Such crises served to weaken the state and its ability to maintain coercive sanctions. It was this, then, that facilitated the rise of agrarian insurrections.

Twentieth-century Mexico functioned as a supplier of raw materials for the dominant capitalist countries, particularly the United States. Such financial problems as an overall decline in agricultural production, a rise in prices and a stationary or declining wage level—all intensified between 1900 and 1911 (Wolf, 1969). A look at Mexico's trade patterns with the United States illustrates the economic problems that result for a country containing major sectors functioning as export zones.

During the period between 1880 and 1910, American capitalism expanded by incorporating the southern and western regions of the United States as suppliers of agricultural and mining resources for the northeastern industrial centers. Mexico became included in this expansion as its northern mines served as important sources of gold, silver, lead, and copper. Other export items included cotton, leather, and meat. American exports to Mexico rose dramatically and consisted primarily of manufactured goods such as machinery for mining operations. The nature of the export-import trade relations clearly became a source for Mexico's economic difficulties (García,

1976). Cumberland (1968) links the downward trend in all staples production between 1877 and 1910 to the concentration by Mexican agricultural enterprises on the production of noncomestibles such as henequen. The worldwide increase in the demand for henequen directly contributed to the destruction of the Mexican cattle industry as henequen plantations expanded. With the crisis in the cattle industry—a major source of domestic food—food prices in Mexico spiraled while wages remained constant (Cockcroft, 1968). Daily wages for the total population in Mexico (in pesos) for the years 1895, 1900, 1905 and 1910 were .34, .33, .34 and .28, respectively. In the same years agricultural workers received even less: .33, .31, .31 and .25. The decrease between 1905 and 1910 should be noted (Estadísticas Económicas del Porfiriato, 1965).

Such economic conditions led to conflicts between various social sectors and the Díaz regime. The middle classes increased their accusations against the Díaz state for fostering foreign concerns. The Mexican bourgeoisie continued to find itself economically stifled by such policies.

Mexico suffered further economic crises in addition to those directly related to the agricultural sector. International monetary problems became severely felt within the Mexican financial structure. Such problems added to the deterioration of the state. Throughout the years of the dictatorship, Díaz had attempted to initiate policies to keep pace with the world monetary standards. With silver as its leading export, the country's money remained based on it. Worldwide silver prices began to fall in the 1880s, reaching the bottom level in 1893 with the demonetization of silver by the United States. With the steady devaluation of the peso, the Díaz government decided to change to the gold standard in 1905. Such a measure proved disastrous. Widespread bank speculations, a decline in the amount of money available for circulation, increases in unpayable debts—all combined to paralyze the Mexican economy. The effects of these conditions were soon felt as the state continued to lose support from previous backers, such as bankers, hacendados, and even the army. The American economic depression of 1907 added to the intensity of the fiscal problems rampant in Mexico (Manero, 1911; McCaleb, 1921; Cumberland, 1952). By 1908 the Mexican bourgeoisie found itself "allied" with some previously pro-Díaz groups. According to Cumberland (1952: 27): "Many of those who turned against the Díaz administration... did so because they detected weaknesses in his government rather than because they opposed the principles on which he stood." Such underlying foundations of the anti-Díaz forces that produced the Revolution were to prove disastrous for the rural sector that joined in rebellion against the regime.

A final contributing factor in the collapse of the Díaz state involves the development of a permissive attitude by the United States regarding the formation of anti-Díaz forces. Prior to 1910, the United States government indicated its favorable attitude towards the Díaz regime. The early 1900s witnessed strikes in several mining centers in Mexico: Cananea, Sonora, Río Blanco. Federal troops relied heavily on the American cavalry's assistance in suppressing these outbursts. American business interests, fearful of economic losses from production slowdowns in the mines, succeeded in exerting pressure on the government to see to it that large detachments of United States forces became stationed along the Mexican border (Cockcroft, 1965; Hart, 1978).

By 1910, however, conditions reversed themselves. A growing uneasiness began to develop among Americans with business concerns in Mexico. The last decade of the Díaz regime coincided with the ascendancy of the United States as a global power. The effect on Mexico, as well as other Latin American countries, was that United States economic interests became more intense and more aggressive. American oil interests felt that the Mexican government in 1909 was starting to favor European business interests. The widespread disillusionment with the Díaz state increased as anti-Japanese hysteria developed in the United States at the end of the Russo-Japanese war. Government officials and businessmen alike feared a Japanese-Mexican alliance under the Díaz regime. Failure to renew the lease of a United States coaling station in Baja California gave support to these fears. As a result, American policy reversed itself; it proceeded to give asylum to anti-Díaz forces, allowing them to establish bases in the United States to launch their attacks against Díaz. More importantly, the United States withdrew its military support of the Díaz state; American troops along the Mexican border began to be recalled (Brandenburg, 1964; Calvert, 1968). Throughout the revolutionary period, American military support, or the lack of it, proved critical in the success or the failure of any given revolutionary group. As will be pointed out later, the peasantry failed to ever benefit from such aid; they became the targets for American-supplied arms in the hands of various anti-Díaz forces.

Peasant Revolts During the Mexican Revolution

The structural weaknesses experienced by the Díaz regime, produced by a combination of national and international pressures, provided a background for the development of peasant revolts. As elements of the various social groups—middle class, hacendados, urban workers—crystallized into opposition factions against the state, the latter struggled to maintain its monopoly of power. To do so, the Díaz regime began to spread thin its repressive forces as it took on the task of suppressing dissent from its one-time supporters. Peasant rebellions developed then as: 1) the state relaxed its coercive powers and 2) attacks against surviving freeholding villages reached more intense levels than ever before. Such attacks were directed at those pockets of freeholding villages that demonstrated the organizational capacity to revolt.

The intensification of peasant land encroachments during the Díaz era reveals two concurrent processes. First, this period of Mexican history witnessed the most complete overlapping of state and landowners' interests. Second, given the existing agrarian structure of the 1900s, land seizures concentrated on Mexico's central area and thus produced unforeseen consequences: peasant mobilization. Although attacks on peasant lands can be traced back for centuries (Tannenbaum, 1933), the Díaz regime developed a national policy aimed at setting the country on the road to "progress." Díaz and his advisors formulated such a plan by using an already accepted anti-Indian sentiment to legitimize land takeovers in the name of progress. The hacendados' desires to increase their land holdings directly aided Díaz's plan for national development (Womack, 1968). Both were a direct answer to the international demand for increased sugar and henequen production: enterprises calling for large amounts of land (Katz, 1974). Díaz manipulated the Reform Laws drawn up by Juárez (1867-1872) to assure the legality of his actions. These statutes were intended, in the then widespread spirit of national anticlericalism, to reduce Church power by undermining its primary source: extensive land holdings. The Leyes de Reforma which under Juárez prohibited corporate holdings were now applied even more vigorously against peasant communal holdings. The Ley de Desmortización (Expropriation) was enforced, making compulsory the division of lands within villages. As a result, the destruction of common land ownership among the peasantry proceeded at an accelerated pace. It is estimated that during the Díaz regime more than two million acres were converted from Indian communities to private hands (Tannenbaum, 1933). Wolf (1969) points out that the Reform Laws had the goal of establishing a middle class through the expropriation of Church lands. The Díaz government used these to strengthen an already powerful landed oligarchy in exchange for its support. Such measures by the Díaz state led to: 1) the transformation of public lands to private use by the hacendados and 2) the removal of peasants from their village communities (MacLean, 1957).

At the time that this national policy began to be implemented, Mexico's agrarian structure continued to reveal significant regional differences. These variations played a critical role in the implementation of the state's land policies. This paper's historical account of the agrarian structure of prerevolutionary Mexico will be augmented by a description of rural conditions during the Díaz dictatorship.

Some statistics on the conditions of Mexico's peasants will illustrate the success with which the landed aristocracy had transformed agrarian patterns to their benefit. By 1910, 1 percent of Mexico's population owned 97 percent of the country's land (MacLean, 1959). Stated differently, fewer than 2,700 families controlled more than one-half of the total land area (Tannenbaum, 1933). As a result, the great majority of Mexico's rural population was landless in 1910 (Whetten, 1948; Parkes, 1950). Stein and Kahl (1968) estimate that close to 80 percent of the population had no land. Southern Mexico comprised that region where such land ownership patterns reached the greatest levels of inequality in distribution. Debt servitude existed on large-scale plantations in this region long before the 1900s. The Díaz government allowed this system to expand. By the time of the Revolution, southern Mexico maintained an agrarian structure based on the coercive system of debt peonage and as such land expansion policies were aimed elsewhere: central Mexico.

Before describing the twentieth century conflict between hacendados and peasants in this region, a brief review of conditions in northern Mexico will serve as a contrast. As mentioned earlier, this part of the country assumed importance primarily as a cattle raising and mining region. Its labor conditions differentiated it from both the southern and central regions. Although large estates similar to southern plantations characterized this area, the existence of nomadic versus village dwelling peasants accounts for the failure of debt peonage to take hold. Large numbers of peasants managed to become sharecroppers or wage laborers. The cattle industry produced the *vaquero* type of rural worker: the cowboy. Having no land ties, this "peasant" cowboy reacted quite differently in response to government policies under Díaz. The struggle between hacendado and the northern rural class was further influenced by the proximity of the U.S. border. Having some degree of mobility, the northern cowboy could often escape conflicts by crossing the Río Grande River. Another alternative was to remain and fight. Such resistance increased during the Mexican Revolution as economic conditions in the U.S. temporarily restricted Mexican immigration. The core of Pancho Villa's "cavalry" of peasants consisted of vaqueros with little land ties who opposed the Díaz state as strongly as their central Mexico counterparts (Wolf, 1969; Goldfrank, 1976). The structural characteristics of each area resulted in different types of rebellion and as will be stressed made alliances between the two groups all but impossible.

With southern Mexico already characterized by hacendado domination and northern Mexico constrained by geographical and social factors, the central region experienced the most powerful attacks by the landowning class in liaison with state forces. Within the central area of Mexico, freeholding peasant villages continued to exist. Such states as Morelos, Mexico, Puebla, Tlaxcala and Guerrero contained higher percentages of their rural population residing in free villages than other states (White, 1969). Although sugar production had been prominent in these states for over a hundred years, it was not until the late 1890s and the early 1900s that international pressures forced the Mexican sugar planters to expand their holdings (Wolf, 1969; Katz, 1974; Goldfrank, 1976). Freeholding villages represented an obstacle to the profit-making enterprises of the hacendados. Between 1908 and 1909 the seventeen main hacendados in one central state, Morelos, produced 52,000,000 kilograms of sugar (McNeely, 1966). Thirty haciendas owned 62% of this state's land (Millon, 1969). The introduction of new expensive sugar refining installations from abroad increased the demand for land. As Womack (1968: 40) points out: "to keep their expensive machines at work, planters needed to grow still more cane—which obliged them to enlarge their landholdings further." The hacendados, thus, began a full-scale campaign to destroy the freeholding villages. Coexistence between a newly modernizing system of sugar production and the communal peasant village inevitably led to protracted conflict in which the former proved victorious over the latter (Whetten, 1948; Coatsworth, 1970; Waterbury, 1975). Such a victory did not come easily. Attacks on peasant landholdings were to be met with resistance. Such villages "ultimately made the social revolution [of 1910] in self defense, rather than become reduced to the same conditions as Indians in other parts of Mexico" (Tannenbaum, 1933: 164).

It is beyond the scope of this paper to deal with the general process and course taken by the Mexican Revolution. The relationship between the peasants that revolted and the other competing revolutionary groups from Madero to Obregón will follow. This paper contends that with the overthrow of Díaz, various political factions struggled against each other in an effort to consolidate sufficient power to direct and shape the rebuilding of the Mexican state. During the years following Díaz's exile in 1911, these groups alternately vied for the support of the peasantry. Relations between peasants and other groups in society have been characterized by the latter's attempts "to soothe the peasants rather than encourage their demands for strong reform measures" (Huizer, 1979: 51). When peasant coalitions could not be formed, or more commonly, when newly formed ones proved no longer necessary to the dominant classes, contenders for state power renewed "Díaz-like" repressive measures against the peasants. Appeasement proved, then, to be a precursor for coercive tactics in subduing peasant uprisings throughout the revolutionary period.

With the outbreak of revolution and the initial attempts by the Díaz government to contain Madero and his followers, peasant uprisings began to develop in central Mexico, particularly in Morelos, home of the most well-known peasant figure, Emiliano Zapata. The regional character of peasant uprisings and its consequences will be dealt with in the next section. A summary of the interaction between Madero and Zapata will first provide an example of the general relationship between urban anti-Díaz forces and the peasantry.

Madero represented the interests of the middle class element in Mexican society that opposed the Díaz dictatorship. This faction viewed as primary the issue of political reform from a corrupt Díaz state to a liberal bourgeois one. To achieve such a transition, the Madero group of liberals believed that a peasant alliance would enable them to emerge as the winner among competing forces on the Mexican political scene. As long as peasants remained outside their camp such consolidation was believed to be impossible (Cumberland, 1952; Callcott, 1963). Although the Madero camp attempted to issue proclamations in support of agrarian demands for land, these remained of little significance. The majority of the middle class opposed the land reforms demanded by the rebelling peasants

(Whetten, 1948; Quirk, 1960; Womack, 1968). As such, the driving force behind the pattern of relations between these two anti-Díaz groups was one of appeasement. The Madero camp adopted an agrarian program as a means to conciliate the peasants (Herzog, 1960). Once such measures failed, Madero used the still intact Díaz army to overwhelm them. Consequently, the Madero faction joined the other contending groups—conservatives, hacendados, top level army men and remnants of Díaz's científicos—to overpower the peasantry (Millon, 1969). Madero and his group ultimately made a trade-off with these elements of the Díaz regime in a futile attempt to consolidate their takeover of state power (Cockcroft, 1968).

Subsequent political factions—Huerta, Carranza, Obregón—struggled to gain a monopoly of power; the peasantry continued to serve as a constraining force in this process. Whichever faction managed to gain control of state power, for whatever length of time, found itself forced to contend with the peasants and their demands. Under the leadership of Huerta, the Church, army, and hacendados proceeded to subdue the peasantry. Carranza's more moderate forces tried, as had Madero, to weaken the peasantry by "implementing" agrarian reforms (Huizer and Stavenhagen, 1973).

Two immediate results developed. First of all, peasant uprisings were eventually contained. Despite the early advances of their "armies," their strength rapidly diminished. Guerrilla tactics eventually became the only means available to them. Such tactics proved unsuccessful against a national army. Second, little land distribution took place, as only lip service was paid to the issue of agrarian reforms (Cockcroft, 1968). The destruction of the hacienda followed only after years from the onset of the Revolution (Chevalier, 1960; Millon, 1966).

In addition to the restraints incurred by the relationship between peasantry and other anti-Díaz forces, other factors contributed to the limitations placed on peasant revolts. One factor was an external one; the other, an internal one. The survival of a nearly intact army posed the major external threat to a rebellious peasantry. Within the peasantry, the internal problems of organization and regionalism added to the eventual containment of rural uprisings.

The early weakening of the army's strength can be explained largely in terms of the dictatorship's faltering attempts to suppress the initial outbreaks of revolt. A crisis of leadership rather than one of strength produced a temporary respite from the armed intervention by the state against the peasantry. Throughout the revolutionary period, the Mexican army stayed intact and represented a potential means for the competing factions to consolidate their power. Like the peasantry, the army became subject to the courtship by one group after another. Madero's decision to maintain the largely pro-Díaz army in order to protect his interim government played an ironic trick on him. Although the Madero-controlled army proved quite effective in disarming Zapata's forces, it also played a significant role in Madero's overthrow (Cumberland, 1952; Calvert, 1968; Cockcroft, 1968). The following revolutionary period produced an even stronger army as the hacendados and the Church collaborated behind Huerta, a militaryman (Callcott, 1931). The army's strength is best understood by pointing out that it took the combined efforts of American intervention and the forces supporting Carrranza to oust Huerta (Cline, 1953; Brown, 1969). Carranza's attempts to transform an army still permeated with "old regime" elements proved ineffective, as once again, a strong military leader, Obregón, successfully led the army to oust Carranza (Callcott, 1931). The consequences for the peasantry stemming from the rivalry between groups supporting or being supported by the army was their movement's continued suppression. Not only did the army remain a cohesive force but also various groups used it to crush peasant revolts that they viewed as threats. A main hypothesis presented by Chorley (1973) states that the success of rebel forces depends to a large extent on the development of circumstances that prevent that army from using full resources. In Mexico, the survival of an intact army represented a major factor in the defeat of the peasantry (Brandenburg, 1964; Womack, 1968).

Two characteristics of Mexico's peasant revolts added, in combination to the military suppression, to their dissolution. The peasant movement lacked a long-range organizational framework. As discussed before, given the agrarian structure, peasant uprisings remained limited to the central area of Mexico and some parts of the North. The organizational skills acquired from participation in village communities proved inadequate in dealing with the demands of a revolutionary situation. Ironically, the same factors instrumental in producing the initial peasant revolts—isolation and autonomy of their villages from hacendados domination—developed into an inhibiting factor. That is, freeholding villages as independent entities remained localized in their particular area. The peasant movement never succeeded in becoming a widespread national force (Wolf, 1969). Chorley (1973: 40) vividly summarizes the strengths, and, more importantly, the weaknesses of mass uprisings similar to Mexico's peasant movement. The mass uprising

... throws itself blindly against the regime which it holds responsible for its sufferings. It commands volumes of violent support which a planned revolt can probably seldom obtain and it goes forward by the sheer impetus of its own tremendous weight ... It has the qualities of the rising floodtide or the mountain avalanche. At the same time it has their defects. The tide turns from flow to ebb and the avalanche expends itself perhaps before any object of real importance has been swept out of its track.

A second characteristic closely related to the limitation imposed by a lack of organizational skill involves the type of issues stressed by the peasantry. As stated previously, freeholding villages mobilized around their concern over land encroachments. The restoration of those lands taken by the hacendados assumed primacy in the goals of the peasant movement. Differential attitudes over the land question prevented alliances between peasants from central Mexico and those from the North. Villa's peasant forces lacked ties to the land. Although his forces did in fact confiscate large tracts of hacendado-owned land, little redistribution took place. On the other hand, Zapata's forces viewed redistribution as essential to their cause. A temporary alliance between the two peasant groups developed only as a result of their mutual distrust of Carranza (Tannenbaum, 1933).

Closely related to the limitation imposed by peasant regionalism was their lack of ability to gain foreign support. A crucial factor in determining the strength of a given revolutionary group involved the extent to which foreign, especially American, supplies could be relied on. Madero depended on the U.S. for both arms and temporary asylum. Wilson's approval of armed intervention at the Mexican port of Veracruz in 1914 directly aided Carranza as it blocked Huerta's forces from receiving German supplies. Furthermore, the Wilson administration's recognition of Carranza practically guaranteed their victory over both Villa and Zapata. The latter were held in low esteem by the U.S. government and as such failed to ever be considered as a recipient of U.S. support (Wolf, 1969). Extreme regionalism, insufficient organizational capabilities and the constant battle fought against them by a superior national army—all led to the disintegration of the peasant movement during the Mexican Revolution. Nevertheless the peasantry did make its impact felt on the course of the revolution and its outcome.

Impact of Peasant Revolts on the Outcome of the Mexican Revolution

As Skocpol (1978) points out, the timing and nature of peasant revolts form an important part of the analysis of any social revolution's outcome. In the Mexican case, both the structural limitations imposed on the peasantry and their relationship with other social groups played a crucial role in determining when and where revolts took place and consequently what shape they took. A central thesis of this paper has been that the survival of freeholding villages became a principal factor in the development of peasant revolts. That these existed in only a specific geographical area in Mexico by the early 1900s proved to be a major drawback. From the beginning, those peasants with the greatest potential to revolt, given other structural and historical configurations, experienced one overwhelming handicap: regionalism. Although many claims are made about the significance of a revolutionary ideology and its role as a mobilizing element (Hart, 1978), the Mexican case stands as a clear illustration that under certain structural conditions peasants remain outside the realm of organized action. Even if the various proclamations issued by the peasants, especially Zapata, had reached the mass group of peasants throughout Mexico, the condition of debt peonage under which most lived constituted a strong inhibitor to collective action. In this way, the peasant revolts that did occur, remained localized; widespread peasant mobilization failed to materialize during the Mexican Revolution. This, in turn, contributed to the type of land redistribution, or rather the lack of it, that developed during and after the course of the Revolution.

Since peasant uprisings never ripened into widespread phenomena, the process of land distribution stayed in the hands of those competing political factions attempting to control state power. Inasmuch as these groups had to come to terms with the peasantry—either by winning their support or subduing them—early land reform policies represented placatory measures. In those areas where groups of peasants had succeeded in taking over some haciendas and redistributing land, such as in Morelos, the national army moved in quickly to "undo" such agrarian reforms and prevent further action. The central government concentrated on pacifying the central area's peasantry for it was there that rural developments posed the most serious threat. Those groups controlling the state firmly believed in the disruptive capacity of Zapata's peasant army, and so, in an effort to circumvent it, they began to initiate land reforms themselves. While the Mexican peasantry never achieved the power to direct this process, their uprisings, though sporadic and limited, exerted sufficient pressure to impose the adoption of some agrarian legislation from above (Whetten, 1948; Chevalier, 1967; Huizer and Stavenhagen, 1970). Most of those laws passed from 1915 on proved to be ineffective due to the state's lack of commitment regarding their implementation. Such legislation, however, became an important basis for agrarian reforms formulated in later years, particularly during the Cárdenas presidency of 1934-1940 (Padgett, 1966).

There is no denying that the Mexican Revolution produced important transformations in the country's agrarian structure. The change in Mexico's land system cannot simply be explained by examining the relationship between elites and peasants. In the long run, agrarian transformation developed as a consequence of various changes within the elite sector and their responses to a changing world economy. When discussing the land reform policies of this period, then, it should be kept in mind that such a process was always part of a larger one which will not be dealt with in this paper. Of concern here is the type of "reform" initiated at the elite level in response to peasant uprisings.

The type of agrarian system that tried to replace the haciendas represented one whose aim was merely to appease the peasantry while insuring the economic and political survival of those groups running the national government. The agrarian measures initiated from above were not developed to create an equitable system of land ownership in Mexican society (González-Casanova, 1965; Stavenhagen, 1970). The peasantry emerged "free" from the haciendas's system of debt peonage but the subsequent conditions often proved nearly as intolerable.

Before describing the ejido system of land ownership, an additional characteristic of the nature of peasant demands needs to be examined. The limited nature of peasant demands for widespread land distribution became instrumental in allowing the central government to impose its own land program. Among those peasants that did revolt, the prevalent concern involved a return to their traditional village communities. The conflict between them and the hacendados revolved around the issue of confiscated peasant land. The demands did not usually contest the legality of property held "legitimately" by some hacendados. On the contrary, attacks against landowners who had not participated in recent land encroachments were rare. Peasant confiscations and expropriations concentrated on those property holders with a recent history of illegal takeovers (Chevalier, 1967). This characteristic of peasant demands partially explains why such limited reforms initiated by the state did not spark more peasant revolts. In addition, the state had managed by this time to regain almost total use of its repressive capabilities. The various revolutionary leaders in control of the central government proved to be astute politicians in dealing with peasant insurrections. Stein and Kahl (1968) point out that during the early years of the Revolution the land distributed by the government was concentrated in areas where peasant pressure was the most intense. The degree with which the Mexican government pursued agrarian reforms is seen by some as a direct reflection of the amount of pressure placed on it by the peasantry (Huizer and Stavenhagen, 1970).

The implementation of the ejido system represented a government measure, beginning with Carranza, to assure peasant stability. The latter Obregón government continued the use of land reform as a means for securing rural tranquility. As a system of communal land holdings, the ejido was to provide for peasant reclamation of usurped land. Ejidos allowed those peasants with legitimate claims to lands to begin working on them. Needless to say, the process of establishing such claims often involved a tedious, if not impossible, task.

By the end of 1926 less than 5 percent of the total rural population had been given ejidos. Less than 2,700 families owned more than one half of the privately owned lands. The amount of land transformed into ejidos by 1927 represented only 3.5 percent of the total land area of Mexico. Not surprisingly, data for the percentage of individual and state recipients of ejidos between 1915 and 1926 reveal that Morelos—the state in which the most intense revolts occurred— obtained the largest amount of land in the form of ejidos. Over 25 percent of the rural population of Morelos received land grants which represented close to 33 percent of the total area of the state (Tannenbaum, 1929). Clearly, land reform became a stabilizing mechanism. For the formerly rebellious peasant, the return of their land, even if it was in the form of small, unprofitable strips, served to foster a sense of "winning" tangible gains (Chevalier, 1967). A more realistic assessment of peasant "gains" indicates several inconsistencies. Ejido lands remained characteristically: 1) dependent on irrigation systems controlled by larger landowners, 2) limited to small properties, and 3) isolated in mountainous areas, past sites of original peasant villages. As such, the peasantry was maintained by the central government at the periphery of Mexican society.

Summary

In explaining the origins and significance of peasant revolts during the Mexican Revolution this paper has adopted a social-structural and political approach. the key variables included: 1) the agrarian structure and its relationship to peasant participation in mass action, 2) the repressive capabilities of the state used to maintain order and 3) the national and international crises which contributed to the attenuation of the state's coercive strength. An attempt was made to establish a relationship between the structural limitations placed on the peasants, the form in which their revolts developed, and the consequent response of other groups in Mexican society to such uprisings. Emphasis has been placed throughout the paper on examining peasant revolts within a larger sociohistorical framework. The case of a postcolonial society such as Mexico illustrates the need to place national developments within an international context. An analysis of the country's agrarian structure and its state political machinery remains incomplete without establishing a relationship between their present condition and their colonial legacy. It is in this respect that this study of Mexico's peasant movement of 1910 differs from most other accounts.

A study of Mexico's agrarian structure of 1910 strongly indicates that given the limited area in which peasant village communities existed, revolts failed to spread throughout the country. The majority of Mexico's rural population—landless, indebted peons—could not be mobilized to join those landowning peasants residing in autonomus villages against whom the hacendados struggled in an effort to expand their estates. More important than a revolutionary ideology, psychological feelings of strain or deprivation, or increasing exploitation, the Mexican village dwelling peasant exhibited the needed within-group solidarity and organizational skills that facilitated revolts as land encroachments threatened to destroy their communal life. As the Díaz state began to weaken, the peasants found themselves in the position to join together and rebel. The struggle among the various anti-Díaz forces to gain control of state power resulted in the initial appeasement and later repression of the peasantry as the Mexican Revolution progressed through the years.

ANTHROPOLOGY/SOCIOLOGY
UNIVERSITY OF SANTA CLARA

References

Alavi, Hamza. 1965. "Peasants and revolution." Pp. 241-77 in *The Socialist Register 1965*. London: The Merlin Press.

Beckford, George L. 1972. *Persistent Poverty*. New York: Oxford University.

Brandenburg, Frank. 1964. *The Making of Modern Mexico*. Englewood Cliffs, N.J.: Prentice-Hall.

Brinsmade, R.B. 1916. *El latifundismo mexicano*. México: Departamento de Imprenta de la Secretaría de Fomento.

Brown, Lyle C. 1969. "The politics of armed struggle in the Mexican revolution 1913-1915." Pp. 60-72 in James W. Wilkie and Albert L. Michaels (eds.), *Revolution in Mexico*. New York: Alfred A. Knopf.

Callcott, Wilfrid H. 1931. *Liberalism in Mexico 1857-1929*. Stanford: Stanford University Press.

Calvert, Peter. 1968. *The Mexican Revolution 1910-1914*. Cambridge: Cambridge University.

Casanova, Pablo González. 1965. *La democracia en México*. México: Serie Popular Era.

Chevalier, François. 1960. "Un factor decisivo de la revolución agraria de México: el levantamiento de Zapata." *Cuadernos Americanos* 6 (November-December), 165-187.

_____. 1963. *Land and Society in Colonial Mexico: The Great Hacienda*, Alvin Eustis (trans.). Berkeley: University of California Press.

_____. 1967. "The ejido and political stability in Mexico." Pp. 158-191 in Claudio Veliz (ed.), *The Politics of Conformity in Latin America*. London: Oxford University Press.

Chorley, Katherine. 1973. *Armies and the Art of Revolution*. Boston: Beacon Press.

Cline, Howard F. 1953. *The United States and Mexico*. Cambridge, MA: Harvard University Press.

_____. 1962. *Mexico*. London: Oxford University.

Coatsworth, John. 1974. "Railroads, landholdings and agrarian protest in the Early Porfiriato." *The Hispanic American Historical Review* 54 (February), 48-71.

Cockcroft, James D. 1968. *Intellectual Precursors of the Mexican Revolution 1900-1913*. Austin: University of Texas Press.

Cumberland, Charles C. 1952. *The Mexican Revolution*. Austin: University of Texas Press.

_____. 1968. *Mexico: The Struggle for Modernity*. New York: Oxford University Press.

Estadísticas económicas del Porfiriato: Fuerza de trabajo y actividades económicas. 1965. México: Seminario de Historia Moderna.

Frank, André Gunder. 1967. *Capitalism and Underdevelopment in Latin America*. New York: Monthly Review Press.

_____. 1969. *Latin America: Underdevelopment or Revolution*. New York: Monthly Review Press.

García, Mario T. 1976. "Out of the desert: The economic modernization of El Paso, Texas 1880-1910." Unpublished paper.

Goldfrank, Walter L. 1976. "Inequality and revolution in rural Mexico." *Social and Economic Studies* 25 (December), 397-410.

Hansen, Roger D. 1971. *The Politics of Mexican Development*. Baltimore: Johns Hopkins Press.

Hart, John M. 1978. *Anarchism and the Mexican Working Class 1860-1931*. Austin: University of Texas Press.

Herzog, Jesús Silva. 1959. *El agrarismo mexicano y la reforma agraria*. México: Fondo de Cultura Económica.

Hu-Dehart, Evelyn. 1974. "Development and rural rebellion: Pacification of the Yaquis in the late Porfiriato." *The Hispanic American Historical Review* 54 (February), 72-93.

Huizer, Gerrit. 1970. "Peasant organizations in the process of political modernization: The Latin American experience." Pp. 49-62 in Arthur Field (ed.), *City and Country in the Third World*. Cambridge, MA: Schenekman Publishing Co.

Huizer, Gerrit and Rodolfo Stavenhagen. 1973. "Peasant movements and land reforms in Latin America: Mexico and Bolivia." Pp. 378-409 in Henry L. Landsberger (ed.), *Rural Protest*. New York: Barnes and Noble.

Katz, Friedrich. 1974. "Labor conditions on haciendas in Porfirian Mexico: Some trends and tendencies." *The Hispanic American Historical Review* 54 (February), 1-47.

McBride, George M. 1923. *The Land Systems of Mexico*. American Geographical Society Research Series.

McCaleb, Walter F. 1921. *The Public Finances of Mexico*. New York: Harper and Bros.

MacLean, Roberto. 1959. *La Revolución de 1910 y el problema agrario de México*. Mexico: n.p.

McNeely, John H. 1966. "Origins of the Zapata revolt in Morelos." *Hispanic American Historical Review* 46 (May), 153-169.

Manero, Antonio. 1911. *El antiguo régimen y la Revolución*. México: La Europea.

Migdal, Joel. 1974. *Peasants, Politics and Revolution*. Princeton: Princeton University Press.

Millon, Robert. 1969. *Zapata: The Ideology of a Peasant Revolutionary*. New York: International Publisher.

Moore, Barrington. 1966. *Social Origins of Dictatorship: Lord and Peasant in the Making of the Modern World*. Boston: Beacon Press.

Padgett, L. Vincent. 1966. *The Mexican Political System*. Boston: Houghton Mifflin.

Paige, Jeffery. 1975. *Agrarian Revolution: Social Movements and Export Agriculture in the Underdeveloped World*. New York: Free Press.

Parkes, Henry Bamford. 1950. *A History of Mexico*. Boston: Houghton Mifflin.

Pletcher, David M. 1951. *Rails, Mines and Progress: Seven Promoters in Mexico 1867-1911*. Ithaca, N.Y.: Cornell University Press.

Priestley, Herbert Ingram. 1923. *The Mexican Nation*. New York: The MacMillan Co.

Quirk, Robert E. 1960. *The Mexican Revolution 1914-1915*. Bloomington: Indiana University Press.

Reynolds, Clark W. 1970. *The Mexican Economy: Twentieth Century Structure and Growth*. New Haven: Yale University Press.

Rippy, J. Fred. 1926. *The United States and Mexico*. New York: Alfred A. Knopf.

Skocpol, Theda. 1978. *States and Social Revolutions in France, Russia and China*. Cambridge: Cambridge University Press.

Stavenhagen, Rodolfo. 1970. "Social aspects of agrarian structure in Mexico." Pp. 225-270 in Rodolfo Stavenhagen (ed.), *Agrarian Problems and Peasant Movements in Latin America*. Garden City, N.Y.: Anchor Books.

Stein, Claudio and Joseph A. Kahl. 1968. "Stratification since the revolution." Pp. 5-30 in Joseph A. Kahl (ed.), *Comparative Perspectives on Stratification: Mexico, Great Britain, Japan*. Boston: Little Brown.

Stein, Stanley J. and Barbara H. Stein. 1970. *The Colonial Heritage of Latin America: Essays on Economic Dependence in Perspective*. New York: Oxford University.

Stinchcombe, Arthur L. 1961. "Agricultural enterprise and rural class relations." *American Journal of Sociology* 67 (September), 165-176.

Tannenbaum, Frank. 1929. *The Mexican Agrarian Revolution.* New York: The Macmillan Co.

―――――. 1933. *Peace By Revolution.* New York: Columbia University Press.

―――――. 1950. *Mexico: The Struggle for Peace and Bread.* New York: Alfred A. Knopf.

Tilly, Charles. 1975. "Western state-making and theories of political transformation." Pp. 601-638 in Charles Tilly (ed.), *The Formation of National States in Western Europe.* Princeton: Princeton University Press.

Turner, John Kenneth. 1911. *Barbarous Mexico.* London: Cassell and Co.

Wallerstein, Immanuel. 1974. *The Modern World System.* New York: Academic Press.

Waterbury, Donald. 1975. "Non-revolutionary peasants: Oaxaca compared to Morelos in the Mexican Revolution." *Comparative Studies in Society and History* 17 (October), 410-422.

Whetten, Nathan. 1948. *Rural Mexico.* Chicago: University of Chicago Press.

White, Robert A. 1969. "Mexico: The Zapata movement and the revolution." Pp. 101-167 in Henry Landsberger (ed.), *Latin American Peasant Movements.* Ithaca, N.Y.: Cornell University Press.

Wolf, Eric. 1969. *Peasant Wars of the Twentieth Century.* New York: Harper and Row.

Womack, John. 1968. *Zapata and the Mexican Revolution.* New York: Vintage Books.

Wright, Harry K. 1971. *Foreign Enterprise in Mexico: Laws and Policies.* Chapel Hill: University of North Carolina Press.

THE MEXICAN AMERICAN MIND:
A PRODUCT OF THE 1930s

Richard A. García

> You Mexican-Americans have been
> taught in those ideals of liberty and
> freedom, justice and equality... and
> you have for inspiration, the patriot-
> ism, self-sacrifice, and valor of Wash-
> ington, Lincoln, Roosevelt, as well as
> Simón Bolívar, Miguel Hidalgo and
> Benito Juárez.... You have an oppor-
> tunity few people of your race possess.
>
> —Manuel C. Gonzales, 1941

> Only through the development of a
> group of well-trained, sincere, and
> earnest leaders can the beautiful ideals
> of the League of United Latin Amer-
> ican Citizens be realized.
>
> —Carlos E. Castañeda, 1940

Introduction*

The intellectual history of Mexicans between 1929 and 1941 is
best understood as the expression of a sociocultural crisis. It was a
decade of an intellectual search for community by the rising middle
class. The Mexican American mind emerged in the 1930s as a product
of social differentiation, the crisis of the Depression, the Americanization role of such institutions as the family, the Catholic Church,
and the educational system, the Mexican and American ethos of the
city, the ideas and ideology of the exiled Mexican "Ricos" and the rise
of the League of United Latin American Citizens (LULAC), as well
as the relative absence of constant immigration.[1]

---

*A version of this paper was read at the ninety-fourth annual meeting of the
American Historical Association, December 28-30, 1979, New York City.

The consciousness of a community is a difficult process to ascertain, but by examining the hegemonic position of the dominant social classes, there is some certainty, nevertheless, of determining when a new set of ideals, values, and opinions begin to become predominant in a community. During the 1930s there began to emerge in San Antonio, Texas, a minute, but viable Mexican middle class. The ideas and ideology of this social stratum were articulated by LULAC. This organization exhibited a new set of ideological tools from which to view the self and society. As a result of LULAC's activities the San Antonio Mexican community began to acquire a new set of ideas and values, in fact, a new sense of ethnicity which defined its forms of social, political, and intellectual life. This new zeitgeist of Mexican-Americanism, which differed from the idea of just being "Mexicano," although it varied from social stratum to social stratum, was by the 1930s and the 1940s a cohesive collective cluster of ideas that permeated the extensive Mexican communities throughout the Southwest.[2]

The development of the Mexican American mind, however, was in crisis during the 1930s in the Southwest, specifically in San Antonio, Texas, which is the focus of this paper. The emerging reality of this new mentality threatened the dominant cultural-intellectual hegemony of "Los Ricos," the exiled Mexican upper class of the community. This paper does not want to suggest that prior to the 1930s there were not any individuals who identified themselves as Mexican Americans, Latin Americans, or Mexicano Texanos. What is being suggested in this paper is that the 1930s was the period in which a whole community, in this case San Antonio, began to become aware of a new mentality—a Mexican American one—that was being advocated, programmed, and institutionalized by the voice of the developing middle class organization: the League of United Latin American Citizens. In order to fully understand the process of this intellectual development we must first focus on the development of the ethos of the city, the social differentiation within the Mexican community, the impact of the institutions on the Mexicans, and finally the ideas and ideology of "Los Ricos" and of LULAC.

Culture, Class, and Community: The Basis for a New Mentality

The emergence of this Mexican American mentality is part of a process that had its origins in two distinct phenomena of Mexican American history: first, the development of the Mexican settlements in the nineteenth century, such as Los Angeles, El Paso, Tucson, and

San Antonio, and second, the immigration patterns that resulted from 1900 to 1930. This immigration was the result of three main factors: the economic development of the Southwest, the economic dislocation of Porfirio Díaz's modernization programs, and the Mexican Revolution of 1910. From the 1880s to the 1930s, over a million Mexicans entered the United States to augment the already existing Mexican population in the Southwest. As a result of these two developments, the 1930s had two distinct intellectual traditions within the Mexican urban communities: an American ethos and a Mexican one. These two dominant clusters of ideas contributed to an uneven pattern of intellectual and cultural development throughout the Southwest. Consequently, there was a constant process of intellectual and cultural continuity and change within the Mexican urban settlements during this period of the Great Migration. Cities like San Antonio, Los Angeles, and El Paso developed as a result, with relatively large Mexican populations and an urban atmosphere of "lo mexicano" and "lo americano."[3]

San Antonio, for example, was a city that had over 82,000 Mexicans within its city limits by 1930. These Mexicans were not only structurally interwoven with the machine politics of the city, but with the economic development as well. Yet, the Mexicans were still separated in the city's West Side: a town within a city. The city was of an American ethos; the town of a Mexican ethos. The Mexicans, regardless of their intellectual orientation, were of vital importance to the economy of the city. By the 1930s San Antonio's industrial and commercial importance was based on its transportation facilities, shipping, construction, military bases, oil, cotton (and other agricultural products), stockyards, packing plants, wholesale and retail trade, pecans, garment manufacturing, and over a thousand different small manufacturing plants. This economic diversity needed labor, but not necessarily skilled labor. Although much of the labor was done by Americans, there were over 275,000 Mexicans in the city and the outlying areas that worked in certain basic spheres of the industrial and agricultural sectors of San Antonio's economy. The manufacturing, industrial, and agricultural development of San Antonio was thus predicated on labor diversity. This created a labor-intense market for semiskilled and unskilled labor. The Mexicans filled this void because of the proximity of the border, because San Antonio was an attraction as a labor center and as a labor funnel to the Midwest and the rest of the Southwest, and, finally, because of the extensive Mexican population that already resided there. San Antonio, in spite of its economic growth never developed a heavy industrial base; it continued to depend primarily on a multiplicity of light industries. This did not affect the Mexican population because it continued to be needed as cheap labor to work throughout the city's military-industrial-commercial economic base.[4]

San Antonio's principal employer by the 1930s was the government through its military bases: Kelly, Fort Sam Houston, Brooks, and Randolph Field. It also had over 310 major manufacturing plants producing goods valued in 1939 at $40,000,000. These major factories supported approximately 63,000 people, including their immediate families. Moreover, the garment industry provided employment for 6,000 to 7,000 Mexican people, including piece workers. The pecan shelling industry, consisting of 12 to 15 pecan shelling and shipping firms, was another major industry in San Antonio, which employed an additional 12,000 to 20,000 Mexican workers during the peak season. In addition to these core industries, there was the large complex of low paying service establishments and the retail trade occupations that employed many semi-skilled Mexicans. Therefore, besides the industrial center, there were over 1,700 establishments in the service sector such as barber shops, beauty parlors, cleaning shops, laundries, automobile repair shops, funeral parlors, and many others. This service sector brought in approximately $9,461,000 per year and employed over 4,200 persons on the average per year. Mexicans, in addition to these sectors of employment, could find jobs in the slaughtering plants, the meat packing plants, the railroad and stock yards, or in the agricultural sector in the San Antonio metropolitan area that extended far beyond the proper. The very economic structure of San Antonio helped to divide the Mexicans economically into the working class, and the lower middle class. The American workplace values were being fused with the Mexican cultural ones. The extent, of course, depended on the occupation. These different American occupations affected the Mexicans' lives by influencing the family's cultural and intellectual matrix. Moreover, because of the extensive Mexican population there had developed since the late nineteenth century an upper middle class of Mexican entrepreneurs and professionals that serviced the Mexican community with grocery stores, barber shops, furniture stores, drug stores, etc. This nascent class was strengthened by the middle class emigrés during the great migration. Each of these classes had their own ideas and ideology, although they still were within the intellectual parameters of "el espíritu de la raza."[5] Both American and Mexican intellectual and cultural traditions, affected their daily lives.

A study done in 1927 showed this social differentiation: out of a sample of 424 native-born Mexicans, 33.5% were laborers, 33.4% were skilled laborers, 29.5% had service jobs, 8.5% were in business, and 5.1% were professionals. This same study also showed that, out of a sampling of 777 foreign-born Mexicans, 50.1% were laborers, 23.3% were skilled laborers, 14.8% had service jobs, 7.5% were in business, and 4.3% were professionals. These figures indicate there was a pyramidical social structure in the Mexican community: a large laboring class and a small middle class of semiskilled workers, businessmen, and professionals.[6] In addition to the laboring class and the sectors of the middle class, there was also a very small number of approximately 100 families of exiled Mexican "Ricos" at the top of this socioeconomic pyramid by the 1930s. The upper middle class Mexicans, socially and culturally, were intertwined with "Los Ricos," and residentially "segregated" themselves in the Prospect Hill area of the West Side or in the San Pedro district, another enclave on the West Side. Others, like some of the "Ricos," moved outside of the "Mexican Quarter." But, regardless of birthplace or residence, the employment situation was difficult during the thirties, although there were some Mexicans, such as the small shop owners, who managed to maintain their shops. Evidence of this is found in *Yearbook of the Mexican Population of Texas* published by J. Montiel Olvera in 1939; it indicated that there were still close to 100 Mexican merchants that had survived the Depression years in San Antonio. This contrasted with the 600 and 700 Mexican merchants listed in a similar annual published in 1924.[7] The very existence of this social differentiation was a prime factor that made possible the emergence of the middle class Mexican American mind.

With the American businessmen's whole-hearted support, these Mexican businessmen, as well as the whole Mexican community, were integrated into the city's political economy, but segregated from the social "economy" of San Antonio. Thus, not only did the Mexicans shell pecans, sew garments, make cigars, but they dug trenches, laid railroad tracks, built streets, drove trucks, gardened, peddled, and did housework. In fact, they did all of the menial work that had been formerly done by other ethnic groups in the city. In addition to this vast pool of surplus labor that resided in the "Mexican Quarter" and other small enclaves throughout the city, there were more than 20,000 Mexican laborers that went through the city each season being funneled from the San Antonio labor center to other parts of the country.[8] The Mexicans that lived in the West Side were not only integrated into the city's political economy, but their

Mexican culture was woven into the very traditions and intellectual "spirit" of the city. Because of this structural integration, in 1940 the San Antonio business community, the religious community, and the political elite appointed a social welfare and fact-finding commission that was representative of the whole community to evaluate the decades' changes in the city's Mexican community. They were aware that the Mexicans were becoming politically and philosophically Americans, yet remaining culturally and socially Mexican, the commission concluded that: "... discrimination against a strong segment of its [Mexican] population is not wise; in fact that it is not healthy, either politically, or educationally, or economically, or socially, to discriminate—in political recognition, or in schools, or in jobs controlled either by labor or capital, or in meeting welfare and health needs—against 40 percent of its Latin American population." The San Antonio establishment needed the Mexicans as participating Americans if the city was to continue its modernization.[9] Yet, San Antonio was not just an American city; it was a city of Spanish-Mexican motifs, of a cosmopolitan comingling of people, and a city of cultural contrasts. Above all the very cultural and institutional structures of the city reflected a weltanschauung of both "Mexicanness" and "Americanness." The very *élan vital* of the city gave the "Latin Quarter" a sense of "Mexican-Americanism," although the economic and political reality did not. Thus, the intellectual culture of the city, regardless of the institutions' efforts, also served to produce a Mexican American mentality rather than just an American one.[10]

Even strikes had an impact on the development of the "new consciousness." The Depression decade forced the Mexican laboring class, often led by individuals such as Emma Tenayuca and Magdeleno Rodríguez, or organizations such as El Nogal Union, the Pecan Shellers Union, the International Ladies Garment Workers Union (ILGWU), the Congress of Industrial Organizations (CIO), or the Communist Workers Alliance of America, to conduct strikes against the pecan industry, the garment industry, the cigar industry, and various other industries. These strikes and this militancy outraged the American community as well as the Mexican middle class community, the Mexican Chamber of Commerce, the American Chamber of Commerce, the League of United Latin American Citizens, the Catholic Church, and the American Federation of Labor. All were opposed to these Mexican strikes, principally because of the "communist" leadership. The strikes and labor agitations had definite repercussions on the Mexican community.[11]

This economic struggle by some of the Mexican workers served to further polarize the Mexican community ideologically, and give impetus to the organizational activities of LULAC and the Mexican American mentality that sought politics within accepted structures, and Americanism not Communism. This ideological polarization occurred during the time when the community was already being polarized socially and economically. The Mexican American mind was also emerging out of the rejection of the Mexican nationalism of the "Ricos" on one side, and the workers' "communism" on the other. Therefore, even though there seemed to be a homogeneous Mexican community in San Antonio's West Side, this was not the case. In short, many factors were serving to separate the emerging Mexican middle class from the Mexican worker and "Los Ricos." Besides the ones already mentioned, there were others: 1) the small, but continuing immigration from Mexico pushed the middle class to disassociate itself from this *gente corriente;* 2) the continuing racial discrimination forced the middle class to attempt to become more Americanized but still try to maintain their Mexican culture; 3) the continuing Americanization of the middle class through the educational, religious, and familial institutions influenced a dual consciousness; 4) the social and political activities of the League of United Latin American Citizens also forced the middle class to adopt a dual Mexican and American perspective; and 5) the daily bombardment by such mediating cultural structures as the American popular culture, through the radio and films, but most of all the middle class's acquisition of the English language, forced an American mentality into daily Mexican thought. All of these factors were affected directly or indirectly by the Depression decade. The Depression not only had an overall economic effect on the Mexican community in general, but in particular it had a direct effect on the cultural and intellectual fragmentation and consolidation of the three groupings in the Mexican society, by causing the extensive laboring class to strike, the small, but influential middle class to focus on itself, and the small comprador class of "Los Ricos" to turn to Mexico. The overall result was an acceleration of the West Side's sociocultural crisis, the political fragmentation of the Mexican class structure in San Antonio, the beginning of the rise of the Mexican middle class' consciousness as a class unto itself with a Mexican American psyche rather than a Mexican one, and the beginning of the building of a Mexican American culture and intellect that would challenge the intellectual cultural hegemony of the "Ricos."[12]

This process of Mexican class and ideological formation in San

Antonio and in many of the Mexican communities in the United States had its inception in the early 1920s, but its clear manifestation in the 1930s. Since the turn of the century, Mexicans in San Antonio had been changing due to the constant waves of new Mexican immigrants, the nation's economic changes, their own need to build a community, and the impact of the city's institutions on their everyday lives.[13] What one literary historian has said of the Jewish people during the early decades of the twentieth century is also applicable to the Mexicans in San Antonio during the 1930s: "A very few years after the mass migration, there . . . began within the immigrant community that process of external social differentiation which is characteristic of American society as a whole."[14] This class differentiation and differing strata consciousness that was apparent in the Jewish community in New York at the turn of the century and the Black community in the same period and in the 1920s became apparent in the Mexican community in the 1920s and highly visible by the 1930s.[15] This process of sociocultural and intellectual change was also occurring throughout the United States. The Depression decade clearly saw the emergence of Mexican American middle class as a conscious social group, through the activities of the LULAC organization, searching for a definite sense of community and a new set of ideas, ideals, and values that would fit their lifestyle in the United States. There were no longer just Mexicans, as "Los Ricos" advocated, or just Americans, as the society proposed, nor were they *gente corriente* as the lower class workers felt. This search for a community and a "new consciousness" was the intellectual and cultural crisis of the 1930s. It was a decade in which the middle class felt pressured by the strike activities of the Mexican laboring class in San Antonio and throughout the Southwest. The Mexican middle class in this decade also rejected the attempt of "Los Ricos" to have the Mexican community in the United States retain its Mexican identity and Mexican allegiance and the philosophy that expected them to return to Mexico to build the *Patria*. It could be said that by the end of the Depression decade the Mexican laboring class was just surviving this era of hunger, unemployment, deportations and repatriations. The Mexican middle class was finding and building its Mexican American community, while "Los Ricos" were losing their intellectual hegemonic hold on the Mexican communities.[16]

Although the culture and society of San Antonio's "Latin Quarter" was divided into three worlds—the laboring class, the middle class, and "Los Ricos"—they intersected on the issues of health, education, immigration and deportation, as well as politics.

In these areas, many times, the two upper classes worked together to help the working class. However, the cultural hegemony was still held by "Los Ricos," although the "counter culture" of the Mexican American middle class was slowly rearing its head. But, regardless of the differences in culture, society, or class, the Mexicans in San Antonio faced the common problems of racism and discrimination. These were unwanted unifying factors that insidiously weaved their way into the core of the community. Like cancer, racism did not respect any class or status group. If nationalism was the positive unifying thread in the West Side, racism was the negative. Both kept Mexicans separated and segregated. If acculturation promised relief, racism did not. Mexicans became Americanized, but discrimination kept them, for the most part, Mexicans. The intellectual dilemma was clear: they were not quite Americans, but neither were they quite Mexicans. The synthesis was Mexican Americanism, although the "Ricos" tried to keep them on the Mexican side of the hyphen by asserting their intellectual role.[17]

Ideas and Hegemony: "Los Ricos"

"Los Ricos" of San Antonio were a *comprador* class. For the most part, they had no economic or political base in San Antonio or throughout the Southwest. These exiled Mexicans always "faced South" toward Mexico and were more interested in the politics of Mexico and the rest of the world rather than in San Antonio. Yet, they still supported any improvement of the economic, the social or the political conditions for the Mexican in the United States, whether they were working class or middle class. In spite of these activities in San Antonio, these "Ricos," who included many of the political refugees who settled in San Antonio between 1908 and 1914 as well as many of the religious refugees who came in the 1920s, were "persons, largely from Mexico's upper classes, [who] looked upon San Antonio more as a refuge than as a permanent home. Some of them left San Antonio as soon as conditions in Mexico permitted, but others remained."[18]

This Mexican comprador class was exemplified by Ignacio E. Lozano and his newspaper, *La Prensa*. The newspaper was referred to as *"un faro del pensamiento"* (an intellectual light). Lozano was referred to at a banquet in 1937 as "the highest representative of Mexico" and a person who "ought to be an example for all Mexicans."[19] These eulogies were from both the middle class Mexicans and "Los Ricos" who were trying to have Lozano elected as the president of the national organization *Alianza Hispano Americana,* which was headquartered in Arizona. This organization rivaled the LULACs and was more representative of Mexicans like "Los Ricos" who identified themselves more as Spanish (Hispanos) than as Mexicans.[20] There were some middle class persons who aligned themselves closer to this sector of the population than to the growing Mexican American one in order not to be identified with the poor Mexicans. For the "Spanish" "Ricos" and the aspiring Mexicano, Lozano was the "Champion of the Mexican People" and the "new Moses," as many referred to him. These statements of praise were made by Americans as well as Mexicans. If Lozano was the personification of "Mexicanism," then *La Prensa* was the vehicle for its expression. Since its inception *La Prensa* had two basic principles: to serve as the voice of the people and the community, and to defend and represent the views of the small nuclear social grouping that came as political refugees. *La Prensa* was a paper, Lozano believed, for all the Mexican community, whether in the United States or in Mexico, and it was to be read in all villages and towns. In fact, Lozano portrayed and advertised *La Prensa* as *"el Paladín de La Raza"* (the champion of the people).[21]

"Los Ricos" felt that they were the "class people" *(gente decente)* that could return Mexico to normalcy, and that they were also the ones who could conserve the "spirit of La Raza" within the hearts of the Mexicans in the United States. Both "Los Ricos" and LULAC agreed on the preservation of this spirit, but LULAC and the middle class were adapting to the Americanization in their lives.[22] The exiled businessmen and writers of *La Prensa,* however, always wanted to return to Mexico; they wanted La Patria. These "Ricos" were only building a feeling and a spirit in San Antonio. They were promoting a Mexican past and a tradition in which they hoped to envelop all the sectors of the West Side community. In juxtaposition, and not necessarily in constant conflict, was the middle classes' everyday activities which were building a "new" sense of community. But, this "new order" was one of American traditions; it was a community based on the present not on the past. Change and time favored the Mexican American middle class since their dreams coincided with reality; the dreams of the "Ricos" did not. Nevertheless, the "Ricos" helped to maintain the Mexican cultural ethos that provided the continuity from the past to the present which the middle class used to support its ideological activities in the present while moving to the future.[23]

This "spirit of La Raza" could best be maintained, the "Ricos" believed, through everyday cultural activities. Therefore, through the cultural activities which emanated from the Casino Social, through the sale of Mexican books, through the sale of Mexican music, and through the speaking and writing of its intellectuals, the "Ricos" of San Antonio continued to maintain the Mexican "spirit" and "soul"—*La Cultura*—despite the sea of acculturation. The "Ricos" were attempting to foster a "high culture" on the Mexicans of San Antonio and the Southwest. They were attempting to develop a sophisticated leadership and a *clase de gente decente*. Mexican leaders and the Mexican *élan vital*, the "Ricos" believed, could be built on the anvil of culture. For the "Ricos," artists were an integral part, if not the cornerstone, of Mexican culture. For the "Ricos" culture and politics were intertwined.[24]

The synthesis of culture and politics produced sophistication, and this was important, "Los Ricos" thought, to *la clase mejor*. This applied to the *mejicanos de adentro* (Mexicans in the United States) and the Mexicans in Mexico. This merger of culture and politics was advocated in *La Prensa, La Opinión,* and through the *Alianza Hispano Americana.* They emphasized "high culture" to the poorer masses as well as to their main readers, the middle class sectors. "Los Ricos" urged the Mexican community to attend the opera, plays, the theater, and listen to classical and popular musical programs on the radio. They urged everyone in the community, moreover, to see Mexican films, read *La Prensa*'s cultural columns, and attend lectures by the *La Prensa* intelligentsia. Especially, they urged everyone to see films in Spanish. Language was a means, they believed, for Mexicans to keep that cultural consciousness viable.[25]

Through their San Antonio newspaper *La Prensa* and its Los Angeles one, *La Opinión,* "Los Ricos" sought to unify the Mexican communities' sense of cohesion in the Southwest. Every Sunday, for example, *La Prensa* carried an entire page entitled *La Vida Cultural Mexicana de Los Estados Unidos.* It carried news from the Mexican communities throughout the United States: Waukegan, Illinois; Cotulla, Texas; Eagle Pass, Texas; El Paso, Texas; Auburn, Alabama; Cheyenne, Wyoming; Colorado; Los Angeles, California; Elgin, Illinois; Chicago, Illinois; Indiana; and many others. Moreover, it carried extensive social news from Laredo, Texas, a city with a large Mexican population. "Los Ricos" hoped to "tie" up the cultural core of the Mexican community with a "string" of nationalism. For "Los Ricos" the Mexicans in the United States were not scattered, isolated individuals, but viable nationalist Mexican communities in exile, and "Los Ricos" felt as if they were the keepers of the cutural tradition. "Los Ricos" hoped not only to have these communities remain culturally Mexican, but uplift them to a "high culture."[26] Because of this belief, "Los Ricos" of San Antonio, through *La Prensa,* sent out its intellectuals and writers on speaking tours, especially to other Texas cities: El Paso, Fort Worth, Austin, Dallas, and the Valley cities of South Texas. Lic. René Capistrán Garza, for example, was sent to speak on nationalist themes such as "Mexico: its Traditions and its People," and "Our Mexican Country and Our Strength" *(Nuestra Patria y Nuestra Fuerza).* Garza and others usually stressed certain basic communal themes: "Mexican Patriotism," "Cultural Unity," and "Our Common Historical Tradition."[27]

Since 1913 when Ignacio E. Lozano began publishing *La Prensa* and 1925 when he started *La Opinión,* "Los Ricos" never deviated from their dual goal of being critics of the Mexican Revolution and of trying to maintain a Mexican cultural hegemony in San Antonio, Los Angeles, and other Southwest communities that had a large Mexican population. Through the use of their press, their intellectuals, their cultural activities, their charitable promotions, their work in the Alianza, and their personal example, they sought to accomplish their goal of maintaining the "spirit of La Raza" and the nationalist allegience within the hearts and minds of the Mexican immigrants and the already residing Mexican Americans. While the Revolution raged in Mexico they concentrated on their hegemonic activities in San Antonio by maintaining their lifestyle at the Casino Social. But in 1930, when the Depression began to affect the San Antonio West Side, when the process of social differentiation began to be accelerated, and when the movement for the *era de concordia* began in Mexico, the "Ricos" once again felt they could go home.[28] Their efforts turned toward Mexico just as LULAC was focusing on San Antonio.

Unfortunately, "Los Ricos" always saw San Antonio through a nationalist ideology, rather than a class analysis. Mexicans, whether they were rich or poor, were Mexicans, according to "Los Ricos." LULAC, for "Los Ricos," was not the expression of an emerging class. It was just a different gestalt. Classes for "Los Ricos" did not exist. Consequently, their wish for a social and cultural homogeneity was idealistic, both for San Antonio and Mexico. They could not have just one culture and one society. Their ideology had no reality; in contrast, LULAC's ideology was based on the emerging reality of the 1930s.

The Mexican American Mind: The League of United Latin American Citizens

The ideas and ideology of the League of United Latin American Citizens were the intellectual waves of the future for the Mexicans in San Antonio's West Side. It was the expression of a new consciousness: in fact, a new order. As the *LULAC News* stated: " . . . in 1929, with the great social upheaval of the Depression just ahead, the Texas wind carried a whisper of hope to the most native of all Texas' sons, the Mexican Americans."[29] Within the extensive Mexican community of "Los Ricos" there was forming a Mexican American mind. It was partially a product of the Mexican middle class' search for community during the 1920s and especially the 1930s. In 1939, J. Montiel Olvera, the compiler of the *Latin American Yearbook of San Antonio,* described this new mentality as one isolated from the intellectual roots that nourished it: the Anglo-American and the Hispano-American minds.[30] This Mexican American mind flourished within the middle class of entrepreneurs: restaurateurs, bakers, barbers, shoestore owners, butchers, furniture store owners, gasoline station owners, jewelers, tailors, druggists, cleaner and laundry owners, and among the over 350 grocery store owners of the Mexican community as well as the small but significant number of professionals, doctors, and lawyers.[31] It was from these Mexican citizens that a culturally cohesive and intellectually conscious Mexican American middle class developed. Their way of thinking and feeling—their lifestyle—was different from "Los Ricos" and "Los Pobres." This class of Mexicans, wrote O. Douglas Weeks in 1929,

> . . . have profited from the superior educational and economic advantages thus afforded [in San Antonio] as well as from contacts with the new [Americans] . . . who have poured in [to the city] from all parts of the South and Middle West, in spite of the fact that these new people have often not understood them. True enough, many of these city dwellers of Mexican extraction have remained ignorant and are constantly drawn to the newly arrived Mexican immigrants who help fill these Mexican quarters, but the fact remains [nevertheless] that there has arisen in their midst a class of prosperous, educated citizenry whose living conditions and attitudes compare favorably with American standards.[32]

The consciousness of this small, but growing middle class was formulated and articulated by the LULAC members who sought, in general, "the promotion of the effective exercise of American citizenship, the cultural advancement of persons of Mexican ancestry, and the effacement of public school racial distinctions. . . . ”[33]

The general basis for the "new consciousness" began in the nineteenth and twentieth centuries, but specifically it began in 1921 when the Order of the Sons of America was founded in San Antonio by a cadre of World War I veterans and other politically conscious individuals: Frank and Melchor Leyton, Mercy Montes, Pablo Cruz, Jr., Leo Longoria, Antonio Tarín, Abraham Armendariz, Vicente Rocha, M.C. Gonzales, and John Solís. All were middle-class Mexicans. Solís explained their effort in the following manner: "we didn't have anything [as Mexicans] in 1921 [;] we decided to organize our people to try and better the condition of Mexican Americans here in San Antonio and Bexar County." The first year, according to Solís, thirty-seven people joined the organization whose general goal was "to develop better American citizens and urge education," and in October of 1921 the Order of the Sons of America, the first consciously Mexican American group, was chartered by the State of Texas.[34] The other goals of the organization were also general, but straightforward: the achievement of economic, social, and racial equality with other Americans, the attainment of social and economic opportunity, and political power. The vehicles for achieving these goals were the Order of the Sons of America Councils that were established throughout Texas. The main membrship requirement, because of their goals, was American citizenship. Also a major emphasis was placed on the members learning and speaking the English language.[35] When one of the members was asked why the Order of the Sons was organized, he responded more specifically than Solís:

> There were a number of Mexican men who had served in the war. Then when they came home, they found that they were not served drinks [at fountains and bars] and were told that 'no Mexicans were allowed': They raised the question then, 'What are we Mexicans or Americans?'
>
> The world wars taught us a lesson. We had thought we were Mexicans. The war opened our eyes. . . . We have American ways and think like Americans. We have not been able to convince some [American] people that there is a difference between us [and the Mexicans from Mexico]. To the average American, we are just Mexicans.[36]

Although the members of the Order of the Sons of America were few, they nevertheless managed to establish organizational councils in many towns and cities outside of San Antonio: Sommerset,

Pearsall, Corpus Christi, Harlingen, Brownsville, Laredo, McAllen, La Grulla, and Encino, Texas. Each council, however, had slight differences in its philosophical and personal emphasis. Even the names of each council reflected this variation from 1921 through 1927: Order of the Sons of America, Knights of America, and the League of Latin American Citizens.[37] In San Antonio, for example, another distinct organization was founded by M.C. Gonzales named Los Caballeros de América. Gonzales even started the *Luchador (The Fighter)* newspaper to voice the organization's ideals. Gonzales and other members traveled throughout Texas establishing clubs, lecturing, distributing manifestos, and overall calling for the improvement of the Mexican communities. Gonzales' "Caballeros" had differences with Alonzo S. Perales' League of Latin American Citizens, although the differences were more personal and tactical than philosophical.[38] Regardless of the differences, all of the organizations, however, probably agreed with the prominent Mexican American who stated:

> We want [Mexicans in the United States] to be proud of their race, but to be loyal to the government [of the United States]. First . . . I tell my people that they should be proud of their race. The Latin race has produced the greatest music, art [and] poetry; the Anglo-Saxon, the greatest government and system of dispensing justice. The superiority of race is not a question of color, but of industry and efficiency, the ability to do more work on less food. The American [for example] eats a big breakfast of eggs and bacon. The Mexican with a cigarette and a cup of coffee goes out and does a morning's work. [It is, therefore, a question of] . . . the ability to save and accumulate—thrift—and to use those accumulations.[39].

The ideology of this "new consciousness" was clear: Be proud of being Mexican in culture, but be American in politics; and most of all be industrious, efficient, and productive. The variations in interpretation of this "Protestant Ethic" reflected the differing councils and organizations of the 1920s: some stressed American patriotism, some racial pride, some financial equality, and some equal opportunity. Nevertheless, the 1920s were the seedbed for the sprouting intellectual strands of the 1930s.

With the closing of the "Roaring Twenties" two things became clear to these Mexicans who aspired to be Mexican Americans. They needed a very clear social and political program and they needed organizational unification. Therefore, in 1927, a call for a unification meeting of the major organizations—Order of the Sons of America, the Knights of America, the League of Latin American Citizens, and

Los Caballeros de América—was issued. This call was made by Corpus Christi leader Ben Garza, the Head of Council IV of the Order of the Sons of America, the largest of the Mexican American organizations. The meeting, which was held at Harlingen, Texas, was the first of a series of meetings toward eventual unification. Such prominent San Antonio leaders as Alonzo S. Perales, Juan Solís, M.C. Gonzales, Maricio Machado, and James Tafolla attended. Three other major leaders attending were from South Texas, Ben Garza, J.T. Canales, and Luis Sáenz. These series of meetings finally culminated on February 17, 1929, at Obreros Hall. At this last major meeting, on May 18 and 19 of 1929, after much discussion, compromise, and argument, Ben Garza, the president of the sessions, and M.C. Gonzales, the secretary, announced that the League of United Latin American Citizens (LULAC) was now the single representative body of the Mexican American middle class. The acronym LULAC contained the central principles of the organization:

L — For *Love* of country and fellowman
U — For *Unity* of purpose
L — For *Loyalty* to country and principles
A — For *Advancement* of a people
C — For *Citizenship,* true and unadulterated[40]

With unification and a common philosophical goal—to make Mexicans into Mexican Americans—LULAC began immediately to spread and attempt to "uplift" cultural pride, increase the rate of American citizenship, and educationally advance the Mexican population to a new Mexican American consciousness throughout Texas, but especially in the San Antonio area. By 1933, LULAC Chapters had spread from Texas to Arizona, New Mexico, Colorado, California and even the District of Columbia and other Eastern States. Wherever there was a Mexican middle class community, LULAC was embraced. Because the organization's growth by 1937 was in part due to the work of the women, the Texas LULAC leadership decided to give them equal leadership privileges and councils. However, their councils were to be composed solely of women. A dual organizational structure, therefore, was established. Mrs. F.I. Montemayor was elected the first woman to the LULAC general office. In addition to this women's section, LULAC established the Junior LULACs between 1938 and 1939 under the sponsorship of the adult councils. The LULAC leadership throughout the thirties sought to incorporate the whole Mexican family within the organizational structure. This would give the organization, they felt, strong social and cultural communal roots while branching out in its economic and political activities. The women, the children, and the men would therefore be unified under a common program, common goals, and a common consciousness: a Mexican American mind that sought hegemonic control of San Antonio's West Siders. The peak of LULAC's growth was reached in 1940-1941. There was considerable work being done in all states and, consequently, there was a great rise in LULAC councils and memberships. This rapidity of growth was due to the organizational tactics formulated in the early 1930s with the formation of the famous *Escuadrón Volante* (Flying Squadron). This was the approach used by a cadre of San Antonio leaders who made sweeps into different areas to organize new clubs and recruit new members as well as take the LULAC philosophy into "todos los rincones del estado y a todos los corazones de la gente." In 1941, however, many of the LULAC members throughout the Southwest were placed on the organization's honor rolls because many had enlisted in the United States military services after Pearl Harbor. This depleted the ranks of LULAC until after the war.[41]

Throughout the 1930s the LULACs were conscious that they had a historical-philosophical mission to accomplish. If the family, the church, the educational system, and the political arena were the institutional transmitters of change for the Mexican American generation, the LULAC members were the active bearers of change via ideas and ideology. In 1932 LULAC President M.C. Gonzales placed LULAC into historical perspective: "We are here on a mission. To make living conditions better for the coming and succeeding generations; not to accomplish that work is to fail in our duties.[42] Then M.C. Gonzales underlined the LULAC's major task as the vehicle of the Mexican American generation of the 1930s. This task was the hegemonic confrontation with "Los Ricos" of San Antonio, who were only building a Mexican consciousness. "'Los Ricos' were never part of our [everyday] life," remembered Gonzales; "their newspaper, *La Prensa,* kept the image of Mexico alive, but never the welfare of Mexican American citizens of the United States or Texas." This role of "Los Ricos," however, was seen as useful by LULAC because it helped to preserve the "Spanish-Mexican culture."[43] Using poetic form, Gonzales described LULAC's historical purpose, which would accomplish what "Los Ricos" did not do.

We are builders of a better race. Tho' brief our time and span, there shall be more of happiness than when our age began and tho' we cannot see it now, when all is understood. We shall leave less of wrong behind. And more of what is good.[44]

Then in less poetic language, he formulated the major political and philosophical tenets of the Mexican American mind:

The minds of the younger generation of [Mexican] Americans, whatever their racial extraction might be, must be trained to be subservient to no one; to feel and act "equal" with all others; to grow into manhood upright, with no complexes of any kind, with loyalty to the [American] flag and respect to the constituted authorities, and an abundance of patriotism in their hearts; that is, if we are to have [future] leaders among the Latin Citizens of this country.[45]

These ideas expressed by Gonzales were in part also expressed by *La Prensa*. Although "Los Ricos" agreed in spirit with the thrust of LULAC's goal to uplift the community, they remained anchored to the idea that Mexicans could live in the United States and co-exist with American culture, but not become part of it. They always remained convinced that all *mejicanos de afuera* must remain Mexican. However, on January 1, 1930, *La Prensa* realized that many Mexicans wanted to remain in the United States rather than return to Mexico; therefore it ran an editorial that attempted to articulate the intellectual mood of the emerging middle sector of the Mexican population in San Antonio and throughout the Southwest. many of the San Antonio Mexicans, "Los Ricos"' advice and LULAC's seemed the same; be good American citizens and, as LULAC said, always "maintain a sincere and respectable reverence for our racial origin."[47] But, there was a difference: "Los Ricos" envisioned the West Siders as Mexicans who could take advantage of living in the United States, but whose loyalties remained to Mexico. LULAC, on the other hand, saw the West Siders as having a dualistic personality, Mexican and American: Mexican in culture and American in ideas and ideology. *La Prensa* could carry an editorial such as the above because it did not contradict its own basic objective: to maintain Mexican cultural hegemony.

LULAC's "uplifting" mission was helped by the fact that by the thirties there were numerous towns and cities in the Southwest, including San Antonio, that already contained a population of Mexicans who were second- and third-generation American citizens. This generational situation was a drawback to "Los Ricos"' philosophy. These Mexicans were being changed by the institutions and their own decisions to change. Many times these native Mexican Americans welcomed their Mexican "relatives," but by the Depression decade they began to establish some social distance between themselves and the poor Mexicans. LULAC, as well as the community institutions, helped them form this distinctiveness. O. Douglas Weeks, who had been one of the few non-Mexicans to be invited to the historic May 18, 1929, meeting of LULAC, observed the phenomenon of this newly forming consciousness. This generationally advanced Mexican American, Weeks noted,

> ... recently awakened to a new sense of the potentialities of his race, views with concern not only these [new impoverished] conditions in the towns, but the older conditions which still prevail in the country. He believes in his people; he believes that what he has [socially and materially] accomplished for himself may be realized in part for his less fortunate [working class] brothers, and he is [also] at present strongly urged by a desire to organize his own [middle class] element for the purpose of hastening the development of their [entire] people and supplementing what an improved school system in the towns at least has been able somewhat to accomplish [making Mexicans into Mexican Americans].[48]

"Los Ricos'" intellectual hold was being weakened.

In addition to pursuing this goal of material progress for all and bringing a new sense of dual consciousness, the San Antonio Mexican middle class led by LULAC sought specifically to eliminate racial prejudice, gain equality before the law, gain equal educational facilities, and gain equal political representation in local, state, and national politics. However, LULAC, as the conscious vehicle of the middle class mind, acknowledged that, as Weeks had noted, "the greatest stumbling block in the way of accomplishing this end is the Mexican American himself, who possesses no clear conception of the significance of the privileges and duties of his American citizenship."[49] In other words, LULAC had to first direct its activities to its own middle class before it could help the rest of the Mexican community. LULAC, therefore, sought to arouse the middle class "to a consciousness of that citizenship," Weeks wrote. LULAC also sought to educate the upper and middle class sectors in their political and civil rights and their obligations. Weeks observed that the LULAC members were the "intelligent class of Mexican Americans" and that they were not necessarily interested in the Mexican national nor the Mexican agricultural transient.[50]

LULAC attempted to make Mexican Americansd aware of their political and civil rights so that they could act as individuals. Many members, however, were aware of the concrete political ramifications of the organization and the fact that they were considered to be "organizers and activists" by the community. As one member stated, "[the] purpose of the Latin American League is to make [Mexicans] better citizens and perhaps they may some day put up candidates for office." Another retorted, when discussing the relationship of LULAC to politics, "[f]rom now on the Mexicans can't be driven like a bunch of cattle" because of this organization.[51] Principally, the League of United Latin American Citizens was trying to avoid politically fragmenting the community. They wanted to be *the* organization and express the "new ideology" for all the classes in the Mexican Quarter. They wanted to unite, not divide, and to uplift rather than downgrade the community. "Los Ricos" objected to the political rise of this middle class organization. One LULAC leader commented on this opposition:

> We have three [kinds of] people to contend with: the American politicians, the Mexican [machine] politicians, who sacrifice their race for their own advantage, and the old Mexicans ["Los Ricos"]. The Mexican politician controls a few voters for what he can get out of them, and is afraid of our society. . . . The Mexican politicians fight us and knock us and call us [LULAC] renegades, but after a while they join. The American politician has the Mexican politician as his voice. . . . The average non-political American of Latin descent calls us renegades. He says, "you are Mexicans, not Americans." Mexican citizens [Los Ricos] in their press even attack us. We are called [by Los Ricos] 'renegades' and 'anti-Mexican'. We call [Los Ricos] visitors [in San Antonio]. [Los Ricos] . . . tell us, [why] . . . are [you] trying to tell the [Texas-Mexicans] to be more loyal to the United States, . . . [since] your forefathers are all of Mexican origin, and you should continue to be Mexicans.[52]

LULAC leaders M.C. Gonzales and Alonzo S. Perales both felt, articulated, and actively sought to change the ideological hegemony of the West Side, and confront these three kinds of opposition. LULAC, whether it wanted to be or not, was a political organization and Perales and Gonzales were their main leaders.

Thus, the "Mexican mind" during the 1930s was pitted against the Mexican American one. During this decade the "Ricos" sought to address themselves to *la época de la concordia*—the time of unification in Mexico. They sought to have "*los mejicanos de afuera* remember that they were Mexican and that they should return to work for Mexico." The LULACs, on the other hand, sought to address their "search for community," also reminding the West Siders to remain Mexican, but to remember they were *mejicanos de adentro,* and thus their loyalties were to their present home, the United States. A LULAC leader forcefully responded to "Los Ricos"' cry of betrayal: "The Mexicans [Los Ricos] say we're trying to Americanize, and get away from Mexican patriotism. We have to be American citizens [since we live in the United States] whether we want to or not."[53] LULAC "faced North" and pursued the reality of their everyday existence in the United States; they looked toward the present and the future. "Los Ricos," however, always "faced South"; they remembered the past and wished to continue it. Regardless of their present exile in the United States, they continued to be Mexicans, from Mexico. Paul Taylor observing this hegemonic confrontation wrote "that if [community] dissensions were avoided, its [LULAC] program followed, and if its appeal to the working class succeeded, the Mexican-American mind would prevail."[54] Taylor observed this, LULAC believed it, and most of the Mexican community, after a decade, accepted it. A continuing sense of cultural ethnicity rather than just a political and philosophical Americaniza- tion persisted with "astonishing tenacity" from 1929 through 1941 in the Mexican community.[55]

In contrast to the struggle with "Los Ricos," LULAC's ideals coincided with the Catholic Church's programs, the educational system's goals, and the families' developmental processes during this decade. These societal institutions were in ideological synchroniza- tion with the community's activist segment, the LULACs. This ideology of the middle class was codified in the LULAC constitution.

From the middle of the 1930s through the 1940s, LULAC members were part of every political, social or welfare activity in San Antonio either as individuals or LULAC members. They were involved in Red Cross drives, Community Chest drives, clothing and food drives, welfare work, Boy Scout and Girl Scout work, Salvation Army work, and city and county health boards.[56] LULAC councils in San Antonio and throughout Texas also lectured and organized around the themes of education, citizenship, the English language, economic opportunities, and civil rights. In particular, LULAC sought to provide educational opportunities and scholarships to Mexican youths as well as adult night schools for the rest of the community. Adult education, LULAC felt, was a method for the entire community to gain self-sufficiency and a higher social standard. LULAC also sought to Americanize the customs and everyday life of the Mexican masses.

The LULAC code exemplified the spirit, the dreams, the ambitions, and the ideals of the Mexican American middle class. It dictated a philosophy of everyday living; it was both the essence of the Mexican American mind and the code for being *gente decente*. It read:

> Respect your citizenship and preserve it; honor your country, maintain its traditions in the spirit of its citizens, and embody yourself into its culture and civilization;

Love the men of your race, be proud of your origin and maintain it immaculate, respect your glorious past, and help to defend the rights of your own people;

Learn how to fulfill your duties before you learn how to claim your rights; educate and make yourself worthy, and stand high in the light of your own deeds; you must always be loyal and courageous;

Filled with optimism make yourself sociable, upright, judicious, and above all things be sober and collected in your habits, cautious in your actions and sparing in your speech.

Study the past of your own, and of the country to which you owe your allegience, learn how to master with parity the two most essential languages—English and Spanish;

Believe in God, love humanity and rely upon the framework of human progress, slow, unequivocal and firm;

Always be honorable and high minded, learn how to be self-reliant upon your own qualifications and resources

In war serve your country, in peace your convictions; discern, investigate, meditate and think, study, at all times be honest and generous.

Let your firmest purpose be that of helping to see that each new generation of your own shall be of a youth more efficient and capable and in this let your own children be included.[57]

As the code indicated, the Mexican Americans did not seek to become assimilated. They sought a duality: Mexican in culture and social activity, but American in philosophy and politics. Within the latter role they sought to adhere to democratic ideals such as civic virtue, equality, right of education, and the right of citizenship. They sought to acquire the use of the English language, but maintain the right to Spanish. LULAC's ideals, intentions, and activities were beyond suspicion: they were for the community.

M.C. Gonzales' and Alonzo S. Perales' philosophies were the central ideas and ideology of LULAC in particular, and the Mexican American mind in general. For Gonzales and Perales, being in LULAC, fighting for the poorer Mexican community, fighting against discrimination, changing Mexicans into American citizens, and developing a love for the United States was being a Mexican American. For Gonzales, specifically, nationalism—unlike with "Los Ricos"—was just a means, not an end. "We used nationalism to organize them [Texas Mexicans] for civil rights and Americanism." We did this, he said, in order for them to have a "share of [American] life, accomplish something [for themselves, and] achieve something. [The] people were hungry for education, for a better life." We wanted to "teach them to be Americans and [we] stress[ed] education since 90 percent of our people were illiterate."[58] LULAC, according to Gonzales, wanted to be classified as an American rather than a Mexican organization in San Antonio, and "we wanted to speak English [in order] to show [that] we were not Mexican [aliens] because to work as a Mexican organization would [have been]... a barrier. [However,] [w]e wanted to remain Mexican [culturally], but take advantage of American life, citizenship."[59]

LULAC was, as a result of this philosophy, the only voice in the 1930s calling for self-identity, seeking to maintain the cultural lifestyle, and working against the Mexican American's problems in education, health, politics, and discrimination. The organization consisted of middle class men and women with a "new consciousness." The LULAC constitution and the LULAC code reflected their desires, their aspirations, their dreams, and their goals. The LULUAC program, in fact, reflected the ideas and ideology of a rising class—a class searching for a new order, a new community. Alonzo S. Perales, M.C. Gonzales, H.T. Manual, Carlos E. Castañeda, and George I. Sánchez were a few of the main articulators of the embryonic Mexican middle class. Reflecting on his personal change of consciousness from Mexican to Mexican American, M.C. Gonzales, stated, "I liked Mexican food and culture, but no matter what, I became part of the American philosophy." Then, speaking of the problem of Americanization, Gonzales remarked, "Mexican culture is in our blood, in our background."[60] The coexistence of this duality was to be tested in the 1960s, but 1929 through 1941 was not the period.

By the advent of World War II many Mexicans in San Antonio and in the Southwest had accepted the new hyphenation of consciousness—a new political and philosophical consciousness, a Mexican American one. Many times, however, until the 1950s, they designated themselves as Latin Americans or Texas Mexicans in order to avoid being categorized with Mexican aliens. They sought to be viewed as *gente decente,* not *gente corriente.* Philosophically, civil rights, equal justice, equality of opportunity, freedom from discrimination, and cultural rights were the core tenets of the Mexican American mind. The American country, flag, service, and honor were the political symbols accepted by the Mexican American middle class. Cultural pluralism and voting were the political pillars, and education was the catalyst and key to their progress, achievement, and prosperity. The Mexican American, in essence, was an American liberal. The Mexican American believed in the virtues of work, not theory. Accordingly, LULAC during this decade fought both for more education and for integration: in swimming pools, in real estate, in hotels, in dance halls and bars, in schools, and in all other spheres of everyday life. Above all they fought for education; it was to be the means to better homes, upward mobility, and better jobs. LULAC and the middle class wanted doctors, lawyers, teachers: not necessarily an intelligentsia, but a managerial class. Not that they were anti-intellectual, they were just pragmatic: basic needs first. From the seedbeds of the 1920s had sprouted the fragments of the Mexican American mind, and the events of the 1930s had fertilized them, while LULAC cultivated and reaped them. The Mexican American mind was, indeed, a product of the 1930s, although it would not be until the 1940s and 1950s that this new consciousness would be hegemonic throughout the Southwest communities.

HISTORY DEPARTMENT
SANTA MONICA COLLEGE

Notes

[1] All of these factors are treated in depth in my dissertation, "The Making of the Mexican-American Mind, San Antonio, 1929-1941: A Social and Intellectual History of an Ethnic Community," unpublished Ph.D. diss., University of California, Irvine, 1980.

[2] A great impetus to the consolidation of the Mexican American mind was World War II, especially the activities of the returning veterans. This was a phenomenon that also occurred after World War I. After World War II in both San Antonio, Texas, and Los Angeles, California, there was a flourish of organizational activity. These new organizations programatically exhibited the "new" cluster of ideas, the Mexican American mentality. For a beginning generational interpretation, see Rodolfo Alvarez, "The Unique Psycho-Historical Experience of the Mexican American People," *Social Science Quarterly*, Vol. 52, June 1971.

[3] For an examination of the development of Southwest communities, see Alberto M. Camarillo, *Chicanos in a Changing Society* (Cambridge: Harvard University Press, 1979); Judith Fincher Laird, "Argentine, Kansas: The Evolution of a Mexican-American Community: 1905-1940," unpublished Ph.D. diss., University of Kansas, 1975; Mario T. García, *Desert Immigrants: The Mexicans of El Paso, 1880-1920* (New Haven: Yale University Press, 1981); Ricardo Romo, "Mexican Workers in the City: Los Angeles, 1915-1930," unpublished Ph.D. diss., University of California, Los Angeles, 1975; Richard Griswold del Castillo, *The Los Angeles Barrio, 1850-1890* (Berkeley: University of California Press, 1979).

[4] Chamber of Commerce, *Manufacturing for Less in San Antonio* (San Antonio: Chamber of Commerce, 1934), pp. 1,2; Frances Woods, *Mexican Ethnic Leadership in San Antonio, Texas* (Washington, D.C.: The Catholic University of America Press,

1949), p. 19; San Antonio Pubic Service Company, *Economic and Industrial Survey* (San Antonio: City Report, 1942), pp. 109, 167; D. W. Meing, *Imperial Texas: An Interpretive Essay in Cultural Geography* (Austin: University of Texas Press, 1969)), p. 24; *San Antonio Express: 100 Years* (San Antonio: San Antonio Express, 1965), p. 22T; *San Antonio Sets the Stage for Industry* (San Antonio: City Document, circa 1910), pp. 1-24.

[5] Federal Writers Project, *San Antonio: An Authoritative Guide to the City and its Environs* (American Guide Series, Clegg Company, 1941), pp. 1-44; *Economic and Industrial Survey,* p. 21; *San Antonio Express,* 5 January, 1930, pp. 1c-2c; *San Antonio Express,* 8 January, 1930, p. 1; Sam Woolford, *San Antonio, A History for Tomorrow* (San Antonio: Naylor Company, 1963), p. 168.

[6] John Williams Knox, "The Economic Status of the Mexican Immigrant," M.A. thesis, University of Texas, 1927). Reprinted by R&E Research Associates, San Francisco, 1971, pp. 21-23.

[7] Woods, *Mexican Leadership,* p. 21; Interview with Rubén Mungía, San Antonio, Texas, June, 1978; Manuel Gamio, *The Life Story of the Mexican Immigrant: Autobiographic Documents* (New York: Dover Publications, Inc. 1971), p. 232; J. Montiel Olvera, *Year Book of the Mexican Population* (San Antonio; published by author, 1939); J.C. Sologaist (ed.), *Guía general directorio mexicano* (San Antonio: n.p., 1924). The issues of *La Prensa* constantly refer to the social and cultural activities of the "Ricos." The society page documents their everyday lives.

[8] Knox, *Economic Status,* pp. 1-12; Woods, *Mexican Leadership,* p. 19; City Report, *Business Interest in Decent Standards,* p. 6; American Corporation, "Our Minority Groups: Two Spanish Speaking People," *Building America Bulletin 8*, No. 5, 1943, p. 146.

[9] San Antonio Government, *Social Welfare Report,* 1940, p. 25.

[10] Frederick Charles Chabot, *San Antonio and Its Beginnings* (San Antonio: Artes Gráficas Printing Company, 1936), p. 15; Marjorie Paulus, "Early Years in San Antonio, 1850-1865," M.A. thesis, St. Mary's University, 1939, p. 9; Meing, *Imperial Texas,* pp. 55-57; Robert Garland Landolt, "The Mexican American Workers of San Antonio, Texas," unpublished Ph.D. diss., Austin, Texas, 1965, p. 41.

[11] See Landolt, "The Mexican American Workers"; *Aztlán: International Journal of Chicano Studies Research,* Vol. 6, No. 2, Summer, 1975. [This issue is devoted to articles on Mexican labor in the United States]. Richard A. García, "Class, Consciousness, and Ideology; The Mexican Community of San Antonio, Texas 1930-1940," *Aztlán,* Vol. 9, 1978; Harold A. Shapiro, *The Pecan Shellers of San Antonio,* Works Progress Administration (Washington, D.C.: Government Printing Office, 1940), p. 23.

[12] See this in more detail in García, "The Making of the Mexican-American Mind," Chapter 2.

[13] There were three parts to this period of the great Migration: 1900-1919 (24,991); 1910-1919 (173,663); 1930-1929 (587,775). Between 1930-1940 only 27,937 Mexicans entered the United States because of the Depression and deportation and repatriation drives. However, Mexican immigration in the 1930s was bolstered by the continued flow of illegal immigration. Gilbert Cárdenas, "United States Immigration Policy Toward Mexico: An Historical Perspective," *Chicano Law Review,* Vol. 2, Summer, 1975, pp. 66-91; Abraham Hoffman, *Unwanted Mexican Americans in the Great Depression: Repatriation Pressures, 1929-1939,* pp. 24-116; American G.I. Forum of Texas and Texas Federation of Labor, *What Price Wetbacks?* (Austin, Texas, 1955), p. 31; also see Arthur F. Corwin (ed.), *Immigrants—and Immigrants: Perspectives on*

Mexican Labor Migration to the United States (Westport, Connecticut: Greenwood Press, 1978).

[14] Irving Howe, *World of Our Fathers* (New York: Harcourt Brace Jovanovich, 1976), p. 117.

[15] See Nathan Huggins, *Harlem Renaissance* (New York: Oxford University Press, 1971); Gilbert Osofsky, *Harlem: The Making of a Ghetto* (New York: Harper & Row, 1966).

[16] This class differentiation in the Mexican community has not really been closely examined by Chicano historians. For the most part they have assumed a certain homogeneity within the Mexican communities and have focused on just the workplace and labor activities.

[17] For a more complete discussion of this see Richard A. García, "Class, Consciousness, and Ideology, The Mexican Community of San Antonio, Texas: 1930-1940," *Aztlán*, Vol. 9, 1978. For a discussion of the Gramscian concept of hegemony as employed in this paper, see Carl Boggs, *Gramsci's Marxism* (London: Pluto Press, 1976), pp. 36-55. For this use of hegemony, but in another context, see Jonathan M. Wiener, *Social Origins of the New South, Alabama 1860-1885* (Baton Rouge: Louisiana State University Press), 1978.

[18] *La Prensa,* which was their major newspaper in San Antonio, was almost completely oriented toward news of Mexico, the United States, and Europe, except for one or two pages of local cultural and societal news. Sometimes, though, a major news story affecting the San Antonio community was placed on the front page. An example of their interests in Mexicans in San Antonio can be seen from *La Prensa,* January 30, 1930, p. 10. For a short discussion of "Los Ricos," see Woods, *Mexican Leadership,* pp. 20-21.

[19] *La Prensa,* 6 April, 1937, p. 1.

[20] Ibid.

[21] *La Prensa,* 29 June, 1959, p. 9; *La Prensa,* 27 September, 1929, p. 3.

[22] Interview with Ignacio Lozano Jr., Los Angeles, California, August, 1978. *La Prensa*'s editorials throughout the 1930s reflected this constant tension between "Los Ricos'" role in Mexico and their role as the *gente decente* in the United States. "Los Ricos," regardless of changes, attempted to remain *mejicanos de afuera* (Mexicans outside the United States) as opposed to *mejicanos de adentro* (Mexicans who now accepted living in the United States).

[23] *La Prensa,* 1 March, 1930, p. 3; *La Prensa,* 12 January, 1930, p. 1; *La Prensa,* 2 January, 1930, p. 3; *La Prensa,* 10 January, 1930, p. 3.

[24] *La Prensa,* 2 February, 1930, p. 8.

[25] *La Prensa,* 23 February, 1930, p. 8; *La Prensa,* 16 February, 1930, p. 8.

[26] *La Prensa,* 1 January, 1930, pp. 3-4.

[27] *La Prensa,* 23 February, 1930, p. 6; *La Prensa,* 29 January, 1930, p. 10; *La Prensa,* 31 January, 1930, p. 7.

[28] *La Prensa,* 4 October 1931, p. 3; *La Prensa,* 5 February, 1930, p. 1; *La Prensa,* 2 February, 1930, p. 8.

[29] "A History of LULAC Part I," *LULAC News,* 36 (1974), p. 10.

[30] J. Montiel Olvera, *Latin American Yearbook* (San Antonio: By Author, 1939), p. 9.

[31] Sologaist, *Guía General,* pp. 211-222.

[32] O. Douglas Weeks, "The League of United Latin American Citizens: A Texas-Mexican Organization," *Political and Social Science Quarterly,* 10 (1929), p. 258.

[33] Paul Schuster Taylor, *An American-Mexican Frontier, Nueces County, Texas* (New York: Russell and Russell, 1934), p. 242.

[34] Solís is quoted in *South Side Sun* (San Antonio, Texas), July 7, 1976, n.p. (Richard Erickson interview with John Solís), John Solís Papers; *La Prensa,* February, 1960 (issue in John Solís Papers).

[35] *LULAC News,* January, 1974, p. 11.

[36] Quoted in Taylor, *An American-Mexican Frontier,* p. 245.

[37] Edward D. Garza, "LULAC: League of United Latin American Citizens," M.A. thesis, Southwest Texas State Teachers College, 1951.

[38] *La Prensa,* February, 1960, n.p. (issue in John Solís Papers); Interview with John Solís, San Antonio, Texas, June, 1978.

[39] Quoted in Taylor, *An American-Mexican Frontier,* p. 246; *La Prensa,* February, 1960 (issue in John Solís Papers).

[40] Garza, "LULAC," pp. 1-11; *LULAC News,* January, 1974, p. 11.

[41] Garza, "LULAC," pp. 10, 15, 24; *La Prensa,* February, 1960; Interview with Rubén Mungía, San Antonio, Texas, June 1978.

[42] Montiel, *L. A. Yearbook,* p. 6.

[43] Interview with M.C. Gonzales, San Antonio, Texas, June, 1978.

[44] Quoted in Montiel, *L. A. Yearbook,* p. 6.

[45] Ibid.

[46] *La Prensa,* 1 January, 1930, p. 2.

[47] Week, "LULAC," pp. 264-265.

[48] Ibid., p. 259.

[49] Ibid.

[50] Ibid., pp. 259-260.

[51] Quoted in Taylor, *An American-Mexican Frontier,* p. 248.

[52] Ibid., pp. 248-249.

[53] Ibid., p. 249.

[54] Ibid.

[55] Edwin Larry Dickens, in "The Political Role of the Mexican Americans in San Antonio, Texas," unpublished Ph.D. diss., Texas Tech College, 1969, suggests this idea by quoting Robert Dahl's *Who Governs?* (New Haven: Yale University Press, 1961), p. 59, "... in spite of growing assimilation, ethnic factors continue to make themselves felt with astonishing tenacity."

[56] George J. Garza, "Along the Trail with Council #12, *LULAC News,* Vol. XIII, No. 7 (January 1947), pp. 9, 14, quoted in Garza, "LULAC," pp. 38-39; Interview with George Garza, San Antonio, Texas, June, 1978. Scout work was instrumental in LULAC activities since 1929. See A. De Luna, "Minutes of Regular Meeting of LULAC," Record Book of the League of United Latin American Citizens, May 20, 1929 (footnoted in Garza, "LULAC," p. 40).

[57] "LULAC Code," in *LULAC News,* November, 1940, n.p.

[58] Interview with M.C. Gonzales, San Antonio, Texas, June, 1978.

[59] Ibid.

[60] Ibid.

CHICANO FAMILY HISTORY— METHODOLOGY AND THEORY: A SURVEY OF CONTEMPORARY RESEARCH DIRECTIONS

Richard Griswold del Castillo

If Chicano history is to develop viable approaches to the study of Mexicano and Chicano families as they evolved under the impact of industrialization and the pressures for assimilation since 1848, the limitations and promise of prior and ongoing historical and sociological research must be assessed. We must learn to distinguish between methodological and theoretical concerns and place proper emphasis on the latter. I hope that as Chicano family history is developed methodologically, we will, at the same time, search for new theoretical approaches which set the family in broader contexts. All this is a long term undertaking which can only be accomplished by a thoughtful review of the relevant literature and the cooperative efforts of many scholars.

My purpose here is to survey the directions that the historical study of the family has taken in American historiography and to consider some of the methodological and theoretical approaches that may serve as useful paradigms in our efforts to construct a Mexican American family history.[1] This study is divided into two parts: a discussion of methodological approaches and an overview of theoretical systems. An attempt is made to evaluate their relevance to the historical study of the Mexican American. My intention is to provide a base line study which will serve as a point of departure for other scholars who are entering the field. Of course, I make no pretentions to exhaust the current literature on family methodology and theory. Others will want to go beyond what I present here to explore certain issues in more detail.

Methodological Approaches

At least four methodological approaches have characterized American family history: (1) the study of household size and composition, (2) the generational model, (3) the family life cycle, and (4) life course analysis.

One of the most ambitious and comprehensive efforts to look at the family from a comparative historical perspective has been that of the Cambridge Group for the Study of Population and Social Structure led by Peter Laslett. The basic thesis of the Cambridge group is that western preindustrial society did not have many families with resident kin and that families have not changed significantly in composition or structure due to industrialization or modernization. They argue that large extended families were not very common types in agrarian societies during the sixteenth century because demographic and economic forces limited the family's ability to sustain large numbers of people.[2] To support their assertions, the Cambridge group draws from their comparative analysis of families in a wide variety of historical settings ranging from Europe to Japan. The thesis of the continuity of family organization and household size from preindustrial times to the present has been supported by independent historical as well as sociological research on the American family.[3]

Despite recent criticism and conflicting findings, the Cambridge thesis raises important questions in relation to the study of the Chicano family.[4] Is the popular view of the large extended family among Mexicanos prior to 1848 in the Southwest more a romantic ideal than a reality? After 1848 did the "traditional" Mexican family remain unchanged in terms of size and composition despite pressures for modernization? If large extended families did exist before 1848, at what point and for what reasons did they change to smaller nuclear units resembling Anglo-American households? And most importantaly what was the significance of these changes?

Today there is little structural difference between Anglo and Chicano families, at least in terms of the proportions of kin residing in the household. Sena-Rivera, for example, has found that the multigenerational household is almost nonexistent among contemporary Chicanos and that the modified extended family model most closely describes the Chicano family.[5] Economic and emotive interdependence and geographical propinquity among members of *la familia* appear to be conditioned by generational distance from the mother country and socioeconomic standing.

In recent years, historians dissatisfied with static and demographically oriented approaches have attempted to view the family from a developmental perspective. An early pioneer in this was Philip Greven, who used a generational model to explain the history of four generations of families in Andover, Massachusetts.[6] There are indications that some Chicano social historians are beginning to utilize a generational approach in social history. In 1973 Rudolfo Alvarez suggested that Chicano history could profitably be studied by this method. Alberto Camarillo and others have studied the G.I. Generation in order to explain emerging political consciousness of the 1950s. Recently, Mario García has posited the Mexican immigrant family as a generation sharing common experiences during the period 1910-1930.[7]

The generational approach may prove to be a popular method to study the Chicano family. There are some problems, however, the main one being the determination of what constitutes a generation. At what point in time shall we begin our analysis of the age group which constitutes a generation? Usually social historians count as a generation a group of individuals who experience as adults some significant event, such as World War I, the Depression, or the 1960s. This approach obviously relies on the arbitrary selection of a "key" historical event. At the same time it deemphasizes the importance of other age cohorts who can be defined as generations and who also experience the event but at a different point in their life cycle. The generational method tends to minimize overlaps between generations as well as the importance of childhood and aging. It assumes that the life experiences of large groups of adults with varying ages are similar. It is obvious that a 20-year-old experiences the world in a quite different way from that of a 40-year-old, yet they are often conceived as being part of the same generation. The generational model will still be useful for family studies but only if its limitations are well recognized.

Another group of social historians has used the family life cycle method to study the family.[8] Pitrim Sorokin first conceptualized the family life cycle in 1931. Since that time various sociologists have elaborated upon his ideas that the family can best be studied through an analysis of its developmental stages. Sorokin hypothesized four stages of family development: (1) the newly married couple, (2) the couple with one or more children, (3) the couple with one or more self-supporting children, and (4) older couples with no children. Each stage suggests that the family should be studied according to different kinds of issues related to function and structure. Later theorists modified and elaborated on Sorokin's scheme. Currently the most widely used life cycle model is an eight-stage one developed by Evelyn Duval and Ruben Hill.[9]

Although the family cycle has been criticized for focusing too much on child rearing functions and for neglecting important social and economic variables related to family development, a number of insightful historical studies have resulted from using this perspective.[10] Chicano historians, however, have not used the family cycle concept to study the household, yet this approach would seem to be ideally suited to comparative research on the similarities and differences between Anglo and Chicano households. Before embarking on an application of the methodology to the study of the Chicano family, however, we should be familiar with the substantive criticism which has surrounded its use. Spanier and Sauer, for example have found that the family life cycle concept has no more empirical value than age or marriage cohort when analyzing family development.[11]

The main value of the family cycle approach is that it can be used to control for the influence of age and household development when discussing questions of family extension, generational assimilation, and socioeconomic status. Marta Tienda's work on economic dependence among Peruvian families illustrates the importance of this method for studying Hispanics.[12] She found that in Peru younger families with children and a high burden of dependence were more likely to incorporate older kin to help with household and economic obligations. Thus kinship systems expanded at certain points in the life history of the family. The same sort of approach applied to Chicano families may show a continuity in function between Latin American and Chicano households.

In the search for a more flexible and comprehensive model to describe family development, some historians have turned to life course analysis. The proponents of this methodology see the family as a collection of life histories with individual members having a complex relationship within the family and to the larger society.

The key focus of life course analysis is the timing of transitional events experienced by individuals. For example, a transitional event might be the decision of a son to marry. This event would have consequences in three spheres, the family of origin, his new wife's family and the new family being formed. The timing of the event is affected by larger historical forces, the historical norms of the particular society, the economic system, role models available and the socioeconomic background of the families involved. Some of the transitions which have been studied using this methodology are entrance into job market, going to school, moving in with relatives and the decision to extend the family. Life course analysis differs from the life cycle methodology in that it centers on the individual's life history in relation to family development while allowing for the influence of social, political and historical factors. Using this method, historians are able to discuss the larger social environment in relation to the family's developmental history.

As developed by Glen Elder, Tamara Harevan, John Model and others, life course methodology is a complex and often confusing approach to family history. Consequently a major problem for social historians will be to understand the terminology and sociologically oriented arguments advanced by the life course proponents.[13]

The value of the life course method for the study of the Chicano family is as yet unclear. In a pilot study of San Antonio Chicano families in 1860, I concluded that the timing of family extension was affected by the violent colonial history of Mexican-Anglo relations in Texas, but that economic factors alone did not explain the creation of large and complex families. Demographic variables such as the age of the husband and wife proved to be more important in the occurrence of this event. While fruitful in revealing some previously hidden aspects of Mexican American family life, the life course methodology proved to be largely esoteric in its results. It is quite removed from larger conceptual or theoretical questions, not to mention the mainstream of American or Chicano historiography.

Theoretical Approaches

The 1970s witnessed a rapid growth in sociological theory dealing with the family, but little of this new research has been incorporated into historical research.[14] There are, of course, many possibilities for articulating a theoretical approach to family history, and Chicano family history in particular. The rest of this paper will discuss four theories which may be relevant for a beginning conceptualization of the field. A critical evaluation of theory is an essential prologue for developing a firm basis for research.

Modernization theories have been developed by social scientists to explain social and economic changes in large geopolitical areas. Generally they hypothesize two historical eras: (1) a traditional or premodern stage, which is characterized by a subsistence rural economy, the lack of developed economic infrastructures, widespread poverty, and nondemocratic forms of government; and

(2) a modern stage, characterized by a developing urban industrial base, the emergence of a sizable middle class, a higher standard of living generally, and increased egalitarianism at all levels of society. Modernization theorists attempt to analyze the social, political, and economic dynamics involved in the transition between these stages. [15]

Many criticisms have been leveled at the proponents of modernization. Scholars of the new left believe that the modernization approach is yet another attempt by western and American imperialists to justify the hegemony of the capitalist economic and social system. Modernizationists, they charge, overgeneralize and stereotype "traditional" nonindustrial societies, tending to discount the value of the latter. Modernization theory lacks precision, expecially when dealing with societies at the micro level. Modernization concepts fail to satisfactorily explain why fundamental changes have taken place, often relying more on descriptive statements of low explanatory value. Tamara Hareven has charged that modernization approaches advance overly simplistic views of the complex processes involved in social and economic change. [16] The theorists, she notes, often do not distinguish between men and women's roles during the process of modernization. Nor do they recognize that so-called traditional patterns often coexist alongside modern ones.

Maxine Baca Zinn has pointed out that for Mexican American families modernization does not result in " . . . a simple substitution of modern patterns for traditional ones." [17] She found that while employed wives in Chicano families demonstrated more egalitarian behavior in conjugal decision making, they still retained many family values labeled as "traditional." Zinn argues that more research must be done on the variation of Chicano family life and that historians as well as sociologists should abandon the simplistic modern-traditional dichotomy.

A critical view of the ethnocentric stereotypes often found in the modernization approach is necessary if we are to use it to explain change in the Chicano family. Modern forms of family life are not inherently better that traditional ones. Changes associated with industrialization and urbanization have not always been uniformly progressive or positive vis-à-vis the family. The complexity and variability of the "traditional" rural Mexican and Chicano family should be recognized. So-called "static" rural societies are always the result of a dynamic and long term historical process. Enough criticism of the social scientific stereotypes of the "changeless" traditional Mexican family has been leveled to make us suspect idealized and overly romantic notions of family life prior to the American conquest.[18]

For all its limitations, modernization may still prove to be useful for the study of the Mexican American family. Few would deny that industrialization and urbanization has had an impact on the structure and composition of the Chicano family. A systematic study of the modernization pressures experienced by the Mexican rural and urban family during the nineteenth century could reveal patterns and processes clarifyng later changes undergone by Mexican immigrant families in the twentieth century.[19] The problems of assimilation and acculturation, both cultural and economic, may be most usefully studied in light of the modernization approach. Further research on the impact of industrial western societies on nonwestern rural peoples may, in the future, produce more sophisticated concepts and theories which will have a greater explanatory value for our understanding of Mexican-American family history.

A central issue that Chicano historians must confront is the relation of economic development to family change. Modernization theory, for reasons already mentioned, is not easily adapted to a study of the social history of the family. Most recently Barbara Laslett has proposed a theory of family history in relation to the economy which may prove to be useful to social historians.[20]

Basically Laslett's approach is to analyze how the historical needs of the capitalist economic system have been in conflict with the needs of families. Since reproduction and production are vital for the continuation of society, a dialectical conflict often exists. This conflict is at the heart of what should be studied by family historians. Capitalists seek cheap factors of production and profits while heads of families seek higher wages, surplus time, and earnings to enable them to raise children and provide sustenance for non-employed household members. The theory revolves around an analysis of "... those actions which families take in order to secure material resources necessary for reproduction of their members... "[21] Using this approach, she suggests that historians concentrate on the ways in which families have responded to uncertainty created by the economic system. A vital part of any historical analysis of family history should be how class conflict affects family change and how social and political institutions affect the well-being of the family.[22]

A problem with Laslett's theory, at least as it is stated in its preliminary form, is that it cannot account for different responses to the same economic exigencies. Why, for example, have Black families responded to poverty and exploitation differently from Mexican,

Italian, Vietnamese, or Filipino families? Families have interpreted and responded to their environment in ways that cannot always be linked to concrete economic conditions. Their responses may not always have a clear relationship to economic self-interest or survival. Take, for example the tendency of some poor and working-class families to have large numbers of children. It has not always been in their economic interest to do so. Some families have reacted to their poverty by encouraging education for their children, while others have not. In general, Laslett's theory, as is true with most Marxian-based theories, cannot account for variations in the working-class family's responses to industrialization.

Laslett's theory offers a dynamic view for explaining very important social processes within the family. Collective family actions, such as the formation of *mutualistas* (mutual aid societies), family-based businesses, and the organization of trade unions and political movements along family lines have been an important phenomenon in Chicano history. When fully developed, Laslett's theory will be an important one, complementing and adding a new dimension to Mario Barrera's synthesis of internal colonialism and class segmentation theory.[23]

A weakness of Marxian-based theories in general is their tendency to discount the importance of psychological or emotional aspects of family life. In perhaps the most sophisticated and challenging theory of family history developed thus far, Mark Poster has attempted to develop a theoretical view which can deal with both the economic and psychological issues of family history.[24] Poster's theoretical formulations emerge out of a critical reading of Freudian psychology, Marxian interpretations of Freud developed by Wilhelm Reich, Max Harkheimer, and the Frankfort School, and a wide range of European and American theorists including Eric Ericson and Talcott Parsons.

From a sweeping and critical review of these theoretical formulations, Poster hypothesizes that family history must be conceptualized from three perspectives (1) the psychological, (2) the reality of everyday life, and (3) the interrelations between the family and society. The family on the psychological level is conceived as being constituted by hierarchies of age and sex, each of which has its own psychological or emotional issues.[25] Relations between children and parents along patterns of identification and authority are the focus of historical analysis. The psychological consequences of child rearing practices are seen as central for understanding the emotional reality of family life.

Prior to an understanding of the family on the psychological level, however, it must be described as a mundane reality from the point of view of everyday life. Categories of family life, derived from a detailed ethnographic study, are used to reconstruct the daily functioning of family participants, their physical environment, and interactions. The study of the family on this level includes an analysis of household compositions, sexual relations, life cycles, residential patterns, and customs.

The final component to Poster's approach is a study of the family in its structural relation to society. Here the family is conceived as influencing and being influenced by political, economic, and legal institutions. Since the psychological structure of the family may not be congruent with the formal hierarchies of society, the results of the family's interactions with society are not predictable and are often a source of conflict.[26]

Poster gives an example of how his critical theory can be used by historians in his analysis of four models of family types: the peasant and aristocratic family in sixteenth- and seventeenth-century Europe, the bourgeois family in the nineteenth century, and the working-class family during the early Industrial Revolution.[27] In each case his analysis reveals a richness of historical detail along with a conceptual unity which is impressive. In order for historians to achieve the same level of analysis, they would have to be thoroughly familiar with a wealth of psychological and sociological literature on the family. Poster's critical theory of the family is a highly sophisticated one which can be applied by Chicano historians only after a great deal of background reading. Of all the theories discussed thus far, it seems the one best suited for a historical analysis of the Chicano family.

Unlike Marxian or cultural approaches, Poster's theory conceives of the family in holistic terms, enabling a more thorough discussion of the socio-psychological dimensions of family life. Using it, for example, we could study Mexicano and Chicano families prior and subsequent to the Mexican War in order to evaluate what was lost and what was gained by the Anglo-American control of the Southwest. We might use the theory to construct historical models of Chicano family life in times past. These would be similar to the ones Poster has given as examples: The Mexicano upper class, rural campesino, and mestizo families prior to 1848; the upper and working class families from 1848 to 1910; the Mexican immigrant families, 1910-1930; and the Chicano middle class family, 1950-1981. Other models could be proposed. In each case, after constructing a detailed profile, we could be able to understand the historical evolution of the family from a multidimensional perspective.

The collective efforts of many scholars over a long period of time will be necessary in order to achieve a solid history of the Chicano family. At present Chicano family studies are largely the domain of the social scientists, not historians. The challenge historians face is to assimilate the wealth of contemporary and past research with historical consciousness. Much work remains to be done. This new direction for Chicano scholarship offers a tremendous challenge for the 1980s.

MEXICAN AMERICAN STUDIES
SAN DIEGO STATE UNIVERSITY

Notes

[1] These have been discussed at length by Maris A. Vinovskis in "From Household Size to the Life Course: Some Observations on Recent Trends in Family History," *American Behavioral Scientist*, Vol. 21 (November-December, 1977), pp. 263-283.

[2] For further discussion of the Cambridge thesis, see Peter Laslett, ed., *Family Life and Illicit Love in Earlier Generations: Essays in Historical Sociology* (London, 1977), p. 13; also in Peter Laslett and Richard Wall, eds., *Household and Family in Times Past* (Cambridge: Cambridge University Press, 1972), pp. ix-9.

[3] See John Demos, "Families in Colonial Bristol, Rhode Island," *William and Mary Quarterly*, Vol. 25 (January, 1968), pp. 40-57; Phillip Greven, "Family Structure in Seventeenth Century Andover," *William and Mary Quarterly*, Vol. 23 (April 1966), pp. 234-256; William Goode, *World Revolution and Family Patterns* (London: The Free Press of Glencoe, Collier McMillan, Ltd., 1963), p. 9.

[4] For criticism of the Cambridge thesis, see: Lutz K. Burkner, "The Use and Misuse of Census Data for the Historical Analysis of Family Structure," *Journal of Interdisciplinary History*, Vol. 5 (spring, 1975), pp. 721-738; "The Stem Family and the Developmental Cycle of the Peasant Household: An 18th-Century Austrian Example," in *The American Family in Social-Historical Perspective*, ed. Michael Gordon (New York: St. Martin's Press, 1973), pp. 34-58; Michael Anderson, "Family, Household and the Industrial Revolution," pp. 59-75.

[5] Jaime Sena-Rivera, "Extended Kinship in the United States: Competing Models and the Case of la Familia Chicana," *Journal of Marriage and the Family*, Vol. 41 (February 1979), pp. 121-129.

[6] Philip J. Greven Jr., *Four Generations: Population, Land and Family in Colonial Andover, Massachusetts* (Ithaca, New York: Cornell University Press, 1970).

[7] Rudolfo Alvarez, "The Psycho-Historical and Sociological Development of the Chicano Community in the United States," *Social Science Quarterly*, Vol. 3 (1973), pp. 920-942; Alberto Camarillo, "Research Note on Chicano Community Leadership: The G.I. Generation," *Aztlán*, Vol. 2 (fall 1971); Mario García, "La Familia: The Mexican Immigrant Family, 1900-1930," in *Work, Family, Sex Roles and Language*, ed. Mario Barrera, Alberto Camarillo and Francisco Hernández (Berkeley: Tonatiuh-Quinto Sol, 1980), pp. 117-139.

[8] For a discussion of the life cycle and family historical research, see Maris A. Vinoskis, "From Household Size to the Life Course," *American Behavioral Scientist,* Vol. 21 (November-December 1977), pp. 263-283. A discussion of the sociological development of the family life cycle concept is in Paul Glick and Robert Parke, Jr., "New Approaches in Studying the Life Cycle of the Family," *Demography,* Vol. 2 (1965), pp. 187-202.

[9] Evelyn Duval and Ruben Hill, "Report of the Committee of the Dynamics of Family Interaction," National Conference on Family Life, Washington D.C., 1948, in *Family Development,* ed. Evelyn Duval (Philadelphia: Lippincott, 1971), pp. 116-117. The family cycle stages are as follows: (1) family formation by newly married couple, (2) married couple with children under three months of age, (3) family with preschool children between thirty months and six years of age (4) family with school-age children between six and thirteen years, (5) family with teenagers thirteen to twenty years, (6) family as launching center with first child leaving to last child leaving, (7) middle-aged parents without children, (8) aging family, retirement, and death of both spouses.

[10] See Laurence A. Glasco, "The Life Cycle and Household Structure of American Ethnic Groups: Irish, Germans, and Native Born Whites in Buffalo, New York, 1855," *Journal of Urban History,* Vol. 1 (May, 1975), pp. 339-364; Howard Chudacoff, "The Newlyweds and Family Extension: The First Stage of the Family Cycle in Providence, Rhode Island 1864-65 and 1879-80," in *Family and Population in Nineteenth Century America,* ed. Tamara Harevan and Maris Vinosvskis (Princeton, New Jersey: Princeton University Press, 1978), pp. 179-205; John Model and Tamara Harevan, "Urbanization and the Maleable Household: Boarding and Lodging in Nineteenth Century Families," *Journal of Marriage and the Family,* Vol. 35 (August, 1973), pp. 467-479; John Model, "Patterns of Consumption, Acculturation and Family Income Strategies in Late Nineteenth Century America," in *Family and Population in Nineteenth Century America,* pp. 206-240.

[11] Graham Spanier and William Sauer, "Empirical Evaluation of the Family Life Cycle," *Journal of Marriage and the Family,* Vol. 41 (February, 1979), pp. 27-40.

[12] Marta Tienda, "Age and Economic Dependency in Peru: A Family Life-Cycle Analysis," *Journal of Marriage and the Family,* Vol. 42 (August, 1980), pp. 639-653.

[13] See Glen H. Elder, Jr., *The Children of the Great Depression* (Chicago: University of Chicago Press, 1974). For a discussion of the life course see Elder's article, "Family History and the Life Course," *Journal of Family History,* Vol. 2 (December, 1977), pp. 279-304. See also John Model, Frank Furstenberg, Jr., and Theodore Hershberg, "Social Change and Transitions to Adulthood in Historical Perspective," *Journal of Family History,* Vol. 1 (1976), pp. 7-32; also Tamara Hareven (ed.), *Transitions: The Family and the Life Course in Historical Perspective* (New York: Academic Press, 1978), introduction.

[14] See Thomas B. Holman and Wesley R. Burr, "Beyond the Beyond: The Growth of Family Theories in the 1970s," *Journal of Marriage and the Family,* Vol. 42 (November, 1980), pp. 729-741; American social historians have developed but not clearly articulated historical theories on the family. For a discussion of this problem, see Lise Vogel, "Rummaging Through the Primitive Past: A Note on Family, Industrialization, and Capitalism," *The Newberry Papers on Family and Community History* (November, 1966), pp. 6-2.

[15] See Richard Jensen's discussion of the characteristics of these idealized stages in "Modernization and Community History," *The Newberry Papers in Family and Community History,* paper 78-6 (January, 1978), pp. 6-20. For a summary of modernization theory, see James T. Fawcett and Marc H. Borstein, "Modernization,

Individual Modernity and Family," in *Psychological Perspectives on Population,* ed. James T. Fawcett (New York: Basic Books, 1973), p. 106.

[16] Tamara K. Hareven, "Modernization and Family History: Perspectives on Social Change," *Signs: Journal of Women, Culture and Society,* Vol. 2 (autumn 1976), pp. 190-206.

[17] Maxine Baca Zinn, "Employment and Education of Mexican-American Women: The Interplay of Modernity and Ethnicity in Eight Families," *Harvard Educational Review,* Vol. 50 (February, 1980), p. 48; and "Chicano Family Research: Conceptual Distortions and Alternative Directions," *Journal of Ethnic Studies,* Vol. 7 (fall 1979), pp. 59-71.

[18] For a representative sample of criticism of stereotypes regarding the "traditional" family, see Miguel Montiel, "The Social Scientific Myth of the Mexican American Family," *El Grito* (summer 1970), pp. 56-63.

[19] For a discussion of the adaptive role played by Mexican immigrant families, see Mario T. García, "La Familia: The Mexican Immigrant Family, 1900-1930," in *Work, Family, Sex Roles, and Language,* pp. 117-139; see also Alberto Camarillo, *Chicanos in a Changing Society: From Mexican Pueblos to American Barrios in Santa Barbara and Southern California, 1884-1930* (Cambridge, Massachusetts: Harvard University Press, 1979), which argues that patterns established in the nineteenth century were formative for later Chicano history.

[20] Barbara Laslett, "Production, Reproduction and Social Change: A Theory of the Family in History," unpublished ms., n.d.

[21] Laslett, p. 14.

[22] Laslett, pp. 27-28.

[23] See Mario Barrera, *Race and Class in the Southwest: A Theory of Racial Inequality* (Notre Dame, Indiana: University of Notre Dame Press, 1979), pp. 212-219.

[24] Mark Poster, *A Critical Theory of the Family* (New York: Seabury Press, 1978).

[25] Poster, p. 155.

[26] See Poster's discussion in Ch. 6, "Elements of a Critical Theory of the Family."

[27] Poster, pp. 166-205.

MEXICAN CINEMA IN THE
UNITED STATES
1940-1952*

Alex M. Saragoza

> In the course of bringing culture to the masses, the advertising industry, the mass media . . . and other agencies of mass tuition took over many of the socializing functions of the home and brought the ones that remained under the direction of modern science and technology.
>
> —Christopher Lasch, *The Culture of Narcissism*

> In Mexico, television is in the midst of an enormous ideological campaign consistent with most reactionary political groups . . . an anticommunist and antidemocratic campaign of tremendous reach.
>
> —Pablo González Casanova, *El estado y los partidos políticos*

Observers of the mass media, as evidenced in the quotes above, have raised several issues regarding the control, purpose and impact of radio, television and cinema. In this vein, the civil rights movement contributed a distinct current of criticism and questioning of the media, particularly their uses to foster racism in American society. Feminists offered their own critique, stressing the inherent sexism found in the portrayal of women and the family in radio commercials,

---

*The author would like to acknowledge the aid of Juanita Saragoza in the collection of data and the assistance of Franciso García, Head Librarian, Chicano Studies Library, UC Berkeley, in the location of research materials.

TV soap operas and motion pictures. In this light, Chicano scholars, among others, understandably called attention to the negative repercussions, past and present, of the media upon minority communities in general, and on children in particular. In this connection, critics noted the increasing powers of the media in the process of socialization. And, in fact, some critics turned to Marxist concepts to explain the role of the mass media in American life.[1]

In the case of the Chicano experience, however, the presence of Spanish-language media in the United States must be considered in addition to the effects of American mass communications. Continuing, substantial immigration from Mexico, moreover, has facilitated the existence of radio and television broadcasting, advertising and moviehouses for Spanish-speaking audiences. Hence, if the media have an impact on Chicanos, regardless of the nature of the effect, the application of that argument plainly entails a critical analysis of Mexican radio, television and film. If Mexican movies, for instance, convey a "message," historians must begin to explore that message in terms of its origins in Mexico and its significance for Mexicans in the United States. In this respect, such an analysis must also be historically specific, that is, the intent and consequences of a movie produced in 1942 may have very different meanings when seen in 1972, whether in Mexico or in this country. Furthermore, an examination of Spanish-language media must also take into account the diversity among Chicanos and its implications for an analysis of the media in Chicano communities.

Finally, given the persistent pattern of Mexican immigration and the recent emergence of an extensive Spanish-language Mexican-controlled television network in the United States, a larger issue underlies the specific focus of this essay: the importance of understanding the interface between Mexico and Mexicans in the United States. As a review of the past proceedings of the National Association for Chicano Studies makes clear, students of the Chicano experience have generally neglected the complexities surrounding the relationship between Mexico and Mexicans in the United States. For the social historian especially, the study of Chicano communities must encompass a Mexican dimension for a complete and penetrating view. In this sense, certain aspects of the Chicano experience must be seen in the context of the intersection of Mexican and American history. Only then can historians fully assess the socialization of Mexican communities in the United States. This essay intends to explore only one facet of this interface. Nonetheless, through this inquiry, we hope to shed light on the significance of the interface between Mexico and Mexicans in the United States as a means to grasp a deeper understanding of Chicano social history.

This paper will focus on the development of Mexican cinema during the period 1940 to 1952. Specifically, our analysis will concentrate on two prominent themes in terms of their sociocultural "messages" and their political implications: (1) the portrayal of the family, and (2) the treatment of poverty and the poor in Mexican film.

The importance of the period 1940-1952 for the Mexican movie industry stemmed from a series of interrelated changes that produced a substantial increase in film production, the consolidation of major studios, and the maturation of various genres within Mexican cinema.[2] Furthermore, a native "star system" appeared in which certain actors, actresses, comedians and singers achieved enormous popularity.[3] Moreover, a group of directors emerged that exercised great influence over the style of Mexican motion pictures.[4] These developments, however, occurred within a political economy marked by an intensifying conservatism, a conservatism that penetrated deeply into Mexican popular culture, including the country's cinematic representations.

Yet, the "messages" contained in Mexican movies were not confined to the people south of the Rio Grande. Mexican film production in the years 1940-1952 provided a reservoir of motion pictures that were repeatedly shown in theaters patronized by Mexicans north of the border. Coincidentally, and especially in the postwar period, the United States witnessed a surge of conservatism. Thus, the intent of Mexican cinema of the 1940-1952 era perhaps paralleled, if not contributed to, the conservatism in America in the Cold War years.

A convergence of forces and events produced Mexico's so-called cinematic "golden age" from 1940 to 1952. Three major factors proved to be particularly significant. First, the strong wave of nationalism regenerated by the presidency of Lázaro Cárdenas (1934-1940); second, the political consolidation of Mexico's dominant party after 1940 and its conservative character; third, the greater opportunities presented to Mexican filmmakers as a consequence of the impact of World War II on the American movie industry. In this context, Mexican movie production grew impressively (see Table 1). Nonetheless, the rise of Mexican motion pictures also included their use to buttress increasingly conservative political regimes.

TABLE 1

Mexican Film Production

Year	Number of Films
1930	1
1931	1
1932	6
1933	21
1934	23
1935	22
1936	25
1937	38
1938	57
1939	36
1940	29
1941	37
1942	47
1943	70
1944	73
1945	82
1946	72
1947	58
1948	81
1949	108
1950	124
1951	101

Nationalism pervaded postrevolutionary Mexico. But European and American influences remained through magazines, advertising, products, and Spanish-language radio broadcasting. The introduction of sound motion pictures initially was restricted to English-speaking audiences. With time, Hollywood added Spanish sound tracks or subtitles to American-made movies and subsequently found an eager market in Mexico. By the 1930s, the American cinematic conquest of its southern neighbor was nearly complete and reached into the remotest corners of the country. As one American anthropologist observed at the time,

> I remember arriving, after three long days of grueling riding into the heart of the great Guerrero mountain range, at the little town of Tlapa. As I dismounted from my horse a native Indian band came marching down the street with a little boy in front holding aloft on a stick a lurid billboard poster announcing to the world that that very night the local movie house would show a "Stirring and Adventurous Drama in Eight Parts Entitled: 'The Reporter of Hollywood.'"[5]

The dominance of American films in Mexico contrasted glaringly with the cultural nationalism of the era. Elected in 1934, the nationalistic Lázaro Cárdenas responded by clamping down on American films, especially those deemed unacceptable to the Mexican government. "Thus we reject movies or scenes that in some form denigrate our nation's history, its people, its institutions and its famous men," a government statement declared at the time; and "we avoid," it went on to say, "the exhibition of movies that contain in their scripts attacks on governments and people friendly to Mexico."[6] The concerns of the Cárdenas administration were understandable in light of the fact, for example, that between June, 1932 to July, 1933, 92 percent of the films shown in Mexico were from the United States.[7] Subsequently, the Mexican government encouraged native producers to make their own movies with Mexican themes and consistent with the interests of the Mexican people.

In the nationalistic atmosphere under Cárdenas, Mexican filmmakers intensified their efforts and their use of elements peculiarly Mexican, e.g. they made films on the Mexican revolution and on Mexico's rural people, and they were willing to employ Mexican popular music. Intellectual currents supported such efforts, created a receptive climate for nationalistic motion pictures, and provided inspiration for cinematic productions. The writings of Martín Luis Guzmán on the revolution, the *indigenismo* of Gregorio López y Fuentes' novel *El Indio,* the musical compositions of Carlos Chávez, and the antiforeign tones of the Mexican muralists such as Diego Rivera and José Clemento Orozco fashioned a nationalistic milieu that found expression in Mexican cinema.[8] *Vámonos con Pancho Villa* (1935) paralleled Mexico's literature of the revolution; *Janitzio* (1934) reflected the *indigenismo* of the era.[9] But it would be a sentimental, musical *comedia ranchera* that set the tenor of Mexican film for several years to come: *Allá en el Rancho Grande* (1936) by Fernando de Fuentes.[10] The singing *charro* (in this case Tito Guízar), melodramatic romances, moon-lit serenades, comic relief and a mariachi-filled, romanticized view of *haciendas, hacendados* and *peones* composed the ingredients of de Fuentes' incredibly popular production.[11] The success of the film astonished Mexicans in general, wealthy businessmen in particular. *Allá en el Rancho Grande* clearly established the popularity of "Mexican" motion pictures, and perhaps more importantly, their profit-making potential. To culminate the period's nationalistic surge, Cárdenas' nationalization of the oil industry in 1938 touched off an explosion of patriotism and effusive *mexicanismo.* In that same year, Mexico produced 57 films, an accomplishment previously unmatched and not exceeded until 1943.

The presidency of Lázaro Cárdenas led to a decisive shift in Mexican popular culture. The record industry, radio broadcasting, and mass publications reproduced in their own fashion the country's nationalist currents. Indeed, the definition of Mexican culture in the 1930s encompassed idealized representations of Mexico's impoverished working class. With the proliferation and accessibility of the forms of popular cultural expression, the cinematic depiction of Mexico's largely poor population took on a new significance, a perspective endowed with a positive, ennobling view of the Mexican masses.[12] The integration of the popular classes (to use the term employed by Mexican officials) into the mass media also reflected the absorption of newly-organized segments of Mexican society into the political system. The marriage of cultural nationalism and politics underscored Cárdenas' administration.

To a large extent, Cárdenas attempted to construct a corporatist state. In 1938, the Mexican president reconstituted the ruling party *(Partido Nacional Revolucionario)* to include representation from the military, labor, peasants and bureaucrats. To indicate the change, the PNR was renamed the *Partido Mexicano Revolucionario* (PMR) and included two organizations that signified the corporatist nature of the Cárdenas presidency: *La Confederación de Trabajadores Mexicanos* (CTM) and *La Confederación Nacional Campesina* (CNC). As Arnaldo Córdova has observed, the PMR "did not emerge precisely as a mass party, rather as a party of groupings (corporaciones), in which its base of support were the organizations, while individuals became secondary."[13] Unfortunately, where Cárdenas' vision produced significant social reforms, he also constructed a political machine vulnerable to uses unforeseen by the most radical leader of postrevolutionary Mexico.

As a result of the Cárdenas-inspired changes, government and party became synonymous with national interest. Consequently, government policies were identified as a product of a consensual political process. A consensus legitimized through the representatives of the various "organized" sectors of Mexican society such as the CTM and CNC. In exchange for influence, the organizations lent their loyalty to the state. In such a corporatist arrangement, nationalism provided a powerful, unifying element, but a force open to manipulation as well. The beginning of World War II coincided with the end of the Cárdenas presidency in 1940. The war and the new administration marked a crucial transition in Mexico that was reproduced in Mexican cinema.

World War II quickly altered the American movie industry. The war effort was translated into film with predictably patriotic results. Moreover, the war meant less money to spend on motion pictures slated for non-English-speaking markets and their attendant costs. As a result, fewer movies were available to Spanish-speaking audiences. Furthermore, American war films were not necessarily popular in Latin America, including Mexico. The subsequent vacuum expanded the national market for Mexican movie producers.[14] In 1940, only 29 films were made in Mexico. Five years later, over 80 movies were produced. As the war stimulated industrialization through import substitution, it also spurred the growth of the Mexican motion picture business.

With its expansion, the Mexican movie industry attracted large capitalist interests (foreign and domestic). These interests signified the emergence of dominant studios with considerable resources. Azteca and CLASA studios soon established their preponderant position over the production of Mexican film. Morever, both companies actively promoted their pictures in the U.S. For instance, in a three-month period in 1948, in Los Angeles, Azteca and CLASA produced 82 percent of the films advertized in the newspaper La Opinión. Azteca alone was responsible for half of the movies that appeared in the newspaper's advertisements. The significance of this development was magnified by the political context in which it occurred.[15]

Mexico entered a new political era in 1940. The presidential administrations of Manuel Avila Camacho (1940-1946) and Miguel Alemán Valdés (1946-1952) inherited Cárdenas' corporatist state, but little of his idealism. "These politicians altered the system, became great bourgeoisie, and began to pass power on to the technocrats in the 1940s," as Albert Michaels and Marvin Bernstein have concluded, "yet, in the end the national bourgeoisie retained power, consolidated their gains and directed Mexico in their preferred direction."[16] The ties between capitalists and the state waxed during and after the war years. This period also served to maintain the economic nationalism engendered by Cárdenas. Mexican industry continued to be highly protected in the name of national interest while profits and benefits increasingly remained in a small number of hands. Foreign investment was allowed to enter the country, especially in the postwar administration, and particularly when such investments furthered the interests of Mexican capitalists.[17]

The intimacy of the alliance between government and businessmen led to a repudiation of Cardenista aims as social policies after 1940 evinced a forceful conservatism. The union of Mexico's ruling party and native capitalists was symbolized in the conversion of the *Partido Revolucionario Mexicano* in 1946 to its present namesake, *Partido Revolucionario Institucional*. The nationalistic substance of the Cárdenas presidency also changed. As Jorge Basurto has noted,

> Of course, the nationalistic rhetoric was not abandoned for a moment; only its content was changed. The nationalism under Cárdenas . . . was essentially leftist . . . As such, that nationalism was unacceptable, for the bourgeoisie that exercised pressures on government so it would be abandoned, but for the government as well that did not resist pressures since it too was so inclined.[18]

Under this arrangement, public acquiescence to governmental policies became especially important as the inequities in Mexican society intensified. While the cost of living more than doubled between 1940 and 1945 (and had tripled by 1950), real wages remained virtually stagnant.[19] Not surprisingly, Mexican cinema reflected the conservatism of the new order. Mexican films increasingly evoked the idealization of obedience and the maintenance of the status quo in Mexican society.

The formation of the government-sponsored Banco Cinematográfico (Film Bank) in 1942 confirmed the linkage between government and movie-makers. The bank made loans to motion picture producers tht met the appropriate criteria. Predictably, as the movie critic Emilio García Riera has observed, "the movie production groups favored by the policies of the Film Bank were precisely those whose major interests indicated support for a nationalist cinema."[20] In addition, the *Departamento de Censura Cinematográfica* (Motion Picture Censorship Department) was inaugurated in 1941 and clearly functioned to promote films acceptable to the dominant order. "It is impossible to permit," stated the head of the censorship department in 1944, "the exhibition of movies that denigrate Mexico whether they are domestic or foreign films."[21] Denigration, of course, included criticism of governmental policies or the promotion of alternative approaches. Cinema became, therefore, an instrument of Mexican conservatism, a conservatism cloaked in nationalist robes.

Between 1940 and 1952, two themes consistently appered in Mexican motion pictures and signalled the conservative nature of the Avila Camacho and Alemán administrations. The cinematic depiction of the family developed into a persistent symbol of the importance and virtues of authority, paternalism, and servility. And, in light of the number of poor in Mexico, it was perhaps understandable that the exaltation of poverty constituted another conspicuous current in Mexican film. In both cases, particularly after 1940, these themes spawned numerous variants with formula plots, stock characters, and similar settings. Moreover, formula films often included the identification of certain movie stars with the roles common to such movies: Sara García, the quintessential maternal figure, Fernando Soler, the premier patriarch, and Pedro Infante as working-class hero were employed frequently by producers to fulfill the requisite roles of formula cinema. The popularity and talent of such actors and actresses only served to enhance the attraction—and profits—of Mexican motion pictures during this era.

In 1941, Juan Bustillo Oro directed *Cuando los hijos se van,* which established the standards for future family films. The movie broke all box office records for that time. The storyline concerned a hard-working father and mother whose children leave the provincial home despite the protestations of their parents and suffer various calamitous experiences. The rebellious offspring return, chastened yet pardoned by the understanding parents. Bustillo Oro's melodramatic motion picture contained a sibling rivalry that ultimately leads to the death of a son (but the guilty brother is later forgiven), a restive, bored daughter who marries to escape the family but finds only abuse, and, lastly, divorce, and the humble, dutiful young man who waits patiently by for the daughter to see the error of her ways, and who finally wins her heart. The message was clear: stay in your place.

Cuando los hijos se van generated a multitude of imitations. In 1942 alone, Sara García played her maternal role in five different motion pictures subsequent to her motherly role in Bustillo Oro's 1941 film as well as her maternal performance in *La gallina clueca* (also in 1941). The title of one film, *Dulce madre mía* (1942), perhaps best summarized the flavor of such movies.[22] In virtually all of these motion pictures, recalcitrant children were invariably selfish, consistently miserable, and always wrong. The essence of such movies was well-captured in the words on a publicity poster for *Cuando los hijos se van:*

> The sanctuary of the Mexican home, rich in tradition with noble customs, serves as the stage of a story of abnegation and tenderness that makes us recall those who gave us life without ever asking for compensation.[23]

One can easily imagine an audience awash with guilt, popped heartstrings, and tear-filled eyes, eager to visit parents after the movie.

Women's roles, especially "wayward daughters," were used regularly to underscore the ill-fated consequences of defiance. Divorce, abandonment, loss of virtue (not to mention virginity), abuse, infidelity, or death were frequent outcomes for restive women; unless, of course, they realized their mistakes and asked for forgiveness (usually in the last reel). In the case of those who died at the end, pardon often occurred in the last gasp of life in the arms of a faithful, virtuous admirer (the guy she should have married), or in the redemptive embrace of a compassionate parent. The gist of such pictures was caught in the publicity statement for *La Abuelita* (1942): "The intense conflict of a modern and tempestuous granddaughter that threatens the purest tradition of a Mexican home, a home of peace and pristine customs defended by a venerable grandmother."[24]

In 1948, Bustillo Oro returned to a familiar theme in *Cuando los padres se quedan solos* (1948). The content of the film scarcely differed from his effort seven years earlier. The message remained the same: uncompliant children continued to be ungrateful, to be victims of their disobedience, and to be sorry for their failure to recognize the wisdom of their parents. Formula family movies persisted in their defense of the status quo, and by extension, of the acceptance of the judgment of sanctioned authority, for example, policies generated by the union of Mexican businessmen and public officials.

If cinema reflected the interests of dominant groups, conditions in Mexico indicated the need for popular culture to provide such support. After 1940, the Mexican government and its capitalist allies apparently required an ideological apologia. Under the administrations of Avila Camacho and Alemán, the amount of national income earned by workers declined from 29 percent to 22 percent, despite a spectacular rise in GNP. Land redistribution fell sharply. Whereas land reform benefitted over 777,000 persons under Cárdenas, only 112,500 people received land during Avila Camacho's tenure in office, and a mere 85,000 *campesinos* gained land in Alemán's presidency.[25] In short, as Roger D. Hansen has concluded, the ruling coalition of politicians and businessmen developed policies "which tightly controlled labor union activity, slowed the pace of agrarian reform, and reduced the relative share of total income of the bottom 60 percent of the Mexican population."[26] Yet, Mexican cinema persistently portrayed the afflictions of affluence and the advantages of poverty. The epitome of this type of film appeared in 1948 and became the most popular movie in Mexican history—*Nosotros los pobres* (1947) with (who else?) Pedro Infante.

In a motion picture filled with subplots and colorful characters, the story basically concerned the efforts of a good-hearted, unpretentious, widowed carpenter Pepe el Toro (Infante) to establish a cooperative carpentry shop while winning the hand of the beautiful and virtuous Celia (Estela Blanca Pavón). The romance was complicated by the rival presence of a wealthy lawyer intent on marrying Celia. By the end of the film, Pepe el Toro had undergone a critical loss of funds, several affronts by his rich rival, false imprisonment for murder and a subsequent stay in solitary confinement, the loss of his home, the death of his paralyzed mother, and a to-the-death fight with three goons. Needless to say, in the end, Pepe el Toro was cleared of the crime, won back his home and shop, and married Celia while strains of "Amorcito Corazón" played in the background. Under the direction of Ismael Rodríguez, the nobility and joy of the poor contrasted frequently with the predictable wickedness and insensitivity of the wealthy. In short, in such movies, "the poor are always better than the rich," as one cultural historian has observed, and "it is preferable to live happy and poor than a millionaire and alone."[27]

Nosotros los pobres had some predecessors, most notably Alejandro Galindo's more provocative, incisive film, *Campeón sin corona* (1945). But the huge popularity of Ismael Rodríguez' vehicle gave birth to a string of motion pictures that retraced the major features of *Nosotros los pobres* and its thematic elements. Indeed, Ismael Rodríguez immediately followed his original, and profitable, success with *Ustedes los ricos* (1948) where Pedro Infante reenacted his part as Pepe el Toro. (A third segment, *Pepe el Toro,* appeared four years later). In Rodríguez' films, and in those of his imitators, the depiction of poverty "was more than an economic condition," rather it became a virtual "social and moral privilege."[28]

Furthermore, the formula poverty movie often conveyed the notion that the "real Mexican" *(lo mexicano)* resided among the poor; and, in fact, *mexicanidad* was frequently identified with poverty. In addition, socioeconomic ascent implied the acquisition of non-Mexican values, attitudes, manners, and dress. In this respect, *agringado* ("americanized") characters were usually treated negatively since such people were flawed by their wealth as well as their lack of Mexicanness. Mobility, or the desire for it, therefore was depicted as a near act of disloyalty. Such a view was suggested, for example, in the portrayal of Mexicans who resided in the United States and who had learned English (or *pochos*) in the film *Primero soy mexicano* (1950). As a satirical song in the movie put it:

If I like 'hot cakes'
I say 'hello' without a handshake
and though I ask for 'ham and eggs'
First I am Mexican!

I don't like those brothers
whose father they call 'daddy'
and their mothers always 'mommy'
all that is vain pride
First I am Mexican![29]

To struggle against poverty, then, courted the anguish of the wealthy, the loss of *lo mexicano,* and the risk of cultural corruption.

Exceptions to the formula movies appeared at times. A few films challenged the motion picture conventions of the era. Nonetheless, in general, Mexican movies remained safely within established cinematic boundaries. Yet, the *cine del pueblo* continued to be popular and usually profitable. While critics frequently lashed out at the bulk of Mexican films, people still poured into theaters. To a large extent, much of Mexico's population apparently identified with the people on the screen. Nearly three decades later, the director Alejandro Galindo recalled the powerful ability of cinema to idealize the *pobre pueblo* (poor people). As Galindo noted to an interviewer, "when the common people have seen themselves reflected in the screen, they respond like you cannot imagine; it is truly moving."[30]

Film-makers possessed the capability to provide a different vision to their audiences. Instead, they chose another path. Most of the movie industry, like Ismael Rodríguez, created a world that pandered to the poor without proposing a solution to their misery. "I believe that the pubic goes to the movies to entertain themselves," as the actress Sara García stated, "nót to see problems, they have enough of them at home, *nor do they go to think* "[31] (my emphasis). Indeed, at its worst, Mexican cinema extolled the splendid acquiescence of the poor to their conditions. It was perhaps an understandable, lamentable failure under the political circumstances of the period. On the other hand, it was also a craven example of the servitude of cinema to the hegemony of political and economic interests. The Mexican experience, however, was not unique.

Across the border, the 1940s and 1950s witnessed a similar relationship between mass culture and political economy. Patriotism obviously and understandably marked American films during the Second World War. The subsequent Cold War decade offered a steady diet of movies that stressed Americanization and conformity. The "communist conspiracy" to take over the world became an undoubted assumption among the American public. Most people presumed that the "wily hand" of communism "reached into every aspect of life in the United States, inculcating attitudes destructive of the truly American way of living and thinking."[32]

In such a milieu, the mass media, especially cinema, attracted the attention of anti-communist zealots, led by Senator Joseph McCarthy. Hollywood quickly succumbed to the pressure with obvious repercussions for American movies. The investigations of the House Committee on Un-American Activities into the American film industry pushed studios to produce "safe" films, i.e. works devoid of controversial or critical content. "Creative work at its best could indeed not be carried on in an atmosphere of fear," Robert Sklar has noted, "and Hollywood was suffused with fear."[33] Redbaiting, innuendo and unsubstantiated allegations proved to be lethal weapons for McCarthy and his right-wing supporters to bully studios, to intimidate actors, actresses, directors and to ruin the careers of resistant individuals. Not surprisingly, conservatism, and its political corollary, McCarthyism, permeated the mass media. As a result, William E. Leuchtenburg has concluded, the period "created an atmosphere which suffocated serious consideration of critical public issues."[34] In short, American wartime movies, and particularly in the post-war era, conveyed a message laced with nationalism, with the importance of consensus, with the dangers of dissent."[35]

The content of Mexican movies reflected views not unlike those seen in American motion pictures of the late '40s and early '50s. After the war, American theaters encountered a great number of movies available to show Spanish-speaking audiences. Nonetheless, with time, the demand for Mexican films exhausted the supply. Not surprisingly, theater managers were forced to exhibit older movies in order to supplement newer releases. In Los Angeles, for example, in a two-month period (March-April, 1948) about 55 films were shown in theaters patronized by Spanish-speaking people. Yet, during that time, several of the motion pictures were repeated, often as second features, and in different movie houses. As a result, between March and April of 1948, 87 percent of the Mexican films advertised in the Los Angeles newspaper *La Opinión* were made prior to 1947.[36] Consequently, the messages of Mexican movies persisted for years beyond their date of production.

Mexicans in the United States found little, therefore, in Mexican or American films to question their status or conditions. Moreover, Mexican cinema worked perhaps to inhibit criticism in Mexico and among Mexicans north of the Rio Grande. The substantial increase in the arrival of Mexican immigrants throughout the war and subsequent years only served to multiply this effect. It is conceivable that exploiters of Mexican labor on both sides of the border benefitted from the alliance of conservatism and nationalism in Mexican motion pictures, an alliance easily appreciated by those who profited from the false consciousness of Mexican workers and their families.

Antonio Gramsci stressed the capacity of ruling groups to shape the consciousness of subordinate sectors of society, i.e. to establish a hegemonic culture that furthered the interests of the prevailing order. In this process, Gramsci pointed out, sources of cultural reproduction (such as religion, schools, media) played a crucial role through their espousal of ideas that attenuated or deflected the ability of the oppressed to perceive the origins of their oppression. According to Gramsci, a false view of social and economic relations ensued and developed. [37] In the case of Mexican cinema, the theme of the family was used as a vehicle to idealize authority. Implicitly, if not explicitly, such a message worked to support Mexico's political and economic elites. Largely subsidized by the government-sponsored Film Bank, Mexican cinema went further in its defense of the status quo. In the midst of an acceleration of the concentration of wealth, Mexican film transfigured the poor and poverty into an embodiment of nationalism, of *patria*. The idealistic nationalism of the Cárdenas years degenerated into a hollow facade manipulated by a coalition of businessmen and government bureaucrats to sustain their position and policies. In its most vulgar form, *lo mexicano* was expressed cinematically as deferential and poor.

The political intent of Mexican cinema emanates clearly from its treatment of the family and poverty. Still, questions remain that require clarification and inquiry. For example, the political connections between filmmakers, party officials, movie-related agencies and businessmen need elaboration. In addition, the pressures of the U.S. also entail study since Mexico was not immune from American influences. Moreover, an in-depth analysis of this period calls for an examination of other forces that contributed to the power of the business-government coalition forged by the Avila Camacho and Alemán administrations. Although it is beyond the scope of this paper, the political environment and workings in which Mexican cinema developed demand further research in order to analyze more fully the political impact of Mexican film between 1940 and 1952.

Furthermore, the socio-cultural effects of Mexican cinema offer a series of additional questions. The situation of Mexicans in the U.S. presents a particularly complex set of issues. For instance, by the 1950s, diversity marked the Chicano community. This differentiation encompassed adherence to Spanish, identification with Mexico, and an association with Mexican cultural symbols or expressions. Thus, many Chicanos increasingly turned to American films and rarely returned to Mexican theaters. On the other hand, Chicanos often encountered American movies consistent with the conservative themes in Mexican cinema where Americanism replaced the *mexicanismo* of Mexican pictures. Yet, recent Mexican immigrants supplanted to a large extent Chicano moviegoers who preferred English-language films. Did such patterns of movie attendance exacerbate divisions within the Chicano community? Did the nationalism and idealization of the Mexican poor alienate more acculturated Chicanos *(pochos)?* Did movie preferences indicate assimilation as opposed to its resistance? And, did the nationalism of Mexican cinema provide an alternative to the pressures of Americanization or a refuge to the cultural isolation of Mexicans in the U.S.? Such questions and others remain to be answered.

Finally, on the portrayal of the family, Mexican films reflected certain realistic elements of parent-child relations. Nonetheless, Mexican film imposed a view where parental authority was constantly vindicated. Moreover, Mexican motion pictures engendered a view where single women were suspect, married women not entirely trustworthy, and female independence usually unfortunate.[38] Possibly, then, such images reinforced conservative parental practices, inhibited change, or reaffirmed sexism. These important issues also need further study.

Through the analysis of representative movies, this paper has suggested the political significance of the content of Mexican popular culture, specifically cinema, and its implications for Chicano communities in the 1940s and 1950s. For in this period, Chicanos faced a society in the grip of reactionary politics and flag-waving extremism. During that era, Mexican film promoted its own version of conformity, a conformity as enervating and conservative as its American counterpart. Hence, the conservatism of the postwar years in the U.S. found an implicit if inadvertant ally in the messages of Mexican films in Chicano communities. Regardless of the source, the consequences for Mexican workers on either side of the border remained: the attempt of capitalist interests to establish or extend their hegemony. Thus, in light of continuing immigration from

Mexico and the persistence of Mexican-based media in the U.S., historians must take into account the Mexican dimension of the Chicano experience and its implications.

CHICANO STUDIES PROGRAM, DEPARTMENT OF ETHNIC STUDIES
UNIVERSITY OF CALIFORNIA, BERKELEY

Notes

[1] See James Joll, *Antonio Gramsci* (New York: Penguin Books, 1977). On the concept of hegemony, see Louis Althusser, "Ideology and Ideological State Apparatuses," in *Lenin and Philosophy and Other Essays* (London: New Left Books, 1971); Pierre Bourdieu, "Cultural Reproduction and Social Reproduction," in *Power and Ideology in Education*, Karabel, Jerome & Halsey, A.H., ed. (New York: Oxford University Press, 1977); R.W. Connell, *Ruling Class, Ruling Culture* (Cambridge University Press, 1977); P. DiMaggio and M. Useem, "Social Class and Arts Consumption: The Origins and Consequences of Class Differences in Exposure to the Arts in America," *Theory and Society* (5: 1978), pp. 141-161; Georg Lukacs, "Reification and the Consciousness of the Proletariat," in *History and Class Consciousness* (London: Merlin Press, 1968); Raymond Williams, "Base and Superstructure in Marxist Cultural Theory," *New Left Review*, (No. 82), pp. 3-16.

[2] This paper relies heavily on the following works: Jorge Ayala Blanco, *Aventura del cine mexicano* (México: ed. Era, 1968); Miguel Contreras Torres, *El libro negro del cine mexicano* (México: N.P., 1960); Eugenia Meyer, ed., *Cuadernos de la cineteca nacional: testimonios para la historia del cine mexicano* (México: Cineteca Nacional, 1975-1976), 7 vols.; María Isabel De la Fuente, *Indice bibliográfico del cine mexicano* (Mécano: Talleres de Ed. América, 1967), 2 vols.; Alejandro Galindo, *Una radiografía histórica del cine mexicano* (México: Fondo de Cultura Popular, 1968); Emilio García Riera, *Historia documental del cine mexicano; época sonora* (México: Ed. Era, 1969-   ), 9 vols. to date; Federico Heuer, *La industria cinematográfica mexicana* (México: Impreso Policiomía, 1964); Carlos Monsiváis, "Notas sobre la cultura mexicana en el siglo XX," in *Historia General de México* (México: El Colegio de México, 1976); Luis Reyes de la Maza, *El cine sonoro en México* (México: UNAM, 1973); Beatriz Reyes Nevares, *Trece directores del cine mexicano* (México: Sec. de Educación Pública, 1974).

[3] Among the most prominent were Pedro Armendáriz, Sara García, Esther Fernández, Fernando Soler, Pedro Infante, Jorge Negrete, Mario Moreno "Cantinflas," Fernando Soto "Mantequilla."

[4] The "big name" directors included Julio Bracho, Alejandro Galindo, Ismael Rodríguez, Emilio "El Indio" Fernández. Note should be taken of the technical expertise developed in Mexican filmmaking over time. In this regard, Gabriel Figueroa became a world-renowned cinematographer.

[5] Eyler N. Simpson, *The Ejido: Mexico's Way Out* (Chapel Hill: University of North Carolina Press, 1937), p. 551.

[6] Cited in Moisés González Navarro, *Población y Sociedad en México (1900-1970)* (México: UNAM, 1974), vol. 2, pp. 91-92.

[7] Ibid., p. 92.

[8] On Mexican nationalism, see Frederick C. Turner, *The Dynamics of Mexican Nationalism* (Chapel Hill: University of North Carolina Press, 1968); on literary trends, Joseph Sommers, *After the Storm* (Albuquerque: University of New Mexico Press, 1968); on musical currents, Claes af Gerjerstam, *Popular Music in Mexico* (Albuquerque: University of New Mexico Press, 1976); on art and nationalism, Justino Fernández, *A Guide to Mexican Art* (Chicago: University of Chicago Press, 1969).

[9] These two films are important benchmarks in Mexican cinema: the first for its realistic portrayal of the human drama of the Revolution; the second for its Indianist sentiment prior to the crass commercialism of Mexican film after the 1930s.

[10] For a brief but incisive commentary, see Carlos Monsiváis, "Notas sobre la cultura mexicana," pp. 443-445.

[11] At the center of the movie was the relationship of two men, one the kind *hacendado* and the other his poor childhood friend and foreman, played by Tito Guízar. Guízar's fiancée, however, is almost seduced by the *hacendado*. A fatal duel is averted at the last minute, both remain friends, Guízar marries his sweetheart, her designing, ambitious mother exposed as the engineer of the seduction, and everybody lives happily ever after.

[12] On the relationship of society and the Mexican state, see the perceptive essay by Carlos Pereyra, "Estado y sociedad," in *México, hoy,* ed. Pablo González Casanova and Enrique Florescano (México: Siglo Veintiuno Editores, 1980), pp. 289-305.

[13] Arnaldo Córdova, *La política de masas del cardenismo,* 2nd ed. (México: Ediciones Era, 1976), p. 148.

[14] On the impact of the war on American films, see Clayton R. Koppes and Gregory D. Black, "What to Show the World: The Office of War Information and Hollywood, 1942-1945," *Journal of American History* 65: 1 (June, 1977), pp. 87-105. On the impact of the war on Mexican movies, see the interview of the producer Raúl de Anda in *Cuadernos de la cineteca nacional,* vol. 3, p. 71. Colin Shindler, *Hollywood Goes to War: Films and American Society, 1939-1952* (London: Routledge & Kegan Paul, 1979); John E. O'Conner and Martin A. Jackson, eds., *American History/American Film: Interpreting the Hollywood Image* (New York: Ungar, 1979), should also be consulted.

[15] The rise of major studios is beyond the scope of this paper; however, the Film Bank made loans to the studios that competed for "stars" and directors. Hence, as the costs of films rose, private investors were able to exercise greater influence as the Film Bank loans were unable to cover the entire costs of production. The information on Los Angeles comes from *La Opinión* for the weeks covering March 1, 1948 to May 30, 1948.

[16] Albert L. Michaels and Marvin Bernstein, "The Modernization of the Old Order," in *Contemporary Mexico,* ed. James W. Wilkie et. al. (Los Angeles: University of California Press, 1976), p. 701.

[17] Lorenzo Meyer, "La encrucijada," in *Historia General de México,* vol. 4, especially pp. 204-208.

[18] Jorge Basurto, "Oligarquía, nacionalismo y política económica," *Revista Mexicana de Ciencia Política* 21 (abril-junio 1975), p. 48.

[19] Roger D. Hansen, *The Politics of Mexican Development* (Baltimore: The Johns Hopkins Press, 1971), pp. 71-77.

[20] García Riera, *Historia documental,* vol. 2, p. 114.

[21] Ibid., p. 208.

[22] For an excellent analysis on this point, see Ayala Blanco, *Aventura del cine mexicano,* pp. 50-52.

[23] Cited in García Riera, *Historia documental,* vol. 2, p. 208.

[24] Ibid., p. 67.

[25] Pablo González Casanova, *Democracy in Mexico* (New York: Oxford University Press, 1970), pp. 222-223.

[26] Hansen, *Politics of Mexican Development,* p. 95.

[27] Carlos Monsiváis, "Notas sobre cultura popular en México," *Latin American Perspectives* 5 (Winter 1978), p. 114.

[28] García Riera, *Historia documental,* vol. 3, p. 298.

[29] Ibid., vol. 4, p. 207. Space does not allow more on this point; *pochos* appeared in Mexican films, but usually in negative terms. The titles of certain films manifested their obvious nationalism, such as *Soy puro mexicano* (1941), *Como México no hay dos* (1944).

[30] Alejandro Galindo in *Cuadernos de la cineteca nacional,* vol. 1, p. 103.

[31] Interview with Sara García, *Cuadernos de la cineteca nacional,* vol. 2, p. 18.

[32] Eric F. Goldman, *The Crucial Decade—and After: America 1945-1960* (New York: Vintage Books, 1960), p. 112.

[33] Robert Sklar, *Movie-Made America* (New York: Random House, 1975), pp. 267-268.

[34] William E. Leuchtenburg, *The Unfinished Century* (Boston: Little, Brown and Co., 1977), p. 705.

[35] The literature on McCarthyism and the conservatism of the 1950s continues to grow. See, among many works, David Caute, *The Great Fear: The Anti-Communist Purge Under Truman and Eisenhower* (New York: Simon and Schuster, 1978), especially pp. 487-538; Larry Ceplair and Steven Englund, *The Inquisition in Hollywood: Politics in the Film Community, 1930-1960* (New York: Anchor Press/Doubleday, 1980); Victor S. Navasky, *Naming Names* (New York: Viking, 1980).

[36] *La Opinión* was consulted for the months of March and April, 1948. The Los Angeles newspaper contained a section on both American and Mexican entertainment, with special attention paid to the movie industry of both countries.

[37] For works on Gramsci, see Phil Cozens, *Twenty Years of Antonio Gramsci: A Bibliography of Gramsci and Gramsci studies published in English, 1957-1977* (London: Lawrence and Wishart, 1977). This section relies particularly on Thomas R. Bates, "Gramsci and the Theory of Hegemony," *Journal of the History of Ideas* 36 (April-June, 1975), 351-366.

[38] Again, film titles often indicated the message of the movies: *Las casadas engañan de 4 a 6* (1945), *Las divorciadas* (1943), *Una virgen moderna* (1945), *La Santa del barrio* (1948), *Perdida* (1949), *Aventurera* (1949).

THE GREASER'S REVENGE TO BOULEVARD NIGHTS: THE MASS MEDIA CURRICULUM ON CHICANOS*

Carlos E. Cortés

Schools are not synonymous with education. They are only part of education. Alongside schools, there operates a parallel educational system, the "societal curriculum"—that massive, ongoing, informal curriculum of family, peer groups, neighborhoods, churches, organizations, occupations, mass media, and other socializing forces that "educate" all of us throughout our lives.[1] Much of this societal curriculum provides multicultural education, both positive and negative, about race, ethnicity, diverse cultures, and foreign nations. Although not always cognizant of it, we are all constantly students of the multicultural societal curriculum.

The media—television, motion pictures, magazines, newspapers, books, and radio—serve as some of the most powerful, relentless educators within the societal curriculum. Expressed another way, all of us—before we enter school, during the time we are students, and throughout the rest of our lives—will "go to school" with the media. Take one example—television. One study reported that young people between the ages of three and sixteen spend one-sixth of their waking hours with the television set.[2] According to another estimate, by the time of graduation, the average high school senior will have spent 12,000 hours in the classroom and 15,000 hours in front of the television set. In other words, teachers may trail the tube in direct contact hours by 20 percent . . . and television is only one component of the media curriculum.

*I would like to thank the Academic Senate of the University of California, Riverside, for an Intramural Research Grant which supported this research.

Moreover, that curriculum is not limited to those aspects of the media which purport to present facts and interpretations—newsmagazines, newspapers, radio and television newscasts, nonfiction books, and documentary films. In addition, the so-called "entertainment media," such as feature films and television series, also have a powerful impact in shaping beliefs, attitudes, values, perceptions, and "knowledge" and in influencing decisions and action.[3] Even advertising, through patterns of depicting selected roles for persons of different societal groups, helps to mold public expectations and a sense of what is "normal" (and, therefore, also what is "abnormal") in society.[4]

According to social psychologist George Comstock, who in 1975 reported that there had been more than 2,300 research papers on television and human behavior:

> Several writers have argued that television is a powerful reinforcer of the status quo. The ostensible mechanisms are the effects of its portrayal on public expectations and perceptions. Television portrayals and particularly violent drama are said to assign roles of authority, power, success, failure, dependence, and vulnerability in a manner that matches the real-life social hierarchy, thereby strengthening that hierarchy by increasing its acknowledgement among the public and by failing to provide positive images for members of social categories occupying a subservient position. Content analyses of television drama support the contention that portrayals reflect normative status.[5]

The Multicultural Media Curriculum

The past decade has brought increasing scholarship on media depictions of various societal groups.[6] In addition, studies have shown that many children develop well-formed attitudes about ethnic people and foreign cultures, including prejudices and stereotypes, early in life, often by the time they reach school.[7] In a pioneering study, Ruth C. Peterson and L.L. Thurstone found that prejudice toward black Americans increased when children saw the classic silent motion picture *Birth of a Nation,* which provides both a southern interpretation of post-Civil War Reconstruction and an appalling caricature of blacks.[8] Irwin C. Rosen determined that viewing the antibigotry feature film *Gentleman's Agreement* actually improved student attitudes toward Jews, even though most of the students were not aware of this change and even stated that the film *had not* affected their attitudes.[9]

Other examples. One survey of fourth-, eighth-, and twelfth-graders found that television had the greatest impact on their attitudes toward foreign nations and peoples. A high school teacher in Massachusetts reported that, when introducing a unit on the Holocaust, she attempted to assess her students' prior knowledge of the subject, only to discover that "Their only encounter with Nazis, it seemed, was while watching *Hogan's Heroes* on television."[10]

A teacher in one of my multicultural education inservice courses encountered an equally dramatic form of media curriculum impact. When introducing an elementary-school unit on gypsies in a city with a sizable gypsy community, she found that her students had deeply rooted preconceptions. When the teacher asked where they had learned so much about gypsies, they responded by citing *Wolfman* and *Frankenstein* movies.

The power of the multicultural media curriculum has not gone unnoticed. For example, during its fall 1977 televised showing of *The Godfather Saga,* NBC repeatedly cautioned viewers that:

> *The Godfather* is a fictional account of the activities of a small group of ruthless criminals. The characters do not represent any ethnic group and it would be erroneous and unfair to suggest that they do.

While such gratuitous posturing probably did little to soften the film's impact on perceptions about Italian Americans, it dramatized an awareness of the power of the media curriculum.

The Media Curriculum on Chicanos

Among the topics covered by the media curriculum is, of course, the Chicano. For tens of millions of people in the United States, the mass media will be their total, or at least their primary, curriculum on Chicanos. This includes the millions who have no or little personal contact with Chicanos (and then usually in a limited variety of situations) and who have little ongoing school study of Mexican Americans.

Moreover, even persons who live in heavily Chicano communities, have considerable personal contact with Chicanos, and study about Chicanos in school will still be influenced by the Mexican American media curriculum. Sometimes the media even outweigh personal experience in educational impact. One study reported that white children felt that TV comedies like *The Jeffersons* and *Sanford and Son* accurately portrayed black family life, even though these same children admitted that the shows contrasted with personal experiences with their own black friends... whom they labeled as exceptions.[11]

The scope, power, and pervasiveness of the multicultural media curriculum, including the curriculum on Mexican Americans, create a challenge for us. To make the media curriculum more of an ally and less of an antagonist, we must take concerted, thoughtful, constructive action. Moreover, to be effective in our actions and avoid the knee-jerk rhetoric of too many well-intended but poorly conceived protest movements, we need to carefully analyze that very media curriculum with which we must deal.

Motion Pictures and Chicanos

For purposes of illustration, let us look at one component of the media curriculum on Chicanos—feature films. I have a speical interest in that topic because of my research for the book I am writing on the history of the themes of ethnicity and foreignness in U.S. motion pictures. Historically, what have U.S. feature films "taught" about Mexican Americans and other Latinos?

During the early years of motion pictures, Chicanos took a real beating. Film titles reflected a widespread Hollywood stance toward and use of Mexicans as film characters—*Tony the Greaser, Broncho Billy and the Greaser, The Girl and the Greaser,* and *The Greaser's Revenge.* Those were movie titles! Yes, progress has been made. Films may still portray Mexicans as greasers, but at least not on the theatre marquee.

Truly, as one scholar has pointed out, in the early days of U.S. motion pictures, the Mexican American did serve as a "convenient villain," particularly in westerns.[12] But lest we feel too sorry for ourselves as being singularly victimized, it should be pointed out that during the same era films were also being made with such titles as *That Chink at Golden Gulch* and *The Wooing and Wedding of a Coon.* Minorities in general, then, were acceptable movie targets as despicable villains, helpless incompetents, or society's clowns.

World War I brought some change. For the first time since the expansion of motion pictures into a form of mass entertainment, the United States had a real enemy. No longer did Hollywood have to trot out minorities for Anglo hereoes to defeat or ridicule for the delight of audiences. The Hun replaced the savage, the greaser, the chink, and the coon as Hollywood's main filmic target. For a brief time, negative minority stereotypes took a back seat to cruel, sadistic, arrogant Germans in such films as *The Hun Within, The Beast of Berlin,* and *The Woman the Germans Shot.*[13]

But not for long! The end of World War I signaled the return of minorities as whipping people. However, times had changed. Latin America, which had become an expanding market for U.S. motion pictures, would not sit still for filmic degrading of Latinos. During the 1920s and 1930s, many Latin American nations spoke out against negative stereotyping of Latinos. Several governments went so far as to ban U.S. films which presented derogatory depictions of Latinos. [14]

To a degree this strategy worked. Hollywood took steps, albeit insufficient and often misdirected steps, to clean up its Latino act. Not wanting to totally bury Latino villains, who had proved to be great box office in the United States, but also not wanting to jeopardize the Latin American market, studios came up with a variety of strategies. One ploy was to invent countries, so governments could not point to these movies as dealing with specific Latin American nations. For example, the nation of Costa Roja in *The Dove*. A second strategy: in films set in Latin America, be sure to include good Latinos (usually light-skinned "Spanish" types) along with the traditional bad Latinos (usually dark-skinned mestizo or Indian types).

The 1932 presidential election of Franklin D. Roosevelt led to the establishment of the Latin American Good Neighbor Policy, in which Hollywood was to play a role. Moreover, social disruption in Europe, culminating in World War II, deprived Hollywood of a major film market and increased the economic significance of Latin American audiences. Once the United States entered the war, Latin America's strategic importance prompted the U.S. government to encourage Hollywood to be an even better neighbor.

Here are a few examples of these changes. MGM obtained Mexican government script approval for its 1934 film *Viva Villa!*, although you would never know this from viewing the ludicrous final product. The U.S. Office of the Coordinator of Inter-American Affairs, under director Nelson Rockefeller, continuously stressed the obligation of U.S. motion pictures to help solidify the Americas in the common struggle against the Axis powers. The Hays Office, Hollywood's official self-censor, even appointed a Latin American expert to help Hollywood avoid filmic blunders which might offend Latin Americans. [15]

Some positive results occurred. Such films as *Juarez*, despite its historical inaccuracies and anti-Indian undertones, and *Bordertown*, despite its patronizing view of Chicanos, at least reflected efforts to provide a more serious examination of Latinos. Later, in wartime-made World War II films, Latinos fought and died alongside their Anglo comrades. Hollywood's wartime "affirmative action" policy called for assigning a variety of recognizably ethnic characters, often including a Chicano, to each filmic military unit in order to demonstrate All-American togetherness. Of course, not all ethnics made it. Blacks, for example, were almost totally segregated from World War II-era war movies, as they were in reality within the military itself, and were not to be admitted into Hollywood's desegregated version of World War II until later in such films as *Home of the Brave* and *The Dirty Dozen.*

The end of World War II brought a decline of U.S. government interest in Latin America and ended Hollywood's Good Neighbor Policy. Thereafter, Chicanos appeared only sporadically in U.S. films, and when they did, the picture was mixed. Some films, such as *A Medal for Benny, Border Incident, Lawless, Knock on Any Door, Trial,* and *Giant,* as well as the long-closeted *Salt of the Earth,* did explore societal prejudice and discrimination against Mexican Americans. But this was paralleled by the filmic resurrection of the Mexican bandito, in films like *The Treasure of the Sierra Madre* and *The Magnificent Seven,* the Chicano buffoon, in films like *The Big Country* and *The High and the Mighty,* and the Chicana prostitute, in films like *My Darling Clementine* and *High Noon.* This was soon followed by the arrival of the Latino urban gang in such films as *The Young Savages* and, with musical embellishment, *West Side Story.*[16]

The mid-1960s ushered in the era of ethnic revitalization, with minority civil rights movements, Black and Chicano Power, the New Pluralism of the white ethnics, and ethnic heritage. Suddenly, it seemed, everybody wanted to be an ethnic.

Hollywood was not immune to this change. Ethnicity was hot. Ethnicity sells. Ethnicity is good box office, particularly when tinged with sensationalism. The result: the greatest boom in ethnic theme motion pictures since the early days of the twentieth century.

Along with other ethnics, Chicanos came more into vogue as a film theme. But was this progress? Numerically and statistically in terms of visibility, yes. But at what cost? Unfortunately, a recycled pattern of negative Mexican American film depictions has developed in the past two decades. If Chicanos are to be presented, color them "violent." Whether good (law enforcers, military people, or prosocial activists), bad (gangs and criminals), or just mixed up, "deprived," or victims of society, movie Chicanos constantly resort to violence and almost always try to resolve issues with physical force, not with intelligence and reason ... *Boulevard Nights, Walk Proud, The Big Fix, Assault on Precinct 13, Back Roads, The Baltimore Bullet.* And not only Chicanos, but other U.S. Latinos as well ... *Fort Apache, the Bronx, Night of the Juggler, The Goodbye Girl, Slow Dancing in the Big City.* Whatever your evaluation of these films as art, as entertainment, or as accurate societal representations, they have one common message—Chicanos and other Latinos are violent.

Other Media

Movies are not alone in sending this message. Commercial television has walked hand-in-hand with motion pictures in portraying Chicanos as violent. Television news "covers" Chicano gangs. *60 Minutes* "explores" Chicano gangs. Drama series from *Police Story* through *Lou Grant* seem to feel the need to present at least one episode which "examines" (and of course "is sensitive to") Chicano gangs. In the fall of 1979 came the TV movie, *Streets of Los Angeles,* in which Chicanos used the threat of violence to influence an Anglo woman, who, of course, was far too stalwart to be stopped by Chicano media machismo. As with motion pictures, some of these programs may individually have had good intentions and artistic merit. But what concerns me is the totality. With so few Chicanos depicted in serious (as contrasted to comic) nonviolent roles and so many depicted as engaging in violent actions, the development of the Chicano media stereotype is obvious.

A recent study of Hispanics on television revealed an ominous pattern. Based on their analysis of network fictional television series from 1975 through 1978, Bradley S. Greenberg and Pilar Baptista-Fernández of Michigan State University reported that Hispanic characters fell almost entirely into three categories—law breakers, law enforcers, and comic characters—with "crook" as the most prevalent Hispanic vocation. In fact, two thirds of all Hispanic characters in television dramatic series (as contrasted with comedy series) were engaged in either law breaking or law enforcing, both areas which involve the use or threat of violence.[17]

To this point I have addressed only the entertainment media. But the analysis of the societal curriculum on Chicanos must extend to other aspects of the media. What sort of news coverage do Chicanos receive from newspapers, from magazines, from radio, from television? How are Mexican Americans presented in or omitted from advertising?

Choose a station or a newspaper. Write down the subject and perspective of each story on Chicanos. Do this for a period of time, and soon the pattern of coverage and attitudinal position should become clear. Compared with the wide variety of stories which could be written about the Chicano community, you are likely to find that two types of stories appear an inordinate number of times—Chicanos committing crimes and Chicanos engaging in cultural events.

I am not issuing a blanket condemnation of all media. Some progress has been made in the past two decades, partly because Chicanos have increasingly expressed their unhappiness about media coverage, partly because of growing awareness on the part of many media people, partly because of the slowly expanding Chicano presence within the mainstream media, and partly because of the development of Chicano media. But the media still have a long way to go before they truly provide the valid balanced coverage which the Chicano community deserves. That quest for balance and validity will depend, to a degree, on the effectiveness of the Chicano media.

The Chicano Print Media

Functioning alongside the mainstream media since the mid-nineteenth century have been the Chicano media, which deserve our attention. However, the Chicano media have faced and continue to face tremendous obstacles. Let us take a look at elements of those media.

Most books on the history of United States journalism devote little, if any, space to the role of the Chicano press. Yet, according to one study, between 1848 and 1958 there were at least 378 Mexican American newspapers.[18] The Chicano press has never been powerful. Historically it has suffered from two major handicaps—undercapitalization and limited readership. Insufficiency of money has forced the Mexican American press to be overly dependent on outside sources, such as Anglo advertisers and government agencies, which could use (or choose not to use) Chicano newspapers to print legal notices. This financial dependence on non-Chicanos, who could sever the monetary arteries at any moment, has tended to moderate editorial policy, mute critical voices, and restrict the militance and social activism of Chicano newspapers. This problem of undercapitalization continues to haunt the Mexican American press today.

One way of overcoming the problem of undercapitalization and the resulting undue influence of government and advertisers is through large readership—making the Chicano press such a good avenue to reach readers that businesses will advertise whether or not they like the editorial policy. Unfortunately, limited readership has also plagued the Chicano press. Low literacy has long been a major Chicano problem. In turn, the traditional low literacy rate has meant that the potential Chicano readership does not measure up to the total U.S. Mexican-descent population.

Not all Mexican Americans read Spanish, nor do they all read English. Part of the Chicano population reads Spanish, part reads English, part reads both, part reads neither. If there is to be a viable Chicano press, the challenge is clear. Chicano literacy rates, in both English and Spanish, must be raised. With literacy comes readership, with readership comes circulation, and with circulation comes advertising. Businesses, even those who disagree with newspaper or magazine policy, will be more likely to advertise if they know they are reaching large numbers of potential customers.

Despite these problems, the Chicano press has managed to survive, if not usually prosper. But what has this press survival really meant? In an article in *Journalism History,* Félix Gutiérrez suggested that Chicano newspapers have played three major roles—as instruments of social control, as weapons of social activism, and as reflections of Mexican American life.[19] To these can be added a fourth role—as preservers and transmitters of Chicano history and culture.

Instruments of social control—spreading official government information about how Americans are supposed to act and socializing Chicanos into the "American way of thinking." Weapons of social activism—protesting against discrimination, pointing out lack of public services for Mexican Americans, raising Chicano social consciousness, and exhorting Chicanos to take action. Reflections of Chicano life—printing poetry, essays, letters, and other types of Chicano expression. Preservers and transmitters of Chicano history and culture—preserving the Spanish language in print, reinforcing its use, and recording the ongoing history of Mexican Americans so that future generations have these documents to learn about their heritage. Throughout U.S. history, Chicano newspapers have fulfilled these roles.

Some newspapers have emphasized the more conservative tacks of U.S. socialization and Chicano cultural preservation. Others have adopted a more militant, social-change orientation. In general, conservatism has proven more palatable for advertisers and government. As a result, many of the "successful" Chicano newspapers in terms of longevity and financial stability have been of this more conservative variety. This is no lament against the conservative Chicano press, because the diverse Mexican American community deserves a broad spectrum of journalistic voices reflecting the multiplicity of Chicano perspectives. However, to build and maintain a broad spectrum of newspaper expression, Mexican Americans must develop more readership and relative economic independence for the Chicano press, so that it can express that wide variety of perspectives, however unpopular some positions may be with advertisers.

The struggle goes on to build a viable Chicano press to provide Mexican Americans with their own media voices. Chicano newspapers are born every year. A few prosper; some simply survive; others die. In addition, recent years have brought Chicano magazines, such as *Somos, Caminos,* and *Low Rider* in California, as well as national Latino magazines, such as *Nuestro, Agenda,* and *La Luz,* dealing with diverse-national-origin Hispanic groups in the United States. Scholarly journals, such as *Aztlán: International Journal of Chicano Studies Research, Hispanic Journal of Behavioral Sciences* and *Revista Chicano-Riqueña,* have challenged deeply embedded academic truisms about Latinos. Finally, Chicano publishers, such as Quinto Sol, Tonatiuh International, Editorial Justa, and Perspectiva Publications, have provided an outlet for books by and about Mexican Americans.

The Chicano press comes in different linguistic packages— Spanish, English, and bilingual—reflecting the diversity of the Chicano reading community and the fact that non-Chicanos are part of the readership. Each newspaper, magazine, and book serves a different role. English-language Chicano publications often contribute to societal analysis, social activism, cultural reflection, and historical preservation, yet they do little to reinforce Spanish linguistic maintenance. Conversely, while the Spanish-language press helps to maintain Spanish-language usage in the United States, some elements of that media contribute little in the area of constructive social change or community awareness.

Chicano Television, Radio, and Motion Pictures

How about the Chicano listening and viewing community, particularly the Spanish-language listening community? Spanish-language television and radio stations now operate throughout the country. In television, as of early 1982 the national Spanish International Network (SIN) numbered ten full-power television stations and 112 affiliates—thirty-nine in Texas, fifteen in New Mexico, fourteen in Arizona, ten in Connecticut, seven in California, five in Florida, four in Oregon, three in Colorado and New York, two in Illinois, Kentucky, and Pennsylvania, and one each in Arkansas, District of Columbia, Idaho, Massachusetts, Missouri, and Washington.[20] By late 1982, SIN had grown by more than 70 percent to 193 affiliates (including cable systems and translators, low-power repeater stations) serving a reported 30 million U.S. households. In addition, as of 1982, there were two independent Spanish-language television stations, and the Spanish-language cable service, GalaVision, had 92,000 subscribers in 102 cities spread throughout fifteen states and Puerto Rico, while in that same year Chicano-owned and operated Buena Vista Cable Television of Los Angeles took its place in the ranks of the growing Chicano electronic media. For radio there is now the National Association of Spanish Broadcasters (NASB)—stations which broadcast exclusively or largely in the Spanish language—and the Southwest Spanish Broadcasters Association, composed of stations with Hispanic ownership.[21] As of 1979, some 159 stations belonged to NASB. Some 100 stations broadcast full-time in Spanish. Howevever, those statistics imply more progress than they truly signify.

First, language does not signify control. For the most part, Spanish-language radio and television stations are owned and controlled by non-Hispanics. While some of these stations may follow socially constructive policies toward the Mexican American community, this still does mean that Chicanos are determining their own media destiny. Widespread Chicano and other Latino broadcast media ownership is a necessary step toward achieving such self-determination. Yet, as of 1981, minorities owned only 164 or 1.8 percent of the nation's commercial radio and television stations and only thirty-two, or 2.3 percent, of the noncommercial stations. Nationally only twenty-five Latinos owned commercial stations and only nine owned noncommercial stations.[22]

Moreover, as in the case of the print media, language and content are distinct matters. Broadcasting in Spanish helps to maintain and reinforce Spanish language usage. However, not all Spanish-language stations are taking the lead in community action or are serving as instruments of constructive social change.

Spanish International Network television programming consists largely of sports, movies, musical shows, and soap operas *(novelas),* with heavy reliance on imported programs. Sports telecasting, in any language, may be a nice placebo, but it hardly increases Chicano community awareness and knowledge. *Novelas,* which comprise one third of SIN's air time, may entertain viewers, but *El derecho de nacer, Dios se lo pague, El milagro de vivir,* and other Spanish-language equivalents of *As the World Turns* and *Father Knows Best* hardly exemplify Chicano power. And while *Disco Fiebre* and *Lucha Libre* may be pleasantly diverting, they cannot be considered indices of Chicano progress. By the same token, Spanish-language music stations and music shows with Spanish-speaking disc jockeys are fine, but they do not usually receive high marks for social change. While I am not critical of Spanish-language television and radio for offering music, sports, movies, and soap operas—after all, these are part of entertainment—such stations need to increase their public service programming, devote more news coverage to the Chicano community, and take stronger pro-Chicano editorial stands.

But if this is to occur, the Chicano community will have to do its part. All Latinos share the obligation of helping to make the Spanish-language broadcast media a viable vehicle for constructive societal change. First, as with the print media, Latinos need to support these stations with their eyes and ears. Viewership and listenership affect advertising rates, and advertising provides the financial base for greater social activism.

Moreover, Latinos need to inform advertisers that they are listening and viewing. The National Association of Spanish Broadcasters has complained that Nielsen and Arbitron, which compile television and radio audience statistics, consistently underrate Spanish-language audiences. According to NASB, among the problems are their measuring systems. However, another problem is the Latino community itself. Arbitron, for example, sends out diaries to selected listeners throughout the country, asking them to keep a record of the programs they watch or hear and to return their completed diaries to Arbitron. Response from Anglo families is about 55 percent; response from Latino families is only about fifteen percent. In other words, Hispanics are partially to blame for their own undercount.[23] Chicanos and other Latinos need to become more activist, even in these small ways.

Finally, let us return to the movies. In the past decade, Chicano film companies and filmmakers have begun creating their own motion pictures—mainly documentaries, but also some feature films. Best-known feature films are *Zoot Suit,* Luis Valdez' film version of his own theatrical success, and the Cheech and Chong movies, starring Chicano Cheech Marín and his Chinese-Canadian sidekick, Tommy Chong. In addition, two major television films, *The Ballad of Gregorio Cortez* (a collaborative effort co-produced by Moctesuma Esparza and directed by Robert Young) and Jesús Treviño's *Seguín* were aired as part of PBS' American Playhouse series in 1982. There is also now an annual Chicano Film Festival in San Antonio. As with motion pictures in general, the quality of Chicano films has inevitably been uneven. However, if Mexican Americans want Chicano filmmakers to continue, develop, and improve, they need to vote with their feet—providing box office support for Chicano films they want to see succeed, avoiding those they feel should not be emulated, and renting and purchasing Chicano-made films for school and community use. Support brings money, and money can mean better Chicano films in the future.

Chicano Media Action Program

I would like to suggest a fivefold plan of action for dealing with the media curriculum on Mexican Americans. First, we need to strengthen the Chicano media—newspapers, magazines, television, radio, publishers, and motion picture companies. We can do so through our support—subscriptions, viewership, listenership, advertising, and patronage of advertisers.[24] But along with support must come input. We should tell the Chicano and Spanish-language media the type of programing we want and need, encourage them to speak out on important Chicano issues, call upon them to provide broader news coverage of the Chicano community, and challenge them to become effective and constructive public educators in spreading a balanced picture of the Chicano community.

Second, we need to bring greater pressure on the mainstream media—compliment them when they serve us well and criticize them when they serve us badly. We must let them know when we are concerned about the way they are depicting us, whether in entertainment programs or through news coverage. In doing so, we must remain aware that we are not the only group concerned with media image, representation, and employment patterns. Other ethnic groups and women's organizations, to cite two examples, can be excellent allies as we seek to pluralize the mainstream media.

Third, we need to work more closely with government—local, state, and federal. We need to take an active role in monitoring and, if necessary and substantiated by evidence, challenging the Federal Communications Commission's licensing and relicensing of television and radio stations. This has been done by various groups in the past, causing the FCC to bring pressure on stations to increase the hiring and promotion of minorities and women and to improve and diversify programing related to minorities and women. We need to support the continuation of the United States Commission on Civil Rights' ongoing examination of minorities and women in the media, as documented in their reports, *Behind the Scenes: Equal Employment Opportunity in the Motion Picture Industry, Window Dressing on the Set: Women and Minorities in Television,* and

Window Dressing on the Set: An Update.[25] Such reports provide evidence we can use to increase pressure on mainstream media to improve Chicano, other ethnic, and women's presence, both in programing and in employment.

Fourth, we need to develop a school curriculum which addresses the structure, content, and impact of the media. This should include the integration of the study of media depictions of Mexican Americans (as well as women and members of other ethnic groups) throughout school, both in the general K-12 curriculum and in teacher education.[26]

From the time they enter school, children should be encouraged and taught to view *all* media analytically. In the elementary grades, students can analyze children's stories, photographs, film strips, and animated films for their depictions of Chicanos and other ethnic groups as well as foreign nations. Advertisements on television, in magazines and newspapers, and even on billboards and bumper stickers can be stimulating sources for studying image formation. High school students can analyze local newspapers and local and national radio and television newscasts for their treatment of Chicanos, other ethnic groups, and women. Feature films and television series can be analyzed for their perspectives and interpretations. In short, media should be used in school to raise the level of student critical thinking about media, to increase student recognition that *all* media presentations reflect attitude and perspective, and to develop student awareness of the content and process of media multicultural education.

Fifth, we need to reach across the border to our sisters and brothers in Mexico and other Latin American nations. Through audience potential, purchasing power, and government pressure, Latin America can influence the U.S. media directly, as well as indirectly through the U.S. government, to provide better treatment of Chicanos and other U.S. Hispanics. Latin America did it before with the motion picture industry in the 1920s, 1930s, and 1940s. It can be done again, this time with U.S. Latinos in alliance with Latin America in the struggle for a just and balanced media curriculum on Chicanos and other Hispanics.

The future of Chicanos will be determined, in part, by their success in dealing with the media. This involves the analytical, active addressing of the media curriculum on Chicanos, on other Latinos, on ethnic groups in general, and on other societal groups such as women, senior citizens, and the physically disabled. Social equity includes media justice, and such justice must be a major Chicano goal.

HISTORY DEPARTMENT
UNIVERSITY OF CALIFORNIA, RIVERSIDE

Notes

[1] Carlos E. Cortés, "The Societal Curriculum and the School Curriculum," *Educational Leadership*, XXXVI, 7 (April, 1979), pp. 475-479.

[2] Wilbur Schramm, Jack Lyle, and Edwin B. Parker, *Television in the Lives of Our Children* (Stanford: Stanford University Press, 1961), p. 12.

[3] Garth Jowett, *Film: The Democratic Art* (Boston: Little, Brown and Company, 1976); Robert Sklar, *Movie-Made America: A Cultural History of American Movies* (New York: Random House, 1975); Lary L. May, *Screening out the Past: The Birth of Mass Culture and the Motion Picture Industry* (New York: Oxford University Press, 1980); Robert Singer and Robert Kazdon (eds.), *Television and Social Behavior. Journal of Social Issues*, XXXII (Fall, 1976); David Thomson, *America in the Dark: The Impact of Hollywood Films on American Culture* (New York: William Morrow, 1977); Stephen B. Withey and Ronald P. Abeles (eds.), *Television and Social Behavior: Beyond Violence and Children* (Hillsdale, New Jersey: Lawrence Erlbaum Associates, Publishers, 1980).

[4] Thomas M. Martínez, "Advertising and Racism: The Case of the Mexican American," *El Grito. A Journal of Contemporary Mexican-American Thought,* II (Summer, 1969), pp. 3-13; James D. Culley and Rex Bennett, "Selling Women, Selling Blacks," *Journal of Communication*, XXVI (Autumn, 1976), pp. 160-174.

[5] George Comstock, *The Impact of Television on American Institutions and the American Public* (Honolulu: East-West Communication Institute, East-West Center, 1977), pp. 20-21.

[6] For example, see Randall M. Miller (ed.), *The Kaleidoscopic Lens: Ethnic Images in American Film* (Englewood, N.J.: Jerome S. Ozer, 1980), and Molly Haskell, *From Reverence to Rape: The Treatment of Women in the Movies* (New York: Holt, Rinehart & Winston, 1974).

[7] For example, see Marjorie E. Goodman, *Race Awareness in Young Children* (2d ed. rev.; New York: Macmillan, 1964), and William E. Lambert and Otto Klineberg, *Children's Views of Foreign Peoples: A Cross-National Study* (New York: Appleton-Century-Crofts, 1967).

[8] Ruth C. Peterson and L.L. Thurstone, *Motion Pictures and the Social Attitudes of Children* (New York: Macmillan, 1933), pp. 35-38.

[9] Irwin C. Rosen, "The Effect of the Motion Picture 'Gentleman's Agreement' on Attitudes Toward Jews," *Journal of Psychology*, XXVI (1948), pp. 525-536.

[10] Roselle Chartock, "A Holocaust Unit for Classroom Teachers," *Social Education*, XLII (April, 1978), pp. 278-285.

[11] Bradley S. Greenberg, "Children's Reactions to TV Blacks," *Journalism Quarterly*, XLIX (spring, 1972), pp. 5-14.

[12] Blaine P. Lamb, "The Convenient Villain: The Early Cinema Views the Mexican-American," *Journal of the West*, XIV, 4 (October, 1975), pp. 75-81.

[13] Richard A. Oehling, "Germans in Hollywood Films: The Changing Image, 1914-1939," *Film and History*, IV, 2 (May, 1974), pp. 4-6.

[14] Allen L. Woll, *The Latin Image in American Film* (Los Angeles: Latin American Center, University of California, 1977), pp. 16-18, 34. A more recent book on Latino film imagery is Arthur G. Pettit, *Images of the Mexican American in Fiction and Film* (College Station: Texas A&M Press, 1980).

[15] Ibid., pp. 34-35, 54-56.

[16] John Whitney, "Image Making in the Land of Fantasy," *Agenda, A Journal of Hispanic Issues*, VIII, 1 (January-February, 1978), p. 10.

[17] Bradley S. Greenberg and Pilar Baptista-Fernández, "Hispanic-Americans—The New Minority on Television," in Bradley S. Greenberg et al., *Life on Television: Content Analysis of U.S. TV Drama* (Norwood, New Jersey: Ablex Publishing Corporation, 1980), pp. 3-12.

[18] Herminio Ríos and Guadalupe Castillo, "Toward a True Chicano Bibliography: Mexican American Newspapers: 1848-1942," *El Grito. A Journal of Contemporary Mexican-American Thought*, III, 4 (summer, 1970), pp. 17-24; Herminio Ríos C., "Toward a True Chicano Bibliography—Part II," *El Grito. A Journal of Contemporary Mexican-American Thought*, V, 4 (summer, 1972), pp. 40-47.

[19] Félix Gutiérrez, "Spanish-Language Media in America: Background, Resources, History," *Journalism History*, IV, 2 (summer, 1977), pp. 38-41, 65-66.

[20] National Spanish International Network Station List (1981).

[21] "Minority Organizations: Looking for Strength in Numbers," *Broadcasting*, October 15, 1979, pp. 45-47.

[22] Lee Marguilies, "Inside TV," *Los Angeles Times*, February 16, 1982, Part VI, p. 9.

[23] Roger Langley, "Hispanic Beat," *Riverside Press-Enterprise*, September 9, 1979, p. D-9.

[24] For an examination of the advertising potential of the Hispanic media, see Antonio Guernica and Irene Kasperuk, *Reaching the Hispanic Market Effectively: The Media, the Market, the Methods* (New York: McGraw-Hill, 1982).

[25] *Behind the Scenes: Equal Employment Opportunity in the Motion Picture Industry* (Report of the California Advisory Committee to the U.S. Commission on Civil Rights) (Washington, D.C.: U.S. Commission on Civil Rights, 1978); *Window Dressing on the Set: Women and Minorities in Television* (Washington, D.C.: U.S. Commission on Civil Rights, 1977); *Window Dressing on the Set: An Update* (Washington, D.C.: U.S. Commission on Civil Rights, 1979).

[26] For a discussion of this process see Carlos E. Cortés, "The Role of Media in Multicultural Education," *Viewpoints in Teaching and Learning*, LVI, 1 (winter, 1980), pp. 38-49.

LOW RIDING IN THE SOUTHWEST: CULTURAL SYMBOLS IN THE MEXICAN COMMUNITY

Luis F. B. Plascencia

Introduction

The presence of highly ornate cars with multicolor paint jobs, crushed velvet interiors, hydraulic suspension systems, and numerous other features—low riders—has become a common sight in the metropolitan areas of the Southwest. Their ubiquitousness in parks, boulevards, and shopping centers, as they ride low and slow, elicits perceptions of either aversion or admiration on the part of the bystanders. These perceptions, despite their antithetical position, share a common basis. They both are grounded in a fragmentary historical understanding of the origins of low riding, the place of low riding in the broader "car culture," its current diffusion, and other related issues. On one hand, the former seems to encompass the perception that low riding is a new, antisocial, gang-related, drug-promoting, crime-inducing, degenerative, self-indulgent, gaudy, and wasteful activity. On the other hand, the latter seems to encompass the perception that low riding is an unbroken historical phenomenon, a conscious rebellion against middle class ideology, a positive cultural assertion and identity, and an activity that will reduce the level of crime and gang fights and thus prepare the path for a lasting peace and brotherhood in the *barrios*. To wholly dismiss or accept both positions is, of course, shortsighted.

The surge in low riding, which began in the late 1970s and surfaced primarily in the Mexican communities within the metropolitan areas of the Southwest, has received little attention outside of journalistic circles. Journalistic coverage of low riding has gradually extended beyond local print media, to national publications such as *Car & Driver, The New Yorker, Road & Track, Life, The New York Times,* and *Natural History.*[1] Social scientists have been slow to heed the lead of journalists.

A discussion of the entire phenomenon of low riding is beyond the scope of this essay. Consequently, this essay focuses on presenting an analysis of the diffusion of low riding from California to the other Southwestern states. Specifically, it presents an interpretation of how certain symbols like "pachuco," "zoot suit," and "cholo" became fused with low riding, and how the entire complex became commercialized. In other words, the process by which certain cultural symbols became integrated into the world of commodities—of products of human labor that are bought and sold. The fusion of these symbols has resulted in the belief that all of these social categories are one and the same, and thus represent the direct historical precursors of the modern low rider. As I shall try to show, the rapid diffusion of low riding received its principal impetus from *Low Rider* magazine, with the support of certain major brewing companies.

In trying to analyze low riding, two conditions became clear. First, that what Marx had noted about the "fetishism of commodities" was an important warning in the analysis of commodities:

> A commodity appears, at first sight, a very trivial thing, and easily understood. Its analysis shows that it is, in reality, a very queer thing, abounding in metaphysical subtleties and theological niceties... A commodity is therefore a mysterious thing, simply because in it the social character of men's labour appears to them as an objective character stamped upon the product of that labour (1906:81,83).

In other words, it is prevalent to look at a commodity and become fixed on how it is used (its use value), or on how much it is bought and sold for (its exchange value), and thus ignore or overlook that a commodity product embodies the labor that was expended on its production and that the production process itself is part of the social relations between the working class and the capitalist class. Second, that in order to decipher this contemporary "social hieroglyphic" (ibid.:85) it was necessary to examine the historical context of the symbols which became linked with low riding.

For the purpose of this essay, "low rider" will refer to a car, truck, van, motorcycle, or bicycle that has been lowered closer to the ground (*bien bajito*—real low), or a person that is associated with a lowered "ride." Low rider vehicles in the Southwest are predominantly associated with individuals of Mexican descent, although not limited to this group since there are a number of Blacks and Anglo-Americans that participate in this expressive form. The lowered cars, or *ranflas,* are for the most part older cars. Some of the collectively desirable and valued cars are the '56, '57, '63, and '64 Chevrolets, as well as 1930s and 1940s models if they become available and affordable. Low riding, in the context of this essay, is defined as a complex social form involving the expression of individual and collective meanings through vehicles such as automobiles, dress, and behavior. Due to the centrality of cars in the current low riding movement, this essay focuses primarily on this type of vehicle.

Origins of Low Riding

Low rider *ranflas* have existed since the late 1930s. According to "Teen Angel," a writer for *Low Rider* magazine, low riding originated in 1938 in a small autobody repair shop in Sacramento, California. The shop's owner, Harry Westergard, customized a 1935 Ford convertible with many of the same features that a large number of contemporary low riders incorporate into their *firme carruchas* ("solid cars"). For example, Westergard was allegedly the first person to have "chopped down" (lowered) the roof of a car, to develop the "smooth look" by removing all the accessories, ornaments, and moldings from the car and then filling the body seams with lead, and inventing the "pop door" (a mechanism for opening and closing the door after removal of the door handle and the door lock).[2]

Prior to the introduction of hydraulic lifts to lower or raise the car for show purposes or to regain legal height when a law enforcement officer is seen in the vicinity (allegedly introduced circa 1957 by Ron Aguirre and his father), or the cutting of suspension coils to lower the car, individuals lowered their cars by placing heavy objects such as bags of cement or bricks in the trunk. Moreover, one could become a low rider by simply moving the front seat as far back as possible while driving the car.

Westergard was apparently well known to the local youth in Sacramento, who:

> used to come around his backyard shop to learn about customizing cars. He always took time to show them how to do things that would help the appearance of their cars (*Low Rider* 1980:12).

His customizing ideas would later gain wider popularity through the work of one of those high school youths who used to visit him—George Barris. George Barris, also known as the "King of the Kustomizers," relocated from Sacramento to the Los Angeles area in the early 1940s, and established a car customizing shop—Kustom

City—in Lynwood. By the late 1940s, George Barris had begun to establish his reputation as a customizing virtuoso with cars such as the "Twin 1940 Mercurys" which have become famous among car customizing circles. An examination of the identical cars reveals the presence of such features as "chopped roof," "dummy [non-functioning] spotlights," minimum use of chrome and moldings, fender skirts (rear tire covers), and a lower rear, features not uncommon among contemporary low riders. Years later, Barris closed his Lynwood shop and reopened Kustom City in North Hollywood, near Studio City. It was not long before Barris began receiving orders from movie actors and film studios for custom cars. Two such cars were the "Batmobile" and the "Munster Koach." Many of the early custom cars made by Barris have become collector's items for the wealthy car enthusiasts, autophiles, who are willing to pay large sums of money to own one of these.

Irrespective of the precise pattern of diffusion or independent invention of car customizing motifs in the 1930s and 1940s, what is clear from an examination of the roots of low riding is that it appears to have first surfaced in Northern California, and that it was part of the broad interest among working-class youth in making cars unique in some way. The interest among working-class Mexican youth in the customizing of cars was coextensive and coexistent with this broader phenomenon. The specific uniqueness and variants, as well as the chronology of the diversions, that appeared in the cars owned by Mexican youth of the period has yet to be documented.

Impetus for Low Riding

The popularity of low rider cars within specific *barrios* in the Southwest has waxed and waned. In some *barrios* it seems to have disappeared altogether, while in others it has exerted a continuity and persistence to the present. The contemporary surge in low riding, particularly within and beyond California (the fountainhead of the movement), has been aided by manifest and latent forces. The impetus for this movement has come primarily from the following sources:

1. The magazine *Low Rider,* produced by A.T.M. (A Toda Madre) Communications Inc. The first issue appeared in January of 1977;

2. The film "Boulevard Nights" by Warner Brothers, and the publicity given to the movie;

3. A film originally titled "Gang," but released as "Walk Proud" by Universal Studios;

4. A documentary special on CBS' "60 Minutes" that focused on low riders in California;

5. The *Zoot Suit* play by Luis Valdez, commissioned by the Los Angeles' Center Theater Group/Mark Taper Forum that became an almost instant success in Los Angeles but failed in New York;

6. The *Zoot Suit* film directed by Luis Valdez (adapted from the play) and produced by Universal Studios;

7. The numerous "Low Rider Happening" custom car shows sponsored by *Low Rider*/A.T.M., as well as other low rider custom car shows that followed the lead of *Low Rider*/A.T.M.;

8. *Q-VO* magazine, produced by National Lowrider Inc., Los Angeles, California. The first issue appeared in May of 1979;

9. *Firme* magazine, produced by the Mexican-American Ventures Corporate Operations Inc., San Gabriel, California. The first issue appeared in the early part of 1981;

10. *Vajito* magazine, produced by Tejano Communications Inc., San Antonio, Texas. The first issue appeared in September of 1981.

From all of the above sources, *Low Rider*/A.T.M. has clearly played the most aggressive role in generating and promoting the acceptance of low riding throughout the Southwestern states, and now the Midwest. Considerable attention is given below to this one source, not because the other sources are inconsequential, but rather, because of the aggressive stance that *Low Rider*/A.T.M. has taken. Moreover, the promotion plan of *Low Rider*/A.T.M. has incorporated some of the other sources, such as the film "Boulevard Nights," and more importantly the symbolism found in the *Zoot Suit* play that the Zoot Suit was an expression of Chicano culture and an example of early Chicano resistance and struggle.

Low Rider/A.T.M. experienced a substantial horizontal expansion in its formative stage. *Low Rider*'s distribution has evolved from an initial sale of 5,000 copies of the first issue which appeared in January of 1977, to its reported sales of over 100,000 copies a month. This relatively high volume of sales has prompted the editor to claim that it is the "Number One Latino Magazine" in the United States. The growth in sales and demand can be attributed to Sonny Madrid, the editor and one of the founders of the magazine, who has carried out with an indefatigable zeal the crusade for low riding. The other two cofounders have never been identified by the magazine. A.T.M., who suddenly and without any notice or comment took over the publication of *Low Rider* from La Onda Communications Inc. beginning with the ninth issue of volume one, also has experienced a substantial growth, as can be deduced from the proliferation of branch offices. After the founding of its principal headquarters in San Jose, California, there soon followed the establilshment of a branch office in Los Angeles (both cities are known as the low riding capitals of the world). Approximately three years later, in February of 1980, the third branch office was established in San Antonio, Texas, across the street from the Alamo. Two months later, in April, *Low Rider* obtained a distribution representative in Austin, Texas; and in May, the Phoenix, Arizona, branch office was inaugurated. *Low Rider* also counts with a distribution representative in Denver, Colorado. The aforementioned is not a complete inventory of the links and nodes of the A.T.M. network, since it lacks the enumeration of the unknown number of distribution representatives that exist throughout the Southwest, and now probably also in the Midwest.

The Fusion of Symbols

A careful examination of the thematic aspects of *Low Rider* reveals the overall development from an exclusive concern with low rider events in Northern California, to a slowly broadening concern with "happenings" in Southern California, then beyond California, and finally to a broader coverage of events in the entire Southwest and Northern Mexico. One also observes the interesting evolution of the fusion of the symbols of pachuco, zoot suiter, cholo, and low rider, a fusion which generates the perception that these social categories are interchangeable and are the authentic and immediate precursors of the modern low rider. In the editor's own words, "Low riders today are the modern Zoot Suiters" (*Nuestro* 1979:16). This affirmation of continuity or roots is part of a broader endeavor to legitimize the diffusion of the social movement, a process that will be discussed below.

The above ahistorical melting of social types is not peculiar or exclusive to the magazine, but seems instead to be a reflection of a popular and academic misunderstanding. The misunderstanding has a long history dating back to newspaper portrayal of "gangs" and "crime" among Mexican youth in the metropolitan areas of the Southwest, such as in the case of Los Angeles, preceding the Sleepy Lagoon case, and stretching across the decades to the present literary and academic writings which discuss pachucos or zoot suiters. The majority of such writings begin with the oversimplified equation between pachucos and gangs, or between pachucos and zoot suiters.

From this unqualified assertion they move to a position where the pachuco is projected and typecast into being either a hero or a villain, the political man or the apathetic man, or more generally, the culture hero or the community cancer.[3]

The paucity in conceptual clarity can be attributed to the fact that these writings have tended to be structured on the impressions of the authors, and thus fail to place each social type within their proper historical context. Among recent attempts to fill the lacuna in our knowledge of the historical context of the Mexican zoot suiter and pachuco have been the outstanding dissertation research done by Mauricio Mazón on the Zoot Suit Riots of 1943 and their intrinsic relation to the labor conflicts of this period and the gradual shift from an external enemy to an internal enemy (1976), and the work of Joan Moore and her collaborators, who focused on the close interrelationship between *barrio* organization, gangs, and the California penal system (1978). Although both of the works made important contributions to our knowledge of zoot suiters and "clubs" in the Los Angeles area, many critical issues still remain to be examined. Two such issues are that of regional diversity (differences among the regions of the Southwest and Midwest, urban-rural differences, etc.), and the role and participation of females in the pachuco, zoot suit, or cholo phenomenon.

The Pachuco

The existence of the pachuco as a social category in the history of the Southwest is widely recognized. However, a detailed historical analysis of the emergence of this character within a specific region or community has yet to surface. This void in the literature has aided the popular and academic misunderstanding of its origins and of the variations that existed in this social type. In discussions of the pachuco, there is very little mention of such critical elements as the urbanization of the Mexican working class; the context of the devlopment of "juvenile delinquency" in the Mexican community; the attempts at forced Americanization; the existence of activist youth organizations in the 1930s and 1940s; the impact of the broader youth "culture" on Mexican youth via music, dress, language, etc.; and others. Moreover, as has been noted by Madrid-Barela: "From his beginning the Pachuco has been endowed with mythic dimensions, a construct of fact and fiction, viewed with both hostility and curiosity, revulsion and fascination" (1974:31).

It is thus understandable, given the mythical dimensions of the pachuco, why this social category has been readily and repeatedly romanticized and made into a legendary hero. Although Grajeda places the blame primarily on social scientists for forging the legend of the pachuco, and adjudges poets as guiltless of this, his own examples as well as his decision to exclude Ricardo Sánchez from his discussion brings into question his interpretation (1980). If it is a matter of placing blame, then it would be more accurate to point out that both social scientists and poets have shared in the legend creation process.

The incorporation of the social category of pachuco by *Low Rider* was manifested in several ways. *Low Rider* reinforced the linkage between the pachuco and low riding primarily through three forms: the development of a section in the magazine titled "Lowriders Pasados" (Old Low Riders); the extensive usage of pachuco dialect or *caló* throughout the magazine; and the interchangeable use of the terms "pachuco" and "low rider" in the magazine. The "Lowriders Pasados" section was devoted to publishing photographs taken in the 1940s and 1950s, "showing the dress styles, hairdos [*sic*], and the caruchitas [*sic*]" of that period. Both title and content of the section served to classify the cars shown as low riders, and the individuals as representative pachucos/low riders. A close inspection of the photographs reveals that although some of the cars appear to have some custom features, the majority of the cars appear to be standard stock and not lowered; and although some of the individuals appear to exhibit some of the dress and hairstyles associated with pachucos, at least half if not more of the individuals reflect more the general styles of the period than anything else. On the question of language, the image presented by *Low Rider* is that *caló* was the unique language of the pachuco movement—the parent of the Chicano movement—and signified the struggle and resistance against cultural domination. The third area of incorporation is the interchangeable use of pachuco and low rider, specifically in discussions related to the history of low riding such as in the section titled "Cruising Into the Past," and features covering some aspect of the history of "Aztlán."

As pointed out above, the social symbol of pachuco was important in shaping the definition and understanding of low riding, as well as its diffusion; however, with the completion of the play *Zoot Suit* by Luis Valdez and its premiere in August of 1978, the pachuco was upstaged by *Zoot Suit*. From that point on, the central symbol became the zoot suit. The symbolic linkage was thus made between the zoot suit and low riding. After the premiere, one encounters first a favorable review in the magazine, followed by the advertising of zoot suit paraphernalia, the appearance of cartoons sporting zoot suits, the use of individuals wearing zoot suits to advertise commodities such as Schlitz beer, and the inclusion of zoot suit contests at the "Low Rider Happening" custom car shows. Because of the centrality of this symbol, and later reinforcement when the MCA/Universal Studios film *Zoot Suit* was released, there is a need to comment on this symbol.

The Zoot Suit

In most of the popular literature on the Zoot Suit Riots or zoot suiters, one notes the formation of the cultural myth that the zoot suit was an exclusive dress style among Mexican youth, and a "cultural expression" or a symbol of "Mexican/Chicano culture." The *Zoot Suit* play and film by Luis Valdez and *Low Rider*/A.T.M. have been prominent in generating this image. *Low Rider* began to project the zoot-suit-equals-low-rider image soon after the premiere of the play, and has continued this tradition up to the present. In most, if not all, of the "Low Rider Happening" custom car shows one finds the incorporation of a zoot suit dance contest as an intrinsic and genuine cultural expression, and as an opportunity for the attendants to reaffirm their cultural roots. The diffusion of the above myth has not been limited to low riders, but can also be found among Chicano/Mexicano university and high school student organizations that have sponsored either zoot suit dances or low rider car shows as concrete Chicano cultural expressions and as a reinforcement of cultural pride.

The existence and promulgation of the zoot suit myth is a curious fact in the context of the numerous sources that document or suggest that the zoot suit was another clothing fashion which was widely imitated among youth in the United States and abroad. Following Simmel (1957), fashion is here understood as a social phenomenon containing antithetical functions such as uniformity and differentiation, and expansion and atrophy. Fashion serves to create uniformity and conformity within a group or class through the process of imitation, which gives the individual "the satisfaction of not standing alone in his actions" and thus "freed from the worry of choosing and appears simply as a creature of the group, as a vessel of the social contents" (ibid.:542-543). Simultaneously, however, the uniformity and conformity created in the group or class acts as a demarcation to differentiate it from another group or class. The second antithesis has to do with the fact that if a fashion is to remain a fashion, it can only be practiced by a portion of the society. The moment that a fashion originally practiced by a few is practiced by a large segment of the population, it ceases to be a fashion and change ensues. Moreover, Simmel also observes that fashion can function as a valve through which an individual may realize the need for "some measure of conspicuousness and individual prominence... when its satisfaction is denied... in other fields" (1957:551). The importance of Simmel's observations is that they draw attention to the need to examine the objects of fashion beyond their surface manifestation, to their socializing and "masking" functions as well as to the fact that fashion "is a product of class distinction(s)" (ibid.:544).

Although the origin of the zoot suit still needs to be fully documented, a *New York Times* reporter claimed that the style originated in Gainesville, Georgia (Berger 1943). According to this account, Clyde Duncan, a Black busboy in Gainesville, ordered his custom suit in February of 1940 (Esquire gives the year as 1939; see 1973), at Frierson-McEver's department store, who sent the measurements to the Globe Tailoring Company in Chicago, where it was made for a cost of $33.50. The "Killer Diller," as the style became known in South Georgia, caught on in "Mississippi, New Orleans and Alabama and leap-frogged to Harlem." Harlem was thus transformed into the axis of diffusion for the East Coast, and presumably for the rest of the country. According to Berger, and reiterated in the *Negro Digest* (1943), Duncan was inspired by the "Civil War garb worn by Clark Gable as Rhett Butler in *Gone With the Wind,* where Gable appears in several scenes in a long coat and peg-trousers" (1943). In fact, however, the pants had stovepipe legs. Another account of the origin is found in a *Newsweek* article, where it is said that the "breeding ground appears to have been Harlem, where the disease appeared about a decade ago," and then spread to the West Coast (1942). Both accounts seem to agree on the importance of Harlem in the diffusion of the fashion. However, if we agree with the latter account, the origins are pushed back to the early 1930s, rather than the early 1940s. Irrespective of the precise source of origin, the fashion seems to have been adopted by Mexicanos in Los Angeles by the end of 1941 (cf. Jones 1969:11). Notwithstanding the limited and perhaps questionable evidence of the origin of the fashion, one nevertheless can conclude that the zoot suit was apparently a Black innovation.

The Zoot Suit, like other clothing fashions, showed a significant amount of individual and group variation. In general, the style consisted of a coat of about midthigh length and heavily padded shoulders and high-waisted trousers with baggy legs—baggiest at the knees—that narrowed to a very small cuff. The full outfit was worn with accessories such as a long goldlike watch chain, a relatively flat hat oftentimes adorned with a feather, and thick-soled shoes. It should be apparent that the description given is the male version of the zoot suit. The reason for this is the fact that most of the literature fails to adequately describe the form worn by female zoot suiters. Bogardus (1943), Griffith (1948), and Jones (1969) provide a brief glimpse of the dress style of the young "pachucas," or "cholitas." The neglect of the female 'pachucas" or "zoot suiters" is perhaps the result of the fact that most of the research has been conducted by males, the exception being Griffith, who has provided the best description, yet even her account is limited in scope.

The fact that the zoot suit was popular among Blacks in the early 1940s is further corroborated by Malcolm X's account of being a zoot suiter in his *Autobiography,* and other sources that point to the style's popularity. One interesting source is the article by Redl, who was writing to dispel the myth that in Detroit "the phenomena [*sic*] is confined... to the Negroes" (1943:259). In the process of dispelling the myth, Redl acknowledges that even though the majority of Zoot Suiters were "Negroes," the "zoot suit cult" was also found among Italian youth and some middle-class youth—presumably white (ibid.; see also Cohen 1943). One also finds that in Baltimore in the early 1950s, there developed a class/racial distinction between youth (we can infer of white, middle-class origins) who wore what resembled a "zoot suit" but referred to it as "drapes" or "black zaks," and youth who were said to sport the "zoot suit" and belonged to a minority group, presumably Black (Barnett 1953:140). The "drapers" perceived a "zoot suiter" as a "bum, a draft dodger, or a guy who hangs around street corners" (ibid.). In the Flatbush section of Brooklyn, it is reported that in a high school attended by students of white middle-class and well-to-do families, four out of ten males wore zoot suits (Banay 1944:82). Mention has also been made that in some of the World War II Japanese relocation camps it was not unusual to see young Japanese males sporting the zoot suit and dancing the jitterbug at the camp dances. Nakagawa and Rosovsky, in their discussion of the disappearance of the *kimono* and the influence of Western style clothing in Tokyo in the early 1960s, point out that in Tokyo one could see "young toughs sporting the local version of the long-forgotten zoot suit" (1965:311). And lastly, one also encounters the reference to the adoption of the zoot suit by Filipinos in California (Bogardus 1943:55).

From the above account, one is led to a clear realization that the zoot suit was a widespread fashion not unique to or created by

Mexicanos, but was instead a widely imitated fashion found among Blacks, middle-class and working-class whites, Italians, Filipinos, and Japanese in the United States and in Japan. One may also infer that the fashion was also present among other ethnic groups, although the necessary documentation is lacking. In short, it should be clear that there is no need to promulgate the spurious myth that the zoot suit was a genuine and exclusive Mexican "cultural expression," or that the contemporary use of one necessarily places an individual in the cultural vanguard.

Having so far repeatedly used the term zoot suit, it is instructive to examine the origins of the term. According to an article that appeared in *Newsweek,* the zoot suits or drapes were originally known in Harlem as "sharpies," and then with the popularization of swing music and the adoption of jitterbug fever among United States youth, the name was changed to "root suit" (the female version was known as "juke suit"); and finally "in late 1941 some Hollywood writers produced the hit 'A Zoot Suit'," from which the modern term is said to derive (1942:48). Lingeman provides us with the lyrics of the song:

> I wanna zoot suit with a reat pleat.
> With a drape shape and a stuff cuff
> To look sharp enough to see my Sunday Sal
> I want a reave sleeve with a ripe stripe
> And a dressed seat with a glad plaid,
> In the *latest fad* to see my Sunday Sal.
> I want to look keen so my dream will say,
> "You don't look like the same beau."
> So keen that she'll scream,
> "Here comes my walkin' rainbow—"
> So make a zoot suit with a reat pleat,
> With a drape shape and stuff cuff
> To look sharp enough to see my Sunday gal.
>   (1970:349; my emphasis).

In evaluating the above etymology one if faced with the question of whether the song was actually written after the term "zoot suit" had been coined, the song taking its name from the "latest fad" rather than vice versa. If one extrapolates from the present song production, however, the former explanation seems the more plausible.

One important area that most writers who have written about the zoot suit have tended to ignore is the fashion context of the early 1940s. From a perusal of popular fashion magazines of the period one notes that many of the elements of the zoot suit were in reality an exaggerated duplication of general styles or forms of the period, the notable exceptions being the length of the coat, the narrowness of the trouser cuffs, and the colors of the materials used in the production of the suits. Otherwise, we observe that the wide V-shaped lapels, relatively baggy pants, deep pleats, and the use of hats were common features of men's wear, up until March of 1942 when the War Production Board (WPB) issued order L-85 (Cf. Blaker 1943; Van Syckle 1943). Order L-85 was aimed at reducing textile-garment production for civilian use, and achieving a fabric saving of 26 percent (ibid.). The order involved setting maximum length specifications for such things as coats, trouser knees, etc., and eliminating trouser cuffs, vests, two-pants suits, pleats, and overlapping waistbands (ibid.). The WPB saw the zoot suit as a "glaring example of wasteful manufacture" and charged that the continued manufacture of the zoot suit would interfere with the war effort (*Esquire* 1973:26). The impact of order L-85 on the entire zoot suit fashion, within the Mexican community and outside of it, remains to be examined by researchers—more specifically, questions of the relation of the order and the media protrayal of "crime" among Mexican youth, the connection between this order and the Sleepy Lagoon incident which took place three months later, and other related issues.

Cholos

The third symbol manipulated in the pages of *Low Rider,* the cholo, stands in contrast to the symbols of pachuco and zoot suit discussed above. This anomaly emerges from two facts. On one hand, some members of the more formal low rider car clubs categorize cholos as *vatos locos* (crazy guys), and thus as deviant low riders who give good, respectable low riders a bad name. On the other hand, some cholos do not have very positive perceptions of the more formal low rider car clubs. *Low Rider*/A.T.M. is thus pressed to reconcile the differences among low riders. The way it achieves this is by limiting the use of the term cholo, or references to this segment, projecting the image that low riders in Aztlán are a homogeneous group, in both thought and action, and devoting more space to the formal car clubs. By following this line of action, *Low Rider*/A.T.M. places itself in the awkward position of potentially alienating a segment of the readership it claims to represent. Before discussing this issue further it will be beneficial to introduce a historical note on the term *cholo.*

The term *cholo* has been used in the Southwest, specifically in California, since the early 1800s. Bancroft's discussion of the term in his work on the history of California, for the years 1821-1824, is one of the earliest references (1885:255). According to Bancroft, cholo

> in American provincial Spanish is the offspring of a Spanish father and Indian mother; but it was never used in California except in an offensive sense, with reference to character rather than to race. It was applied only to vagabonds who came from Mexico (ibid.).

From the letters cited by Bancroft one notes a clear antipathy toward the behavior and dress of the cholo. Cholos, such as the men in Navarrete's infantry company—the "soldados de la otra banda"— were referred to as individuals "sin disciplina y sin religión," "of mixed race and worse than mixed character, vicious and quarrelsome . . . Small in stature, wearing the hair short in contrast with presidential troops," and who should be housed in "separate quarters" (ibid.; cf. also Francis 1935:338-345).

More contemporary references to the term *cholo* can be found in the works of Victor Clark (1908) and Manuel Gamio (1930). In his research on Mexican workers, Clark notes that "cholo" was a reference to individuals who had "recently" immigrated to the United States from Mexico (1908). A slightly more complex observation of the usage of the term *cholo* was noted by Gamio, who states that in the 1926-1927 period there existed an antithesis between *cholo* and *chicamo* [sic], a recent immigrant, and *pocho,* someone with a longer residence in the United States (1930). The differentiation involved the degree of "Americanization" (ibid.:19; also reiterated by McWilliams 1968:209-212).

The contemporary use of the term *cholo,* in contrast to the above, is generally found in reference to a youth of Mexican descent residing in a low income area within one of the principal metropolitan areas of the Southwest, who may or may not belong to a formal club (or "gang"). Cholos are often associated with popular and stylized forms of dress, such as khaki pants, a sleeveless white T-shirt, a bandanna, a plaid long-sleeved shirt (similar to that produced by Pendleton), and possibly a tattoo in the hands, arms, or face. Cholos, moreover, are also associated with living *la vida loca* (the crazy life), as a *vato loco.* *La vida loca* is considerably varied and may range from the normal, rebellious acts of youth, to more serious activities involving several levels of drug use (including alcohol) and possibly offenses involving property or persons. Some writers have classified the cholo as the modern day version of the pachuco. This assertion however needs to be presented in more detail and with greater sociohistorical specificity.

From the above three descriptions of the reference of the term cholo, one observes both continuity and discontinuity. The continuity is reflected in the fact that in all three periods the term embodied a negative connotation for the broader population. The discontinuity is reflected in the disassociation with referents to heritage, immigration, and cultural assimilation.

Low Riding and Low Riders

The development of low riding, like other social phenomena, evolved within a broader historical context. An examination of the contemporary manifestation of a particular social form, such as low riding, in comparison to a parallel form may suggest that the two are antithetical. However, an analysis of the historical context of the forms may reveal homologous antecedents for the two. Low riding and hot rodding appear to conform to this pattern. Although the specifics of the influence of one form upon the other and the gradual diversification has not been addressed to date, the general parameters can be pieced together.

Both low riding and hot rodding were influenced by the general, though short-lived, wartime affluence which youth experienced in the early 1940s and was channeled into the consumption of records, entertainment activities, cars, clothes, and other commodities. By the early 1950s, hot rodding, or the act of "hopping up" (modifying the motor to increase its potential speed), was well established and became part of a larger movement. Car customizing, especially through the influence of George Barris, was an important element in this development. Low riding, on the other hand, appears to have receded in some areas, and in others apparently disappeared.

In the 1950s, the United States experienced not only the surge of hot rodding, but of several car-related activities such as drag racing, custom car shows, antique car shows, demolition derbies, and slot car racing. Moreover, there soon followed a flood of hot rod and car customizing magazines to meet the emerging market demand. All of these individual elements became part of the broader context which created what some have dubbed the American "car culture" (cf. Wolfe 1965; Dettelback 1976; and Flink 1975).

America's car culture, or the existence of autophiles, is not a thing of the past. Evidence of this is clearly apparent in the contemporary existence of numerous national car clubs with state and local chapters, independent local car clubs, as well as the occurrence of multitudinous auto shows throughout the United States. As an example one can note the various Mustang car clubs, exotic car clubs, and antique car clubs, such as the Horseless Carriage Club of

America which has chapters in most larger cities. The membership in the majority of the aforementioned auto clubs is recruited from the "professional" segment of the population—lawyers, doctors, businessmen, and others.

Low rider cars, despite their perceived distinctiveness from other car forms, share a number of links with other customized cars, hot rods, and antique cars. Firstly, they all draw from the same pool of auto technology—auto parts and accessories suppliers. Secondly, they often appear in the same auto shows. Thirdly, the club events or auto shows are often sponsored by the same corporations—tobacco or brewing companies. This, of course, should not be interpreted to mean that the majority of the participants in each of the car forms view themselves as sharing similar interests or having any intrinsic links with members in other car forms. An example of this is the antipathetic relationship between low riders and high riders (either hot rodders or four-wheel drive vehicle owners) in some areas of the Southwest. In some cases this underlying relationship has led to physical confrontations between the two groups.

Low rider cars vary considerably in ornateness and decoration. Because of the impossibility of describing in detail the diversity that exists, one can list some of the common and desired features in low riders. One method of describing a low rider is to contrast it to a parallel form, such as a high rider. The table below presents some of the contrasting preferences of owners of each type of vehicle.

LOW RIDERS	HIGH RIDERS
1. Lower the body.	1. Raise the body. (The rear is raised higher than the front.)
2. Minimize the use of chrome.	2. Maximize the use of chrome.
3. Emphasize slow speeds.	3. Emphasize high speeds.
4. Emphasize collective performances. (E.g., caravaning. The exceptions are car "hopping" contests and show competitions.)	4. Emphasize individual competition (drag racing).
5. Have high valuation of and desire for hydraulic lifts, though a small number actually own them.	5. Have low valuation of hydraulic lifts, and no general desire for or use of these. Preference is given to heavy duty shock absorbers.
6. Prefer wire wheels or "tru-spokes" wheel covers/rims.	6. Prefer "mag" wheel covers/rims.
7. Prefer the use of narrow tires.	7. Prefer the use of wide tires, particularly the rear tires.
8. Emphasize streamlining or the "smooth" look.	8. Minimally emphasize streamlining.

9. Put prominent emphasis on customizing the interior (e.g., crushed-velvet upholstery, swivel seats, chain link steering wheel, chandeliers, etc.)

9. Give minimal emphasis to customizing the interior (vinyl upholstery, vinyl/leather or wood steering wheel, VDO gauges, etc.). Greater emphasis on the performance of the engine and related parts.

10. Often engrave windows.

10. Seldom engrave windows.

11. Emphasize the use of multiple colors and designs such as murals on the exterior.

11. Emphasize the use of one or two colors, minimal use of designs, and rare use of murals.

12. Value highly multiple-layer lacquer paint jobs.

12. Make limited use of multiple-layer lacquer paint jobs.

A low rider *ranfla,* however, may contain only one of the elements listed above and still be referred to as a low rider. The number and quality of the features found in a low rider will depend on a number of variables regarding the owner, such as age, sex, marital status, number of dependents, employment, salary, etc. In other words, the person's ability to consume the desired commodities (articles and services) will vary with the owner's socioeconomic position, and thus the rate of acquiring a majority of the features also varies.

A range in diversity such as that found among low rider cars is also present among the owners. Although *Low Rider* magazine seems to create the impression of homogeneity among low riders, the opposite fact emerged from the research conducted in San Antonio, Texas. From interviews conducted with car club members and non-car club members, and from observations made at gathering places and car shows, a fourfold classification emerged. Each "type" is a heuristic tool to organize the variability observed. Additional field research in Austin, Texas, has generally supported the classification. However, significant modifications may be needed to make the classification more precise. In addition to specifying the four types, the list below points out some of the key areas that emerged as important in describing the heterogeneity observed, such as age, technical knowledge, and centrality of cars in that person's life.

I.   TECHNICIAN OR CRAFTSMAN

1. Older individual—in the forties age range or older.
2. Extensive technological knowledge.
3. Capable of doing almost all work on the car, with the possible exception of the upholstery work.
4. Began to work on cars at an early age.
5. Has participated in the hot rod tradition and possibly in the antique auto show sphere.
6. Owns several cars.

7. Cars are an intrinsic element of his life—no clear segregation between work and leisure when it comes to cars.
8. Rapid rate of conversion or modification of car in the process of customizing it.

II. LIMITED TECHNICIAN

1. Not as old as the technician; late twenties and thirties.
2. Limited technological knowledge.
3. Capable of doing a significant amount of work on cars. Paint, upholstery, lift work and other areas may be paid or bartered for.
4. May have been employed in a car-related shop or industry.
5. Has most likely participated in the hot rod tradition.
6. Probably owns more than one car.
7. High interest and preoccupation with cars, but cars are not necessarily an intrinsic element in this person's life.
8. Slower rate of conversion.

III. STYLE CONSCIOUS

1. Late teens or early twenties age group.
2. Limited technological knowledge.
3. Capable of doing some of the work on the car; will purchase services for all or most of the major work needed to customize or maintain the low rider, or may purchase a completed product.
4. Probably has a permanent job with a relatively high wage, or a semiskilled occupation with a moderate remuneration for work performed.
5. Relatively marginal to the hot rod tradition.
6. Generally owns one car.
7. Work and leisure spheres are segregated.
8. Strong interest in cars and the status obtained through them; cars are not an intrinsic element in his life.
9. "Overnight" rate of conversion when completed commodity is purchased; otherwise, rate of conversion may equal that of the limited technician.

IV. PRIMER

1. In the twenties and thirties age-group range.
2. Limited technological knowledge.
3. Capable of doing a significant amount of work on cars; paint, upholstery, lift work and other areas may be purchased or bartered for.
4. Employment status not as permanent.
5. Participated in the hot rod tradition.
6. Owns one car—for work and leisure.
7. Work and leisure minimally segregated.
8. Slow rate of conversion; the primer on the body of the car may be present for a considerable period of time.

The above list draws attention to two important issues. First, there are critical differences among the class of individuals that are labeled low riders and upon whom a notion of homogeneity is often imposed. Two differences that emerge as particularly important are those of socioeconomic status and technological knowledge. Second, that the age of the person and the centrality of cars in that person's life places the individual in a different relationship to the development of low riding. An examination of the five low rider car clubs that were formed in the latter part of 1979 and the early months of 1980 in San Antonio suggests how the juxtaposition of these issues was critical in the diffusion of low riding.

The year 1979 was an important period in the contemporary evolution of low riding in San Antonio and other cities in the Southwest, specifically outside of California. Working class Mexican youth from the Westside and Southside of San Antonio, ranging in age from preteens to early twenties, became attracted to the "new" social movement that was spreading like wildfire—a term sometimes used by *Low Rider* staff (cf. 1980; February). The younger individuals, pre- and early teens, focused their energies in customizing their bicycles; the older age set, late teens and early twenties, focused their energies in the formation of low rider car clubs and the customizing of their cars. The San Antonio low rider car clubs, like most of the car clubs that exist elsewhere, are predominately male oriented. Membership size in the four clubs that emerged in the latter part of 1979 ranged from fifteen to thirty-five members; the ages ranged from nineteen to twenty-five years of age. An important dimension of the car clubs was that, like other social groups, they appeared to provide a significant degree of small-group solidarity and were a source of identity for the individual members. For some of the members the car clubs reinforced kinship and friendship ties previously established. The low rider cars provided the central focus of status for the individual as well as for the entire club. This fact was most evident in the formal and informal competitions for status or trophies among the car clubs.

From the initial interviews, it became evident that the diffusion of low riding in San Antonio had its greatest impact among the male youth in their late teens and early twenties, who had a limited technological knowledge of car customizing and did not perceive cars as central to their lives. Moreover, it was reported that *Low Rider* was key in developing their interest in low riding. All five clubs would best be characterized by the classification of "Style Conscious." It thus became clear that *Low Rider*/A.T.M. was having its greatest success in the promotion of low riding, not with the older low riders, many of whom had been low riders or hot rodders or even "bikers" in the past, or with older individuals such as the "Primer" who had a limited disposable income, but instead with youth who had a relatively higher disposable income and who could participate more actively in low riding activities. In other words, the juxtaposition of certain critical variables such as age, disposable income, centrality of cars in that person's life, and technological knowledge about cars and car customizing shaped to a significant extent the diffusion of low riding in San Antonio, and presumably in other cities in the Southwest where low riding has been actively promoted by *Low Rider.*

The Promotion of Low Riding

In the investigation of a social movement it is much easier to describe the manifestations of the movement than it is to describe the process that stimulated and sustained the diffusion of the movement. One important reason for this is the lack of access to information that would verify the hypothesis under consideration. In such cases the researcher must assemble the bits and pieces that surface randomly and are oftentimes scattered. The analysis of the promotion of low riding by *Low Rider* encountered these limitations.

The investigation of the diffusion of low riding began with a few seemingly simple questions: Who owns *Low Rider?* Is there a formal promotional plan? What interests does *Low Rider* have in the diffusion of low riding? Are there any other interests in the promotion of low riding?

In reference to the question of ownership one notes an unexpected development in the January of 1980 issue of *Low Rider.* Toward the beginning of the issue one finds that a full page was devoted to the following:

COMING NEXT ISSUE
1. Who is Lowrider Magazine?
2. Is it Chicano Owned?
3. Are they Lowriders?
4. Is it a non-Chicano Front?
FIND OUT IN FEBRUARY

From this set of statements one can deduce that someone must have begun to ask certain questions, and the magazine felt some obligation to provide some answers. In the February issue, at the end of the editor's two-page letter, the reader is told:

> I apologize for not running Who is Behind Low Rider Magazine, but we didn't have enough room, and my '52 didn't get out of the shop in time. I have a T-bird but the '52 is my pride. However, the article will run in the March issue, and this will be an even bigger issue with no increase in price (*Low Rider,* February 1980).

When the March issue came out it contained the exact same number of pages as the February issue (76 pages), and no mention of the matter promised. Moreover, the April issue also remained silent on this question. One is left to wonder why the editor chose not to answer the questions promised. It may be that the omission was motivated by other factors not mentioned in the apology, such as the fact that Mr. Madrid was sedulously working in Texas making preparations for the first "Lowrider Happening" held at the San Antonio Convention Center in March 1980. In addition to the time spent in preparing for this event, he traveled extensively throughout South and Central Texas locating distribution representatives and simultaneously promoting the magazine and low riding. With such an active schedule it is understandable why he would not have had time to answer the questions noted in the January issue. The explanation given by the editor thus appears to have been an effort to avoid answering the question "Who is behind *Low Rider?*"

The question of ownership was briefly answered not in the magazine but in a one-sheet flyer that was inconspicuously placed on one of the tables surrounding the *Low Rider* booth at the San Antonio show. Under the heading of "Chicano Ownership" one is told:

> Perhaps the key to our success lies in the fact that we are a Chicano-owned publication with employees who have come out of the barrios of Aztlán. As such, our goal is not to exploit, but to communicate—in a way that our readers understand. And we've succeeded. Since its inception three years ago Low Rider Magazine has emerged as the largest selling Chicano magazine in Aztlán (*Low Rider,* n.d.).

The relevance of the statement lies not in the answer it provides concerning the ownership of the magazine, since it does not really accomplish this, but rather in its effective manipulation of certain nationalistic symbols such as "Chicano" and "Aztlán." By juxtaposing the concept that it is "Chicano-owned," with that of "barrio" and "Aztlán," it is able to gloss over the question of ownership by providing a symbolically proper generic answer. After all, who would question the ownership of a business that consisted of Chicanos who came out of the barrios of Aztlán? By selecting the generally positive symbol of "Chicano," in place of "Mexican

American," "Spanish American," "Hispanic," etc., which may not have as positive connotations among working-class Mexican youth in the Southwest and Midwest, in combination with the quasi-political symbols of "barrio" and "Aztlán," *Low Rider* was able to create a symbolically positive cluster that would be difficult to question.

Moreover, by explicitly denouncing that the goal of the magazine was not to "exploit but to communicate," it aimed at divorcing the profits generated by the magazine from any notion of exploitation, and thus deflect any suggestions that the magazine may be exploiting the phenomenon of low riding. Although *Low Rider* attempts to absolve itself from any concern with the commercial potential of low riding, it nevertheless shows concern with the emergence of promoters who "are getting hep to the popularity of lowriding" and "are only concerned about the commercial money-making side of lowriding and are not even lowriders themselves" (*Low Rider,* July 1981:6-7). The message is clear: if low riding is to be promoted by anyone other than *Low Rider,* they shold at least be low riders.

In order to secure their position and to "help protect the car show scene, ATM Communications has started a Union of Car Shows de Aztlán" (ibid.). The Union, via *Low Rider*/A.T.M., following the structure of the International Show Car Association, would establish a circuit of "official" car shows per population area. The winners of each show would then be allowed to participate in the national show, on the basis of the number of points accumulated in the local shows. It thus appears that the unstated motive behind the idea of a Union is an attempt by A.T.M. to secure their investment in the growth of low riding and to maintain their control on the present and future growth of low riding.

The above leads to the question of whether *Low Rider* operated with a formal promotion plan to spread low riding or, as suggested by the magazine and many low riders, low riding was a spontaneous, self-generating expressive movement that *Low Rider* was reporting on. In the interview conducted with Sonny Madrid and Ray Canales, the field representative in charge of the San Antonio office, both individuals suggested that *Low Rider* was principally reporting the growth of low riding, and secondarily providing support and assistance to the low rider clubs that were emerging in Aztlán. Moreover, the magazine was being marketed to meet the emerging demand among low riders for such a magazine. Specific answers about the accuracy of the two interpretations remained moot until the release of the August 1980 issue of the magazine. In the

introduction to a story about the "Taste of Latin" low rider car club
of Corpus Christi, Texas, one finds the following disclosure:

> Low Rider Mag. has spread from coast to coast as Corpus Christi,
> Texas, develops into a Low Rider city. Corpus is the easternmost city
> on the Gulf coast of Aztlán to have low riders and local distribution
> of Low Rider Magazine. In [a] short year low riding in Texas has
> spread like wild fire from El Paso to Corpus and from the Rio
> Grande Valley to the Panhandle. To the staff of Low Rider we have
> reached our three year goal, to spread low riding throughout Aztlán.
> Si se puede raza, y hay vamos raza del Mid-West and East Coast
> [sic]. (Low Rider, August:34).

The admission of the three-year goal, and by implication of a plan
that probably accompanied the goal, was somewhat surprising, since
its existence was so closely guarded before. The author's suspicion of
such a plan was not the product of great epistemological insight but
rather was based on the close observation of the spread of branch
offices, the choice of location for the branch offices, the growth of
distribution representatives, the extensive traveling of the editor
throughout the Southwest in general, and South Texas in particular,
and a detailed reading of the magazine.

The specifics of Madrid's excursion in Texas remained
hypothetical until its confirmation over a year later in one of the rare
editorial letters, wherein it is noted that he spent nine months in
Texas, from January to November, promoting low riding (Low
Rider, July 1981:6-7). The promotional plan included the
importation from California of a 1962 Impala, a 1954 Sedan
Delivery, and a 1973 Thunderbird, all fully customized, for the
purpose of giving "the homies from Texas some ideas on lowriding"
(ibid.). Mr. Madrid's evaluation of his efforts is relatively accurate
when he reports that with "the help of Texas lowriders, Lowrider
Magazine, and the carruchas for promotion, the lowriding scene in
Texas grew ten times" (ibid.). His statement embodies two important
issues. First, it acknowledges the promotional role of the California
low rider cars, and, more importantly, the role of Low Rider in
promoting low riding. Second, it acknowledges the link between the
growth of low riding in Texas and the magazine. The information
provided by the two disclosures noted above, the three-year goal to
spread low riding from coast to coast, and the activities of the editor,
clearly indicate the role of Low Rider in the impetus of the spread of
low riding throughout the Southwest and presumably beyond the
Southwest.

If one accepts the argument that Low Rider was central in the diffusion of low riding, then one needs to ask what it gains from spreading low riding throughout Aztlán. There are at least three possibilities: 1.) *Low Rider* is strictly interested in increasing the number of actual low riders for its own sake; 2.) *Low Rider* feels a philanthropic obligation to spread low riding and thus "provide people with a unique way to communicate with each other—to experience a sense of brotherhood"; 3.) *Low Rider* aims to generate a consuming market for the products it produces or it markets and thus establish a profit level for the existence and growth of the corporation (cf. *Low Rider*, n.d.). If one accepts the first possibility, questions still remain: Why does *Low Rider* feel the need to conduct such a zealous crusade in the recruitment of adherents to low riding? What will the rapid increase in low riding accomplish? Who will benefit most from such a rapid diffusion? The second possibility gives one something more to go on. If one grants the "brotherhood" argument as logical, despite its somewhat simplistic idealism, one ends up with a question similar to the one above: who will benefit most from the "sense of brotherhood"? Moreover, one then has to raise the issue of why *Low Rider* has carried out such an aggressive promotion from coast to coast, when in fact it has not achieved this sense of brotherhood among low riders in Los Angeles or San Jose, the low rider "capitals" of the Southwest? A related issue is the question of why it has paid so much attention to the promotion of the magazine when, in fact, it is the sense of brotherhood that demands attention. The third possibility seems to offer at least a partial explanation for the questions of what is to be gained, who is to gain the most, and why *Low Rider* has carried out an aggressive crusade in the spread of low riding from coast to coast. In short, *Low Rider* appears to be primarily interested in generating, cornering, and securing a potentially large market for the sale of its products and services, which can generate sufficient profits. The reference to services is to the advertising services it provides for the numerous and increasing number of auto-related and other industries that advertise in the magazine.

It is important to also recognize that it is possible that when the magazine was first created it may have been oriented toward a different set of goals. Perhaps like the political organizations discussed by Robert Michels in his classic work *Political Parties* (1959; orig. 1908), *Low Rider* experienced the process of "goal displacement," wherein an original goal was displaced by another goal. In the case of *Low Rider* the change may have been from a concern to "communicate" or to establish a "brotherhood" to a concern with the commercial potential of low riding. The questions of whether in fact the change did take place, and if the change coincided with the change in the name of the parent corporation from La Onda Communications to A Toda Madre Communications, awaits further study.

The observation that the magazine "somehow changed" in its emphasis, scope, and direction is not an observation limited to the author, as evident from the statements of a perceptive *pinto* (prison inmate) who wrote the following letter to the editor of *Low Rider:*

QUE PASO, LOWRIDER? QUE PASO?

Dear Low Rider Magazine,

Somehow I feel you have changed, or is it me? I don't know, but I knew you when! And you don't seem the same to me! A few years back you used to reach out to your gente. I felt a part of you, you were our magazine then. Our voice to Aztlán. Now I open your covers and I see more ADS than anything else! Carnales, I understand that the bills must be paid, pero, don't the 15 bolas a year do that? You are Numero Uno!! Doesn't this mean you sell un chingaral de magazines??

I doubt that you sell because los vatos want to read "ads." For that We can look into the yellow pages and let out fingers take a stroll! Que no?

I don't know, Low Riders, I just don't know!! I hate to think you vatos are going capitalist on your own Raza, but that's all you leave me to think. What I do know is that I buy the magazine to check out las rucas, las ranflas, las rucas, the happenings, and that before I could turn your pages and see mis homeboys y homegirls tirando party at Kelly Park, Story and King, or at the Disco East parking lot, but now all I see is where they got their T-tops, Tru-spokes, paint jobs, interiors, "lift," zoot-suits, and chrome polish!

Okay, Low Rider, okay! So now we know where we can take our ranflas to make them look a toda madre! Now can you give "us" (la gente that these same shopkeepers used to call the placa on, just for parking in their parking lot) back our magazine? Carnales, like I say, I know the bills must get paid! and believe me I know about overhead y todo ese pedo! Pero you are now trying to cover four states, and if you truly need all those ads to make ends meet, go ahead on ese! But at least you could put a few more pages between the covers and let us (la gente that made you a star) become a part of you once more! And if anyone can unite the Lowriders of Amerika it's you (LRM), but then I hate to think of how little coverage each state will get, since you seem to be spreading yourself pretty thin with just Aztlán! . . . And now, Low Rider, I leave you with a word of warning . . . Playboy was once number one too—until the perverts found out they couldn't get off on advertisements! Es todo al rato.

El Trinito de San Jo
José Trinidad #299469
Ellis Unit C5-10-1
Huntsville, Texas (*Low Rider,* August 1980).

Although the author initially had some reservations about the authenticity of the letter, the letter gained credence after the discovery that the inmate number given in the letter corresponded to a José Trinidad, who was serving a prison sentence in the Texas Department of Corrections.

Trinidad's letter contains several significant observations and statements. Within the larger topic of change, the letter covers three critical issues: the change in the relationship between certain businesses and low riders, the role of advertising in the magazine, and the ownership and control of symbols. In the letter Trinidad makes the keen observation that businesses which in the past used to call the police about low riders now were advertising in the magazine and considered low riders important buyers of their products. The letter also clearly notes the increasing importance of advertisements in the pages of the magazine, to the point that they appeared to him as being the priority of the magazine. He also makes the analogy to *Playboy,* which, it is suggested, became so concerned with advertisements that they lost their sales position; by implication *Low Rider* may suffer the same fate if they do not alter their direction. The third, and most important, issue raised is the subtle question of ownership and control of symbols. Through the repeated reference to the notion that the magazine used to be "our magazine," "our voice," and the demand to "give 'us'. . . back our magazine," what is being questioned is the right of a magazine to take and control particular symbols and use these for commercial gain—in other words, the right of capital to appropriate certain symbols of the working class, the right of capital to control the sphere outside of the place of direct production, the factory, and the society at large. Other analysts who have discussed related issues have referred to the process or "plan" on the part of capital to expand its control beyond the factory, as the formation of the "social factory."[4] The utility of this concept rests on drawing attention to the need to view the spheres of "consumption" and "production," not as separate realms as they are usually treated, but as two integrated subprocesses within a larger process. Moreover, it also directs attention to the need to examine conflict and struggle not only in the factory but outside the factory, and at the same time to examine the impact of struggle in one sphere upon the other.

In spite of the fact that Mr. Trinidad's letter is not typical of the letters sent to the magazine, or at least of the letters printed by the magazine, his letter underscores the fact that the creation, manipulation, and diffusion of cultural symbols as commodity forms, is a fertile arena for conflict. The response to the establishment of the commodity form, or to what Hebdige subdivides as the two forms of "incorporation," semantic/ideological and 'real'/commercial (1979:96), can represent an instance of potential class struggle. In the present case the struggle is over the question of whether low riding "belongs" to "La Raza," the "gente," or to a commercial institution. However, to positively assert on the basis of Mr. Trinidad's letter that the struggle is presently being waged would be a naive position, and an extrapolation beyond the available data. On the other hand, it would be equally shortsighted to a priori dismiss the critical issues noted in the letter.

An issue closely related to the unflagging effort to promulgate low riding throughout the Southwest has been the attempt to alter the image of the low rider held by non-low riders. This effort is a critical element in the legitimation of the movement, which if accomplished can facilitate its diffusion by neutralizing some of the opposition and establishing the perception that the movement is a positive phenomenon. The extensive public relations campaign has included a vast number of activities. In each of these activities low riders have either initiated the event or have been a very visible part of it. A brief summary of some of these public relations events are as follows: a "Chicano Voter Registration" drive in San Jose; a fundraiser for muscular dystrophy (Jerry's Kids); a Walk-A-Thon in Albuquerque for cerebral palsy; providing low rider cars for state and local politicians, such as Henry B. González, at the 1980 Cinco de Mayo parade in San Antonio; participating in the California Golden 500 Club banquet in honor of Senator Alan D. Cranston; a fundraiser for the building of El Santuario de San Martín de Porres church in Albuquerque; and numerous other events.

The final question regarding the promotion of low riding still needing to be discussed is: are there any other interests in the promotion of low riding? This question, like the related question of ownership, is one that is somewhat difficult to answer because the documents and information needed to satisfactorily answer it are not readily accessible, and due to their potentially sensitive nature, may never be. On the basis of the monologue generated in the January and February issues referred to above and the interview with the editor it seems unlikely that the full picture will become public.

Although the full picture of the financial interests in the magazine is not available, one can piece together some of these interests from the advertisements in the magazine and from the identification of the cosponsors of the "Low Rider Happening" custom car shows. An examination of the advertisers in the magazine reveals that the auto-related industries, such as auto parts, tire stores, hydraulic lift shops, body and paint shops, etc., are the most consistent buyers of space in the magazine. A second group of interests is that represented by sellers of stereos, records, tapes, T-shirts, and beer. The third and last group of interests is a miscellaneous cluster of small businesses such as restaurants, jewelry stores, hair styling shops, and clothing shops.

On a closer examination of the patterns of advertising and corporations sponsoring "Low Rider Happenings" one encounters an interesting partnership, that between *Low Rider* and the Joseph Schlitz Brewing Company of Milwaukee, Wisconsin. Starting with the January 1979 issue, Schlitz has consistently occupied the entire back cover of the magazine. The themes of the ads have progressed in the following fashion: a photograph of a male dressed in a zoot suit and a second person holding a six-pack of Schlitz in front of the zoot suiter, with the caption "Beer Makes it Good, Schlitz Makes it Great"; a photograph of a Schlitz bottle and the caption "Que Bien Te Ves"; a photograph of Little Joe y La Familia under the name Schlitz.

A second link in the partnership, and perhaps the more important of the two, has been the cosponsoring of "Low Rider Happenings." Even though it is probable that Schlitz has cosponsored a significant number of car shows and low rider events, the evidence at hand is limited to those instances where it was explicitly advertised that Schlitz was formally cosponsoring the event. The most important of these shows was the "Super Show" held in the Los Angeles Convention Center in September 1979. The entire ceiling of the convention center was draped with green, white, and red banners (the colors of the Mexican flag) supporting a Schlitz or *Low Rider* banner. In Albuquerque, Schlitz cosponsored a low rider event in which it donated a car to be raffled. As expected, Schlitz cosponsored, along with KONO radio station, the San Antonio "Low Rider Happening" held at the city's convention center. Schlitz' interest at the San Antonio show, and presumably at the Super Show and other shows, became readily apparent when it was observed that Schlitz was the only brewer operating a beer booth. Through the monopolization of the sale of beer, Schlitz encouraged the attendants to "go for it" and seek their "gusto."

The decision on the part of Schlitz to promote low riding and participate in low riding events was an economically rational one. It was a logical, and perhaps expected, decision grounded on factors such as the following: the Hispanic population, as evident after the 1970 Census, was becoming an increasingly important buying market and thus a population with great profit potential; Hispanics, and

Mexicans in particular, according to national surveys funded by the federal government and local market studies by consultants, by the late 1970s were reported as having relatively high rates of heavier drinking and were possibly the ethnic group with the highest beer consumption (cf. De Luca 1981); and the fear that after Schlitz lost its number one sales position in the 1960s to the "King of Beers," Budweiser, made by the Anheuser-Busch Brewing Company, and after it lost sales following a change in brewing procedures in 1974, that profits would continue to decline unless it tapped into new markets. This decision to invest in low riding was shaped by events within the brewing industry in the 1970s.

The 1970s were a turbulent period for the brewing industry, a period characterized by one of the cyclical "beer wars." The major casualties of the "war" were Schlitz' sales and profits. The major beneficiary of the "war" was the Miller Brewing Company, a subsidiary of the Phillip Morris Tobacco Company. After Miller's introduction of the Miller Lite and Löwenbrau brands in the mid-1970s, and their sales strategy to capture greater control of the blue-collar beer-drinker market, Miller smoothly moved into second position behind Anheuser-Busch. The result was that by 1979 Schlitz found itself in third place in overall sales, and sixth place in brand sales, behind Budweiser, Miller, Pabst, Miller Lite, and Coors, and recording its first deficit ($51 million). By 1980 Schlitz was pushed to fourth place by the Pabst Brewing Company.[5]

Given the gradual decline of Schlitz' economic position among the brewing industries, and the demographic facts about the Hispanic population (largely a young population), as well as the recorded high consumption of beer by this population, it is not surprising to discover Schlitz' concern with the promotion of lowriding. Low riding appeared to contain all the elements of a profitable investment, and "Low Rider Happenings" became important vehicles to materialize the profit. The fact that the discussion so far has been limited to Schlitz' involvement with low riding should not obscure similar efforts on the part of Anheuser-Busch, Miller, and Coors to follow the lead of Schlitz in promoting "Hispanic" events, or advertising in local, regional and national "Hispanic" newspapers and magazines (e.g., *Latino, Caminos, Nuestro, Q-Vo, La Luz, Hispanic Business,* and so on). Oftentimes the support goes beyond a single event, such as the 53rd Texas League of United Latin American Citizens' Convention on the part of Schlitz, Anheuser-Busch, Miller and Coors, to more long-term support of groups such as the League of United Latin American Citizens on the part of Coors (Coors also contributes substantially to the Heritage Foundation, an ultraconservative research organization). Irrespective of the form or medium employed, the principal concern of these companies is not to ensure the viability and welfare of the Hispanic population or their cultures, but instead a much more precise concern to first increase the consumption of their products on the part of this population and thus generate profits for the welfare of the corporation, and second, and more abstractly, to continue the relationship between capital and the wage worker. The implication of this is that capital needs to exert control not only in the factory, or the place of production, but also outside of the factory, in the society at large.

The diffusion of low riding in the Southwest was thus a complex process involving the effective selection and transformation of certain symbols, and their promotion in a package pregnant with cultural metaphors. *Low Rider,* as the principal promoter of low riding, perceptively selected a phenomenon that had waxed and waned in different communities and carefully superimposed the symbols of pachuco, zoot suits, and, to a limited extent, cholos, and then set out to promote it with an indescribable zeal throughout the states in the Southwest, and later beyond the Southwest. The promotion plan consisted of the promotion of the magazine, the promotion of low riding in general, the establishment of distribution representatives, the establishment of branch offices, and the promotion of "Low Rider Happenings." The magazine played a central role in the entire process. It served not only to communicate events that were taking place and to advertise certain commodities, but more importantly to create the perception of a movement that was spreading on its own behalf like "wild fire." After three years it could, and did, claim that it had reached its goal of spreading low riding from coast to coast. The task, however, was not achieved without the aid of certain corporate interests. Early in the process Schlitz became an important confrere in the promotion. Schlitz appears to have perceived low riding as a partial savior from their financial crisis. Whether low riders will make a substantial profit for the company has yet to be determined; however what emerges from this venture is the often ignored, or at least underestimated, fact that capital needs the working class either in the form of their labor (more precisely their labor-power) or as buyers of capital's commodities.

Analysis and Conclusion

This essay has sought to provide an interpretation of the diffusion of low riding in the Southwest. In order to accomplish this the essay began by discussing the origins of low riding, to the extent documented, and then moved to a discussion of how *Low Rider* selected, transformed, and fused a number of individual symbols into a product that would be accepted by a broad segment of the Mexican population. Moreover, by framing the promotion of low riding in terms of a set of positive cultural qualities it was able to increase the potential of its acceptance. An important part of the promotional plan was to establish a positive perception of low riders, by initiating or participating in socially approved events.

The essay also described the process by which symbols are redefined and then diffused. This redefining process involves the selection and elaboration of certain aspects of their historically derived meaning, such as in the case of the pachuco and the zoot suit, and then their projection into the present—thus the illusion of historical continuity and the legitimation of their present use as objects that reinforce cultural pride or solidify cultural identity. For example, wearing a zoot suit is a Chicano cultural expression, or low riding is an example of cultural pride. This is not to suggest that cultural forms or symbols do not, or should not change in meaning, but rather, that in the case of low riding an expressive form was appropriated and transformed into a commodity. The appropriation and its manipulation, however, did not go unnoticed, as is evident in Trinidad's letter. As pointed out in the essay, Trinidad's letter and his incisive observations can be interpreted as an example of the negation of the perception of the working class as passive observers; his comments clearly raised the question of the ownership and control of symbols perceived as belonging to "La Raza," the "gente." In sum, Trinidad was questioning the right of capital to establish its control beyond the factory; he questioned the establishment of the social factory. In other words, he was questioning whether if Low Riding is good, does Schlitz make it great, and whether Miller Time is Low Riding Time.

CENTER FOR MEXICAN AMERICAN STUDIES
UNIVERSITY OF TEXAS, AUSTIN

Notes

[1] See West (1976), Trillin (1978), Steinfort (1980), *Life* (1980), King (1981) and Gradante (1982), respectively. A listing of the articles that have appeared in local newspapers and magazines in the states in the Southwest would not have contributed substantially to the point under discussion, and thus was omitted.

[2] *Low Rider* (March 1980:12). It should be noted that the full accuracy of the historical account of Mr. Westergard's work and his contact with George Barris has not been verified to date. The account provided on the origins of low riding, hot rodding, and related facts has relied on the information found in some of Teen Angel's columns, such as the one in 1978 (vol. 2, no. 11) and the above-cited issue, as well as on *Low Rider: Technical* (a special issue in 1982), Wolfe (1965), Carter (1982), and general information gathered from a perusal of hot rod and car customizing magazines. The discussion of the themes in *Low Rider* is based on an examination of the majority of the issues from 1977 to 1982. An important source for issues not owned by the author was the collection found at the Benson Library, The University of Texas at Austin.

[3] See the following writings: Carey McWilliams 1943a, 1943b, 1943c, 1943d, 1964, and 1968; George I. Sánchez 1943; *Newsweek* 1942 and 1943; *Time* 1943; *Life* 1943; Banay 1944; Griffith 1947 and 1948; Coon 1948; Harvey 1948; Barker 1950; Turner 1956; Braddy 1960; Octavio Paz 1961; Heller 1966; Steiner 1969; Jones 1969; Salazar 1970; Scott 1970; Morales 1972; Gómez 1973; Ricardo Sánchez 1973; Hinojos 1975; Corona 1976; Thomas Sánchez 1978; Murphy 1978; Grajeda 1980; and others. The inclusion of a detailed commentary on each of the aforementioned was not feasible within this essay. Consequently, with regret, this endeavor was put aside.

[4] The reader is referred to the following sources for a fuller discussion of the concept of "social factory," "social capital," and correlate arguments: Baldi (1972); Tronti (1973); Cleaver (1979); and the collection of articles found in *Zerowork*, Volume One (1975) and Volume Two (1977).

[5] For information about the brewing industry the reader is directed to sources such as Standard and Poor's *Industry Surveys: Beverage and Tobacco* (1981, April and December), Moskowitz (1980), and Louis (1981). The *Wall Street Journal* is an excellent source for current changes within the industry.

References

Baldi, Guido. 1971. "Theses on the Mass Worker and Social Capital," in *Radical America* 6:3-21.

Banay, H.G. 1944. "A Psychiatrist Looks At the Zoot Suit," in *Probation* 22:81-85.

Bancroft, Hubert H. 1885. *History of California: 1801-1824*, Volume Two (Volume 19 of the collected works). San Francisco: Bancroft and Company Publishers.

Barker, G. 1950. *Pachuco, An American-Spanish Argot*. University of Arizona Bulletin #21; Social Science Bulletin #18. Tucson: University of Arizona.

Barnett, H.G. 1953. *Innovation: The Basis of Cultural Change*. New York: McGraw-Hill.

Berger, Meyer. 1943. "Zoot Suit Originated in Georgia," in *The New York Times*, June 11, 1943.

Blaker, Mimi. 1943. "Fashions in 1943," in *Journal of Home Economics* 35:73-76.

Bogardus, E.S. 1943. "Gangs of Mexican Youth," in *Sociology and Social Research* 28:55-60.

Braddy, Haldeen. 1960. "Pachucos and their Argot," in *Southern Folk-Lore Quarterly* 24:255-271.

Carter, Geoff. 1982. "Big Daddy and the King," in *Street Rodder,* May.

Clark, Victor. 1908. *Mexican Labor in the U.S.* Bureau of Labor Bulletin #78. Washington, D.C.: U.S. Bureau of Labor Statistics.

Cleaver, Harry. 1979. *Reading Capital Politically.* Austin: University of Texas Press.

Cohen, Haskell. 1943. "Mellow Like a Cello," in *Negro Digest* 1:7-9.

Coon, Gene. 1948. "Pachuco," in *Common Ground* 3:49-52.

Corona, Bert. 1976. "Interview," in *Mexican American: Movement and Leaders,* Larralde, C., ed. Los Alamitos, California: Hwong Publishing Company.

De Luca, John, ed. 1981. *Alcohol and Health.* Washington, D.C.: U.S. Department of Health and Human Services, National Institute on Alcohol Abuse and Alcoholism.

Dettelbach, Cynthia Colomb. 1976. *In The Driver's Seat: The Automobile in American Literature and Popular Culture.* Westport: Greenwood Press.

Esquire. 1973. *Esquire's Encyclopedia of 20th Century Men's Fashions.* New York: McGraw-Hill.

Flink, James J. 1975. *The Car Culture.* Cambridge, Mass.: MIT Press.

Francis, Jesse Davies. 1935. *An Economic and Social History of Mexican California: 1822-1846.* Reprinted by Arno Press in 1976.

Gamio, Manuel. 1930. *Mexican Immigration to the U.S.* New York: Dover Publications (1971 edition).

Gómez, David G. 1973. *Somos Chicanos: Strangers in Our Own Land.* Boston: Beacon Press.

Gradante, William. 1982. "Low and Slow, Mean and Clean," in *Natural History* 91:28-39.

Grajeda, Rafael. 1980. "The Pachuco in Chicano Poetry: The Process of Legend Creation," in *Revista Chicano-Riqueña* 8:45-59.

Griffith, Beatrice. 1947. "The Pachuco Patois," in *Common Ground* 7:77-84.

_____. 1948. "Finger-Tip Coats are the Style," in *Common Ground* 8:61-67.

Harvey, Louise. 1948. "Delinquent Mexican Boys," in *The Journal of Educational Research* 42:573-585.

Hebdige, Dick. 1979. *Subculture: The Meaning of Style.* London: Methuen and Co., Ltd.

Heller, Celia S. 1966. *Mexican American Youth: Forgotten Youth at the Crossroads.* New York: Random House.

Hinojos, Francisco. 1975. "Notes on the Pachuco: Stereotypes, History and Dialect," in *Atisbos: Journal of Chicano Research,* Summer.

Jones, Solomon J. 1969. "The Government Riots of Los Angeles, June 1943." Thesis, UCLA.

King, Wayne. 1981. "Chicanos Riding Close to the Ground But Going in Style," in *The New York Times,* May 9.

Life. 1943. "Zoot Suit Riots," in *Life* 14:30-31 (June 21).

_____. 1980. "Lowriders of the Urban Range: A Chicano and His Car Are a Fiesta on Wheels," in *Life* 3:88-94 (May; new series).

Lingeman, Richard R. 1970. *Don't You Know There's a War On?: The American Home Front 1941-1945.* New York: Putnam's Sons.

Louis, Arthur. 1981. "Schlitz's Crafty Taste Test," in *Fortune,* January.

Low Rider. The majority of the issues between 1977 and 1982, including the "Technical" issue and the flyer.

Madrid-Barela, Arturo. 1973. "In Search of the Authentic Pachuco: An Interpretive Essay," in *Aztlán: International Journal of Chicano Studies* 4:31-60.

Malcolm X. 1965. *Autobiography of Malcolm X.* New York: Grove Press.

Marx, Karl. 1906. *Capital: A Critique of Political Economy, Volume One.* (1st German edition, 1867.) New York: The Modern Library.

Mazón, Mauricio. 1976. "Social Upheaval in World War II: Zoot Suiters and Servicemen in Los Angeles, 1943." Unpublished dissertation, UCLA.

McWilliams, Carey. 1943a. "The Forgotten Mexican," in *Common Ground* 3:65-78.

_____. 1943b. "Los Angeles 'Pachuco' Gangs," in *New Republic* 108:76-77.

_____. 1943c. "Race Tensions: Second Phase," in *Common Ground* 4:7-12.

_____. 1943d. "Zoot Suit Riots," in *New Republic* 108:818-820.

_____. 1964. *Brothers Under the Skin.* Boston: Brown and Co. (orig. 1942; revised in 1951 and 1964).

_____. 1968. *North From Mexico.* New York: Greenwood Press (orig. 1949).

Michels, Robert. 1959. *Political Parties.* New York: Dover Publications.

Morales, Armando. 1972. *Ando Sangrando.* La Puente, California: Perspectiva Publications.

Moore, Joan W., et al. 1978. *Homeboys: Gangs, Drugs, and Prison in the Barrios of Los Angeles.* Philadelphia: Temple University Press.

Moskowitz, Milton, et al. 1980. *Everybody's Business.* New York: Harper and Row Publishers.

Murphy, Suzanne. 1978. "A Year with the Gangs of East Los Angeles," in *Ms.* 7:56-64.

Nakagawa, K. and H. Posovsky. 1965. "The Case of the Dying Kimono," in Roach, M. and J.B. Eicher, eds. *Dress, Adornment, and the Social Order.* New York: John Wiley & Sons.

Negro Digest. 1943. "Origins of the Zoot Suit," in *Negro Digest* 1:69-70. (Condensed from *The New York Times,* see Berger.)

Newsweek. 1942. "Drape Shape," in *Newsweek* 20:48-49.

_____. 1943. "Zoot Suits and Service Stripes: Race Tensions Behind the Riots," in *Newsweek* 21.

Nuestro. 1979. "Lowrider is Just Warming Up," in *Nuestro* 3:16-17.

Paz, Octavio. 1961. *The Labyrinth of Solitude.* New York: Grove Press (orig. 1950; rev. and expanded in 1959).

Redl, Fritz. 1943. "Zoot Suits: An Interpretation," in *The Survey Monthly* 79:259-262.

Salazar, Rubén. 1970. "Pachuco Folk Heroes—They Were First to be Different," in *The Los Angeles Times,* July 17.

Sánchez, George I. 1943. "Pachucos in the Making," in *Common Ground* 4:13-20.

Sánchez, Ricardo. 1973. *Canto y Grito Mi Liberación.* New York: Anchor Books (orig. 1971).

Sánchez, Thomas. 1978. *Zoot Suit Murders.* New York: E.P. Hutton.

Scott, Robin F. 1970. "The Zoot Suit Riots," in *The Mexican-Americans: An Awakening Minority,* Manuel P. Servín, ed. Beverly Hills: Glencoe Press.

Simmel, Georg. 1957. "Fashion," in *The American Journal of Sociology* 62:541-558 (orig. *International Quarterly* 10:130-155, 1904).

Standard and Poor's. 1981. *Industry Surveys: Beverage and Tobacco* (April and December).

Steinfort, Cissy. 1980. "Lowriders: The World of Cruising, Hydraulic Suspension and Throwing Scrapes," in *Road & Track* 31:146-149.

Steiner, Stan. 1969. *La Raza: The Mexican Americans*. New York: Harper and Row.

Time. 1943. "Zoot Suit War," in *Time* June 21:18-19.

Trillin, Calvin and E. Koren. 1978. "Our Far-Flung Correspondents: Low and Slow, Mean and Clean," in *The New Yorker* 54:70-74.

Tronti, Mario. 1973. "Social Capital," in *Telos* 17:98-121.

Turner, Ralph and Samuel J. Surace. 1956. "Zoot-Suiters and Mexicans: Symbols in Crowd Behavior," in *American Journal of Sociology* 62:14-20.

Van Sycle, Calla. 1943. "The Clothing Fashion, 1943," in *The Journal of Home Economics* 35:80-83.

West, Ted. 1976. "Low and Slow," in *Car & Driver* 22: 47-51; 74-76.

Wolfe, Tom. 1965. *The Kandy-Kolored Tangerine Flake Streamline Baby*. New York: The Noonday Press (orig. 1963).

NEWSPAPER COVERAGE OF UNDOCUMENTED MEXICAN IMMIGRATION DURING THE 1970s: A QUALITATIVE ANALYSIS OF PICTURES AND HEADINGS*

Celestino Fernández

Although Mexicans have been coming across the U.S.-Mexican border continuously since its political creation with the signing of the Treaty of Guadalupe Hidalgo in 1848, this movement has not always been viewed in the same way. Historically, as internal economic conditions change, so too does the way in which undocumented Mexican immigration is perceived, defined, and resolved (Bustamante, 1972; Gamio, 1930; García, 1980; Samora, 1971).

In periods when the American economy is in a state of growth, illegal Mexican immigration is mostly ignored by the majority of Americans. However, as the country enters periods of economic decline, the phenomenon surfaces in the mass media as a major news item and is perceived and defined as being out of control and highly problematic. This was certainly the case during the economic Crash of 1929, the Great Depression of the early thirties, and again in 1954. The result in each case was tighter enforcement of immigration laws. For example, "Operation Wetback," a major Border Patrol effort to round up and deport illegal Mexican immigrants was conceived and implemented in 1954.

Yet, at other points in time when the country experienced periods

*Part of this work was supported by a grant from the University of Arizona Foundation. The views expressed herein are those of the author and do not necessarily reflect the position, policy, or endorsement of the funding agency.

of economic expansion or when it needed a source of cheap labor—during the early part of the twentieth century and again during World War II, for example—Mexican *campesinos* were actively recruited and encouraged to enter the country. Almost five million Mexican nationals were contracted to work in the United States between 1942 and 1964 under the Bracero Program (a bilateral agreement between the Mexican and U.S. governments). Historically, the need for cheap labor in the United States has been continuous. The railroads, agriculture, mining industry, service occupations, and clothing industry have all benefited from Mexican labor.

Independent of the need for cheap labor expressed by employers, during periods of economic decline Mexican undocumented immigration is viewed as a serious problem requiring a drastic and immediate solution. Undocumented Mexican workers are defined as the cause of the economic problems and the "logical solution" is to deport as many as can be rounded up.

During the 1970s the U.S. again experienced internal economic difficulties resulting in high rates of inflation and unemployment. Although this internal economic decline did not decrease the need for Mexican workers, it did, however, serve to call national attention to the phenomenon of undocumented immigration from Mexico.

During the 1970s illegal Mexican immigration became a major news item. All forms of mass media—television, radio, newspapers, magazines—featured items on this phenomenon. The public was bombarded with "information," albeit not necessarily accurate information, on undocumented Mexican immigration. On a regular basis, one could pick up a newspaper or magazine, listen to the radio, or watch television and encounter an item on illegal immigration. Whether they were identified as *illegal aliens, undocumented workers, illegal immigrants, undocumented immigrants, wetbacks,* or just plain *illegals* or *aliens,* the phenomenon captured the attention of the mass media and in turn of the American public.

Even "entertainment" programs on television dealt with this topic. Several popular programs, such as "CHIPs" and "Lou Grant," devoted entire episodes to the theme of Mexican undocumented immigration. By the end of the decade even a feature-length commercial film appeared, entitled "Borderline," starring Charles Bronson as a Border Patrol Agent.

Illegal immigration became an issue of such importance that even the Gallup Poll began to report on public attitudes towards immigration. In a poll conducted for the Immigration and Naturalization Service (INS), the Gallup Organization (1976) found that nationally over half of the sampled population had recently read or heard something about "the problem of illegal aliens." Respondents living in the West and particularly those living in states bordering with Mexico were especially likely to have read or heard about "the problem." Over two-thirds of the respondents living in this region indicated that they had read or heard something about illegal immigration. Undocumented immigration became such an issue that almost everyone knew something about it or at least thought they knew something about it. But what image did the public have of this complex social phenomenon?

This paper reports on a quantitative content analysis of images of Mexican undocumented immigrants as portrayed in the news media. Berelson (1952:18) provided an early definition of content analysis as "... a research technique for the objective, systematic, and quantitative description of the manifest content of communication."

Our sample consists of the total universe (N = 949) of articles dealing with undocumented Mexican immigration published in four newspapers—*Los Angeles Times, New York Times, Washington Post,* and *Arizona Daily Star*—during a seven-year period in the 1970s (1972 through 1978). In this paper we report specifically on the analyses of the headings and photographs that accompanied these articles.[1] We believe that these two items are important in and of themselves (i.e., apart from the articles) because newspaper viewers often read the headings and view the photographs without reading the articles. Thus, headings and pictures can leave an image in the reader's/viewer's mind. It has been found, for example, that pictures add to the recall of news items and information (Katz, Adoni, and Parness, 1977). Moreover, it is the heading and the picture that often leads one to read the article.

Theoretical Discussion[2]

Two theoretical frameworks guided the research reported herein: a) the sociology of knowledge (Berger and Luckmann, 1966); and b) conflict sociology (Collins, 1975; Dahrendorf, 1959; Mills, 1956). In the case of the sociology of knowledge, it is a well-documented fact that the mass media do not simply mirror social reality; they mold and shape images, perceptions, and interpretations of social reality (Altheide, 1976; Altheide and Snow, 1979; Gans, 1979; Lester, 1980). In terms of the conflict approach, several studies (e.g., Altheide and Snow, 1979; Gans, 1979; and Lester, 1980) have shown that there are a series of decisions and interpretations involved in the process of selecting and presenting news to the public that systematically bias the "facts" in favor of the dominant group.

In theoretical terms, then, we asked basically two questions of the data. From the theoretical perspective of the sociology of knowledge, what image or more generally, what social reality was constructed by photographs and headings appearing with newspaper coverage of undocumented Mexican immigration? From the perspective of conflict sociology, what competing interest group dominated the image and interpretation that was represented in these photographs and headings?

Procedures

Two samples were used in the analysis reported herein, the first consists of all pictures (N = 179) that appeared alongside articles dealing with the topic of undocumented immigration from Mexico between 1972 and 1978 in the *Los Angeles Times, New York Times, Washington Post,* and *Arizona Daily Star* (published in Tucson, Arizona). The other subsample comprises all the headings (N = 949) of those articles. (The procedures used in the selection of those articles are more fully described in Fernández and Pedroza [1983].) Undoubtedly we missed a few photographs and headings over the seven-year period studied and across the four newspapers. However, that would be a very small number. We are confident that our samples are very close to the full universe of cases for that period and for those newspapers and that any missing cases would not systematically bias the data.

The unit of analysis consists of both themes and categories that were developed using the techniques of grounded theory (Glaser and Strauss, 1967). That is, the themes and categories emerged from the data (pictures and headings) themselves. The data were analyzed using descriptive statistics.

Findings: Photographs

Frequency

Overall, only 13 percent (N = 101) of the 949 articles analyzed were accompanied by a picture. However, several of the articles contained more than one photograph, some as many as four or five, bringing the total number of pictures to 179. This latter number, then, is the sample used for the study reported herein.

Minor differences were found in the frequency of pictures among the four newspapers studied. The *New York Times* and *Washington*

Post tended to print more photographs with their articles on illegal Mexican immigration than the *Los Angeles Times* and *Arizona Daily Star*. For example, 10 percent of the articles in the *Los Angeles Times* were accompanied by pictures compared to 19 percent of those found in the *New York Times.*

Although the first and last year studied had the same proportion of pictures (15 percent of the articles in both 1972 and 1978 were accompanied by photographs), we found a steady decrease in the proportion of articles that included photographs from 1972 to 1976 (from 15 to 6 percent). This pattern reversed in the latter part of the decade so that the last two years studied (1977 and 1978) accounted for 61 percent of the pictures of the seven-year period included in our study.

Controlling for reporters' ethnicity, 13 percent of the stories written by Spanish-surnamed reporters were accompanied by pictures compared to 20 percent of those written by non-Hispanic reporters. However, since most reporters do not take their own photographs, we analyzed photographers' ethnicity as well. A mere 6 percent of the pictures were taken by Spanish-surnamed photographers compared to 66 percent by non-Hispanics. A large number of photographs, 27 percent, did not include a by-line while 1 percent was identified as having been supplied by the Border Patrol.

Anonymous stories (those without a by-line), as reported in Fernández and Pedroza (1983), tended to be less objective about and more distant from the phenomenon that they were reporting on. This pattern is further evidenced by our finding regarding the number of pictures found with articles not containing a by-line; a mere 5 percent of the anonymous reports were accompanied by photographs.

Interestingly enough, although letters to the editor accounted for only 11 percent of our sample of articles, almost one-fourth of the photographs found were printed alongside letters to the editor. These pictures obviously had not been mailed in by the authors of the letters; rather, they were selected and included by the editors.

Contents of Photographs

In this section we report on the contents of the pictures found accompanying our sample of newspaper articles on undocumented Mexican immigration. Table 1 presents a typology and breakdown of the general categories that emerged. Overall, the majority of the photographs (63 percent), although not as high as might be expected given the phenomenon being reported on, were of humans (undocumented immigrants, politicians, Border Patrol). Over one-fourth (27 percent) were of inanimate objects (cars, fences) and 10 percent were drawings (Statue of Liberty, people) or illustrations (tables, figures).

TABLE 1

Breakdown of Pictures by Category and Newspaper

	Humans*	Inanimate Objects*	Drawings**	Totals
LA Times	.60	.25	.15	100 (52)
NY Times	.63	.29	.08	100 (49)
Washington Post	.67	.26	.07	100 (46)
Arizona Daily Star	.63	.28	.09	100 (32)
Totals	.63 (113)	.27 (48)	.10 (18)	100 (179)

*Descriptions of these categories are found in Tables 2 and 3 and in the text.

**Drawings included everything from the Statue of Liberty to the U.S.-Mexico border as depicted by one strand of barbed wire with a drawing of a bare foot on the Mexican side stepping on thorny cacti awaited by a shoe over the smooth American flag on the U.S. side. Another drawing showed a Border Patrol agent being overrun by a swarm of flying illegal Mexican immigrants.

As can be seen in the same table, there was very little variation among the four newspapers studied in the proportions of pictures in each of the three categories. The *Washington Post* tended to print slightly more pictures of humans (67 percent of its pictures were of people) than the other newspapers, while the *Los Angeles Times* included more drawings with its articles. The differences, again, were not large.

Border Patrol, INS, and Politicians. In another paper (Fernández and Pedroza, 1983) we reported that the Border Patrol and other Immigration and Naturalization Service (INS) officials were cited as references more often than any other group and much more frequently than undocumented Mexican immigrants. The contents of the photographs were consistent with this pattern (see Table 2). The Border Patrol and other INS officials (particularly the Commissioner) were the central focus of 37 percent of the pictures in which humans were the main object.

The most common picture in this category showed one or more Border Patrol agents in the process of performing their job, e.g., patrolling the border in their cars, four-wheel drive vehicles,

TABLE 2

Breakdown of Photographs In Which Humans Were the Main Focus

	INS-Border Patrol	Undocumented Immigrants	Politicians	Others*	Totals
LA Times	.42	.35	.13	.10	100 (31)
NY Times	.35	.39	.23	.03	100 (31)
Washington Post	.32	.23	.23	.22	100 (31)
Arizona Daily Star	.40	.45	.00	.15	100 (20)
Totals	.37 (42)	.35 (39)	.16 (18)	.12 (14)	100 (113)

*This category included pictures such as that of a researcher, smuggler, restaurant owner, and newspaper reporter.

airplanes, or helicopters, checking for footprints in the dirt, checking electronic sensory devices to make sure that they were operating properly, or in the process of apprehending one or more undocumented border crossers. Following is a list of captions taken from our sample that serve to illustrate the type of photograph just described.

First, some from the *Los Angeles Times:*

> HOLE IN THE BORDER — Border patrolman Carl Fisher with walkie-talkie reports on barbed-wire fence cut so vehicles could cross border. (12-17-72)
> ON-THE-SPOT SEARCH — Border Patrolmen frisk a suspect at the San Onofre checkpoint on Interstate 5. (8-19-74)
> CAUGHT IN CROSSING — Border patrol officers talk with aliens before sending them back. (9-18-77)
> GOING HOME — Santa Fe agent James Sutor frees two illegal aliens who were taken back to Mexico. (8-14-78)

From the *New York Times:*

> Members of the Border Patrol checking the U.S.-Mexican border near Laredo, Tex., as patrol plane scans area. (6-25-73)
> Bill Eatman, Border Patrol agent, with Mexican captured in attempt near Tijuana to enter U.S. illegally. (7-22-73)
> Preparation: A Border Patrol jeep smooths a dirt road surface—the better to show up footprints of the night's wetbacks. (3-10-74)

> Border patrol helicopter hovers over band of illegal aliens after they were captured entering the United States at spot near San Ysidro, Calif. (4-22-77)

> Border Patrol officer keeping radio contact with helicopter crew as they search for Mexicans attempting night crossing. (11-9-78)

A couple of examples from the *Washington Post:*

> Border patrolman, seeking illegal aliens, questions a lemon picker in Yuma, Ariz. (2-3-75)

> Guard examines break in the fence at the U.S.-Mexican border. (8-17-75)

And finally, from the *Arizona Daily Star:*

> U.S. Border patrolmen still make use of their keen eyesight to spot tracks like the patrolmen of the 1930s are doing below, but today they also have the help of modern electronic equipment. Ralph Binder, radio supervisor, and Richard E. Heidt, patrol agent, man the patrol's Tucson office. (5-31-74) [This caption describes several pictures.]

> Along the Rio Grande, a bunch of hopeful crossers on the Black Point railroad bridge cross back to Mexico with the arrival of U.S. Border Patrol. (5-15-77)

As the reader may have noticed, in some cases there was an overlap in categories, that is, a picture may have included both the Border Patrol and undocumented Mexican immigrants. Such pictures were categorized on the basis of both the caption and careful viewing . For example, most of the captions listed above make it unmistakably clear that the focus of the photograph was on the Border Patrol. In some cases, however, the caption implies that the focus was on illegal border crossers when, in fact, anyone viewing the picture would conclude otherwise. The last caption listed above, for example, may lead the reader to believe that that picture should have been more appropriately categorized under the heading of "undocumented Mexican immigrant." However, anyone viewing this photograph would reach a different conclusion since it is self-evident that the central focus of the photograph was on the two Border Patrol agents and their car (found in the forefront and much larger than the potential illegal immigrants). In fact, the "hopeful crossers" described in the caption were found in the background and barely visible. The patrolmen and their car were between the photographer and the potential border crossers who were standing on the railroad tracks, at a considerable distance from the Border Patrol.

While the overwhelming majority of photographs of the Border

Patrol showed them working and usually included other people or objects, those of bureaucrats, politicians, and INS officials tended to be close-ups (mug shots) of the head and shoulders of a single individual. The captions under such pictures usually only gave the person's name, e.g., "Leonel Castillo," "Representative James H. Scheuer," "President José López Portillo," "President Nixon," "Former Immigration Commissioner Leonard F. Chapman, Jr.," "Rep. Peter W. Rodino, Jr.," and so forth.

Overall, 16 percent of the photographs in which humans were the central focus were of politicians and other bureaucrats (see Table 2). As would be expected, given their proximity to such individuals, the *New York Times* and *Washington Post* had significantly higher proportions of pictures of politicians and bureaucrats than the *Los Angeles Times* and *Arizona Daily Star* (see Table 2).

Undocumented Mexican Immigrants. As shown in Table 2, undocumented Mexican immigrants were the central focus of 35 percent of the photographs in which humans were pictured. In terms of the four newspapers studied, the widest variation was between the *Washington Post* and the *Arizona Daily Star.* In the *Washington Post*, undocumented Mexican immigrants were the focus of only 23 percent of its pictures compared to 45 percent of those in the *Arizona Daily Star.*

The most common photographs in which undocumented Mexican immigrants were the central focus showed one or more such individuals while being apprehended (captured), sometimes even handcuffed or behind the fence of a Border Patrol detention center. Rarely were the pictures of these individuals close-ups (like those of politicians) nor were the people in the pictures identified by name. This lack of personal identity, one could argue, may have been intentional on the part of reporters and photographers in an effort to protect the names of the undocumented from the Border Patrol. However, given the findings we report in Fernández and Pedroza (1983) regarding the relatively small use of undocumented Mexican people as sources of information, we believe that undocumented Mexican immigrants were not the focus of more pictures, and certainly of more photographs in natural settings, because Anglo reporters and photographers did not have access to them. Furthermore, even when pictured, these photographers simply did not take the time to learn their names. The findings regarding the contents of pictures taken by Spanish-surnamed photographers lend further support to this explanation. Interestingly enough, of the ten pictures taken by Spanish-surnamed photographers, nine focused on undocumented immigrants in natural settings. For example, one man was pictured eating, several men were pictured working, one was shown juggling oranges (in the orange grove where he worked), and some were pictured walking to work. Moreover, some of the individuals pictured were even identified by name in the captions. But these kinds of pictures were rare among non-Hispanic photographers. Clearly, language and ethnicity play a role in the access reporters have to undocumented Mexican workers.

Following is a list of captions that serve to illustrate the negative and more common type of photograph in which undocumented Mexican immigrants were the central focus. We begin with some from the *Los Angeles Times:*

> WALKING AND WAITING — Alien inmates stroll behind chain link fence and under eye of guard at El Centro Alien Detention Center. (2-24-74)
>
> EIGHT WHO DIDN'T MAKE IT — Illegal aliens stopped at the checkpoint near San Onofre by the Border Patrol are marched into office for processing. More than 100 more detained during one eight-hour shift recently. (8-19-74)
>
> BORDER-BOUND — Illegal aliens, many rounded up in factory "surveys" conducted by the U.S. Immigration and Naturalization Service, board a bus for Chula Vista Border Patrol station. From there many of them will be returned (but not deported) to Mexico. (1-30-77)
>
> Illegal aliens being taken in handcuffs into detention area of federal building here. (12-15-78)

From the *New York Times:*

> Caught near a cabbage patch: Two young Mexicans apprehended near Tijuana about a half mile inside the United States. (3-10-74)
>
> Aliens captured near the Texas border. (5-1-77)
>
> Captured illegal aliens about to be taken to Border Patrol headquarters at San Ysidro, Calif. (6-1-77)
>
> Mexican aliens are apprehended by immigration officials. (12-24-78)

This type of photograph leads the viewer to conclude that undocumented Mexican immigrants are criminals, since when pictured they are often shown handcuffed, with their arms stretched over their heads, or as prisoners in a detention center, and always with the hunters (Border Patrol) who have stalked and tracked them down. It is almost like viewing some of the pictures in the sport pages of newspapers that show hunters and their "prize kill" or fishermen with their "prize catch." In any case, there are exceptionally few pictures of Mexican undocumented immigrants that would lead a viewer to a more balanced perception and interpretation of the immigration phenomenon. To be sure, exceptionally few pictures of illegal immigrants in our study arouse compassion or empathy in the viewer.

Inanimate Objects. Unexpectedly, well over one-fourth (27 percent) of the photographs accompanying newspaper items on undocumented Mexican immigration were of inanimate objects. Table 3 presents a breakdown of the categories that emerged from our analysis of these photographs. Automobiles and fences were the two inanimate objects most frequently photographed. Overall, 35 percent of the photographs in which inanimate objects were the center of attention were of fences, fences that sit on the U.S.-Mexico border. Automobiles were photographed almost as frequently, 30 percent of the time. The category of "Other" included a hodgepodge of pictures of various inanimate objects, e.g., a mural, a Border Patrol badge, the front of a restaurant, etc.

TABLE 3

Breakdown of Photographs In Which Inanimate Objects Were the Main Focus

	Fences	Automobiles	Others*	Totals
LA Times	.38	.24	.38	100 (13)
NY Times	.22	.21	.57	100 (14)
Washington Post	.17	.50	.33	100 (12)
Arizona Daily Star	.78	.22	.00	100 (9)
Totals	.35 (17)	.30 (14)	.35 (17)	100 (48)

*This category included pictures of various kinds of inanimate objects, such as the front of restaurants, a mural, an airplane in Tijuana, a "green card," the Rio Grande, and a Border Patrol badge.

We did find considerable variation in these categories among the four newspapers studied (see Table 3). For example, only 17 percent of the photographs of inanimate objects printed in the *Washington Post* were of fences compared with 78 percent of those found in the *Arizona Daily Star*. On the other hand, the *Washington Post* had the highest proportion of pictures of automobiles (50 percent) while the *New York Times* had the lowest, 21 percent.

Following is a list of captions of some photographs from each of the four newspapers studied that serve to illustrate the type of picture included in each of the three categories of inanimate objects (fences, automobiles, and other). We have included one caption for each category, beginning with the *Los Angeles Times.*

> NO MAN'S LAND — Where border fence ends at the ocean; Mexico is to the left, U.S. to the right. (3-15-76)
>
> END OF THE ROAD — Illegal aliens are ordered out of a car that was halted by suspicious patrolmen. (8-19-74)
>
> HOLDING AREA FOR ALIENS — Enclosure in a Bell warehouse for detainment of illegal aliens awaiting deportation to Mexico. (11-11-77)

From the *New York Times:*

> The barbed but porous U.S. border: Despite efforts of the Border Patrol, thousands have entered illegally each month. (3-10-74) [Picture of a chain-link fence with rolled barbed wire on top.]
>
> Smuggled Mexican and tequila caught by the Border Patrol behind a false trunk partition. He'll no doubt try again and again—and may well eventually succeed. (3-10-74) [Picture of the back of a car with the trunk open.]
>
> No caption. (6-25-73) [Picture of Border Patrol badge.]

Also from the *Washington Post:*

> A barbed wire fence—easily stretched or cut—guards the U.S.-Mexico border near San Luis, Ariz. The view is toward Mexico. (2-2-75)
>
> A pickup truck hides foreigners sneaking into the U.S.: About 3 million enter illegally every year, and the government catches only a few of them. (2-29-76)
>
> The butterfly-shaped fishing nets of Huercorio's Lake Pátzcuaro. (12-4-77)

And finally, from the *Arizona Daily Star:*

> Steel curtain — The U.S. Border Patrol has had strips of steel like this welded to the existing fence along the U.S.-Mexico border in an effort to curb smuggling. (2-1-77)
>
> Beefed-up barrier — Steel strips welded to the international boundary fence in Nogales, Ariz. present a better barrier to illegal entrants than does the fence alone, border officials say. Prior to the installation, some holes could be driven through. (6-20-77)
>
> The Back Of This Van Hid 18 Aliens Who Tried Unsuccessfully To Sneak Across A California Border Checkpoint. (9-5-76)

The reader may have noticed that the first two captions under the *Arizona Daily Star* seem to describe the same photograph. The picture printed February 1, 1977, appears to be a blow-up of a section of the photograph printed later in the year, although we cannot be certain since the first photograph is identified as having been taken by John Woestendiek while the second does not have a by-line and is simply identified as a "*Star* photo." We suspect, in any case, that the photographs, if different, were taken at the same time and one was stored in the files for later use. According to several reporters and photographers we interviewed, this is common procedure in the modern production of news.

We are certain, however, that one photograph was printed at least twice in the *Arizona Daily Star,* once on December 12, 1971, and again on March 20, 1977. The picture shows the profile of two young males looking through a chain-link fence. The viewer assumes, since there were no captions, that the fence sits on the U.S.-Mexico border and that the two males are potential illegal border crossers. In 1971 this photograph was printed with a story entitled, "Why A Border Fence? United States-Mexico Debate The Merits Of A Weak Dividing Line," by Bill Walters and in 1977 it appeared alongside a story by Tom Turner with the heading, "Mexican immigration laws need change."

Another photograph, with the caption, "An alien wades across the Rio Grande into the United States," was found in both the *New York Times* and the *Arizona Daily Star*. On April 22, 1977, it appeared in the *New York Times* with a story by John M. Crewdson entitled, "A Night on Patrol for Illegal Mexican Aliens." The identical photograph was printed in the *Arizona Daily Star* almost a month later, on May 15, 1977, alongside basically the same story by the same reporter but with a different heading, "Border patrol is a 'big game.'"

Findings: Headings

Intensity

Headings were coded for intensity (emotionalism/sensationalism/sentimentalization) using a three-category variable (positive, neutral, and negative). Following is a list of examples of the headings included in each of the three categories.

Positive   *Date*

"Mexican Immigration No Threat to U.S."
   (Los Angeles Times)   4-24-77
"Bandit Gangs Prey on Mexican Aliens Crossing
   Border to Seek Work in U.S." *(New York Times)*   6-6-76
"Native-Born American Xenophobia" *(Washington Post)* 5-24-78
"In Search of a Better Life" *(Arizona Daily Star)*   6-29-75

Neutral

"Illegal Aliens — Where to Draw the Line"
   (Los Angeles Times)   11-11-78
"The Illegal Immigrants" *(New York Times)*   1-14-75
"Why Mexican Villagers Keep Heading North"
   (Washington Post)   12-4-77
"Panel to Discuss Illegal Aliens" *(Arizona Daily Star)*   3-12-72

Negative

"Illegal Aliens Blamed for Increasing Crimes"
   (Los Angeles Times)   1-30-77
"TB Rise Sparked by Illegal Aliens" *(New York Times)*   5-18-75
"Illegal Aliens: A Choice of Evils" *(Washington Post)*   4-18-75
"Flow Called 'Uncontrollable'" (kicker)
"Illegal Aliens Flooding Yuma, California Areas"
   (Arizona Daily Star)   2-3-73

Of the 949 headings in our sample, fully 41 percent were found to
be alarming, those that immediately created a negative image of
undocumented Mexican immigrants (see Table 4). Only 12 percent of
the headings, on the other hand, portrayed these people in a positive
way, while 47 percent were coded as neutral (without a clear
emotional overtone).

TABLE 4

Intensity of Headings by Newspaper

	Positive	*Neutral*	*Negative*	*Totals*
LA Times	.13 (53)	.55 (217)	.32 (128)	100 (398)
NY Times	.16 (33)	.43 (91)	.41 (87)	100 (211)
Washington Post	.04 (5)	.35 (50)	.61 (86)	100 (141)
Arizona Daily Star	.13 (25)	.43 (85)	.44 (89)	100 (199)
Totals	.12 (116)	.47 (443)	.41 (390)	100 (949)

As Table 4 shows, we found considerable variation in the intensity of the headings among the four newspapers studied. The *Los Angeles Times* had both the lowest proportion of alarming headings (32 percent) and the highest proportion of neutral ones (55 percent). The *Washington Post* was at the other extreme, it had the highest proportion of negative headings (61 percent) and the lowest proportion of both neutral (35 percent) and positive (4 percent) headings. The differences between the *Washington Post* and the *Los Angeles Times* reflect, we believe, the regional variation in access to and contact with undocumented Mexican immigrants. The *Los Angeles Times,* being closer to the phenomenon, was less likely to present an unbalanced view. On the other hand, the *Washington Post* is located at a great physical distance from the phenomenon being reported on. Moreover, it is situated in a community that abounds with politicians who, because they have to maintain an image and their popularity, often misrepresent the "facts." Thus, the *Washington Post* presented a more slanted and negative image of illegal Mexican immigration. (This pattern was also found, as noted above, with the photographs and in the contents of the articles as reported in Fernández and Pedroza, 1983).

Although some variation was found in the proportions of headings in each category over the seven years studied, it was not systematic, i.e., no pattern could be identified. On the other hand, controlling for reporters' ethnicity yielded clear differences (see Table 5). Articles written by Spanish-surnamed reporters had the highest proportions of both positive and neutral headings, 18 and 53 percent respectively. Articles written by non-Hispanics were more likely to have alarming headings (45 percent) and least likely to have neutral ones (43 percent). Headings of articles without a by-line tended to fall somewhere in between the two (see Table 5).

TABLE 5

Intensity of Headings by Reporter's Ethnicity

	Positive	Neutral	Negative	Totals
Spanish-surnamed	.18 (17)	.53 (50)	.29 (28)	100 (95)
Non-Hispanics	.12 (56)	.43 (206)	.45 (215)	100 (477)
No By-line	.11 (43)	.50 (187)	.39 (147)	100 (377)
Totals	.12 (116)	.47 (443)	.41 (390)	100 (949)

Numbers and Influx

Although there was a great deal of variation in the themes

highlighted in the headings, a substantial proportion of the headings made references to an "influx" or "increase" in the number of undocumented Mexican immigrants crossing the border, often mentioning a specific number. Overall, 134 or 14 percent of the headings fell into this category. The proportion varied from 11 percent in the *Los Angeles Times* to 21 percent in the *Arizona Daily Star*.

Following is a list of examples of the types of headings that "informed" the reader of an influx in the number of Mexican workers entering the U.S. illegally.

Los Angeles Times	*Date*
Arrests of Illegal Aliens Rise Nearly 500% in Last 5 Years	11-9-72
600,000 Illegal Aliens Apprehended by U.S.	1-17-74
701,000 Aliens in Southwest Arrested in '74	2-5-75
Influx of Illegal Aliens Termed 'Out of Control'	1-9-77
The Silent Invasion	1-11-77
Border Patrol Notes Rise in Illegal Aliens	3-15-77
Illegal Alien Apprehension Increases 25%	8-3-77
Alien Arrests Along Mexican Border Up 35%	5-3-78
Colby Calls Mexico Bigger Threat Than Russia to U.S.	6-6-78

New York Times	
Electronic Vigil Fails to Stem Mexican Alien Influx	7-22-73
Illegal Aliens Pose A Growing Problem	4-24-77
100 Border Patrolmen Rushed to California	5-24-77
Increase in Illegal Aliens Linked to Amnesty Plan	7-7-77
More Than Million Caught at Mexican Border	11-24-77

Washington Post	
Patrol Can't Keep Aliens Out	2-3-75
Can We Stop the Invasion of Illegal Aliens?	2-29-76
Problems of Snowballing Illegal Immigration Cited	1-9-77
The Illegal Influx	2-12-77
One Million Aliens Caught	11-24-77

Arizona Daily Star	
19,000 Aliens Enter State Illegally	2-11-72
More Aliens Crossing Mexican Border	5-16-73
Illegal Alien Cases Rise Dramatically	9-14-73
200,000 Massed to Slip Into U.S. at Tijuana	8-9-77
Bumper Alien Crop in Cochise	10-3-77
Border Patrol Corrals 3,042 Aliens	9-16-78
3,042 Aliens Arrested	10-10-78
Alien Arrests Increase	12-15-78

The reader may have noticed the coincidence in the number reported in two headings found in the *Arizona Daily Star* (September 16, 1978 and October 10, 1978). In both cases, 3,042 "aliens" were reported to have been apprehended by the U.S. Border Patrol. The stories under these headings are very short, particularly the second, and thus it is difficult to understand what exactly is going on. Both stories reported that this was the number of "aliens" apprehended by the Tucson sector of the Border Patrol "last month." The "information" in the articles was based on data released by the Border Patrol. Taking it at face value, one would have to conclude that indeed the exact same number of individuals were apprehended by the one office in both August and September. (Although the stories were printed in September and October they were reporting data for "last month," i.e., August and September.) This seems highly unlikely. We suspect that the two stories are based on the same news release from the Border Patrol and that through some confusion on the part of the newspaper staff the same information appeared in two separate stories on different months. The daily reader, however, would probably not have recalled the first item upon encountering the second almost a month later and would view the latter story as containing "news," i.e., up-to-date information. It is also possible that the item was used the second time as a filler story that the editors felt would be of some interest to the readership. In any case, one should question this type of reporting and wonder about its impact on the readers.

Before moving on to another theme, it is interesting to note that while 134 of the headings made reference to an "influx" of undocumented workers, only five stated the opposite view, i.e., that there was a decrease or no change in the number of undocumented border crossers from Mexico. Four of these were found in the *Arizona Daily Star* and the other appeared in the *Los Angeles Times*.

Jobs and Social Services

One of the issues that surfaced during the 1970s regarding the impact of undocumented immigrants on the U.S. economy was whether they displaced American residents and thus contributed to unemployment. Some of the headings studied reflected this concern, mostly implying or concluding that illegal Mexican immigrants did in fact take jobs away from American workers. Following are a few examples of the types of heading that gave the reader an impression that U.S. citizens were losing jobs to illegal immigrants.

New York Times	*Date*
Job Rise is Linked to Curb on Aliens	9-22-74

Washington Post	
Aliens Said to Cost U.S. Jobs, Taxes	7-18-76
Are Imported Migrant Workers Taking U.S. Jobs?	8-12-78

Arizona Daily Star	
15,000 Illegal Aliens Hold Jobs Here, Patrol Says	3-18-76
Send Not Workers to Take Our Jobs	8-31-77

Interestingly enough, the tone of these headings was inconsistent with the social science research conducted during the same period which continuously found that undocumented Mexican immigrants were *not* displacing American workers (Cárdenas, 1976; Cornelius, 1978; Fagomen, 1973; Human Resources Agency, 1975, 1977; North and Houstoun, 1976). In fact, the great majority, about 85 percent, of illegal Mexican immigrants work in unskilled occupations (North and Houstoun, 1976), for the most part work shunned by Americans. To be sure, the data do not support a cause-and-effect relationship between the presence of undocumented immigrants and domestic unemployment. This notwithstanding, the American public believed what they read in newsprint. Fully 51 percent of those questioned in a Gallup Poll in 1976, for example, responded that illegal aliens take jobs away from residents when asked, "What problems, if any, result from the presence of illegal aliens in this country?"

Just as the public believed the myth regarding jobs, they came to believe that undocumented Mexican immigrants were enrolled in public relief programs. The Gallup Poll (1976) mentioned above found that 77 percent of all respondents felt that illegal aliens often collect unemployment or welfare and are a drain on the taxpayer. The news media contributed to this contradictory image of the illegal immigrant; i.e., on the one hand he is displacing an American worker and on the other he is collecting welfare. Following are a few examples of headings found in the newspapers studied that perpetuate the image of the illegal immigrant as a social parasite.

Los Angeles Times	*Date*
Aliens Reportedly Get $100 Million in Welfare	1-27-73
U.S. Taxes Lost on Illegal Aliens' Income	
Estimated at $100 Million	6-15-74
Alien Health Bill Put at $50 Million	7-19-77
Aliens' Abuse of Welfare Cited	11-14-77

New York Times

Wetbacks and Social Security	4-14-74
U.S. Study Says Illegal Aliens Create $16 Billion Tax Burden	12-1-75
Dollar Drain Laid on Illegal Aliens Estimated in the Billions Annually	5-27-77

Conclusions

The 1970s parallel two earlier periods of downturns in the U.S. business cycle (the early 1930s and 1950s) when Mexican workers were viewed as a threatening labor surplus. In both of these earlier periods we saw an extremist media campaign that portrayed undocumented Mexican immigrants as jeopardizing the employment status of American citizens. Such images lead to increased enforcement and large increases in the number of apprehensions. During the Great Depression an estimated half-million Mexican nationals were repatriated (Hoffman, 1974). "Operation Wetback" during the early 1950s has been credited with the expulsion of nearly 4 million Mexican workers (García, 1980).

The escalation of Border Patrol enforcement during the 1970s is now history. The number of apprehensions of undocumented immigrants steadily increased from slightly under 390,000 in 1971 to over one million in the latter years of the decade. During this period, the media were very active in their reporting of "news" on the issue of illegal immigration from Mexico. As reported in Fernández and Pedroza (1983), the number of articles on this topic in just the four newspapers used in the present study increased from 54 in 1972 to 267 in 1977.

Our findings show that the Mexican undocumented immigrant was basically portrayed as a criminal who took jobs away from Americans and at the same time was a drain on the nation's social welfare programs. Never mind that this image contradicts itself, it was still the one most commonly perpetuated during the 1970s.

The photographs and headings in the four newspapers studied assisted in defining the undocumented Mexican as undesirable. Yet, the "influx," "increase," "invasion" reported in the news media was based on questionable evidence. Estimates of the number of undocumented Mexican immigrants in the U.S. were derived largely from figures released by the Border Patrol and other officials of the Immigration and Naturalization Service. These figures in turn were based on rates of apprehension of "aliens." It is true that the number of apprehensions increased dramatically during the 1970s and that most (about 90 percent) of those apprehended in the Southwest were people from Mexico. This increase in the number of apprehensions may not necessarily reflect an influx in the number of border crossers. It may only reflect Border Patrol activity. We know, for example, that: a) the Border Patrol escalated its night patrol during the 1970s; b) additional agents were assigned to the U.S.-Mexico border region; and c) the use of electronic sensors and other modern technological devices increased. All three measures would lead, of course, to an increase in the number of apprehensions even if the actual number of border crossers remained the same. Thus, the number of apprehensions does not necessarily reflect an increase in the volume of border crossers nor is it a reliable guide to the number of undocumented immigrants in the country at any specific time.

Hence, the "crisis" of illegal migration may be in large part rhetoric. Yet, one can see that the negative image of the "illegal alien" that emerged during the 1970s and was perpetuated by the news media had an impact on immigration policy. Both the Carter Commission on Immigration and Refugee Policy and President Reagan's Task Force on Immigration recommended a more restricted immigration policy and increased enforcement along the U.S.-Mexico border by the turn of the decade.[3]

Note that we are not implying a conspiracy on the part of reporters and newspaper editors to "get the Mexicans." Our analysis, however, shows that reporting on the issue of undocumented immigration was not balanced. The "news" and "information" printed in the newspapers studied promoted a rather negative image of the undocumented Mexican immigrant. Furthermore, we believe that the American public accepted this slanted view and as a result exerted pressure on legislators to enact a more restrictive immigration policy. In this way, then, the news media were not just reporting the news; they were indirectly effecting immigration policy.

DEPARTMENT OF SOCIOLOGY
UNIVERSITY OF ARIZONA

Notes

[1] The analyses of the contents of the articles are reported in Fernández and Pedroza (1983 and forthcoming).

[2] For a more fully developed theoretical discussion see Fernández and Pedroza (1983).

[3] The Commission appointed by President Carter turned in its final report in March, 1981, after Carter was already out of office. President Reagan established his Task Force shortly after taking office and its first report was released through the Justice Department in July, 1981.

References

Altheide, D.L. 1976. *Creating Reality: How TV News Distorts Events.* Beverly Hills, CA: Sage.

Altheide, D.L. and R.P. Snow. 1979. *Media Logic.* Beverly Hills, CA: Sage.

Berelson, B. 1952. *Content Analysis in Communication Research.* Glencoe, IL: Free Press.

Berger, P.L. and T. Luckmann. 1966. *The Social Construction of Reality: A Treatise in the Sociology of Knowledge.* Garden City, NY: Doubleday.

Bustamante, J. 1972. "The 'wetback' as deviant: An application of labeling theory." *American Journal of Sociology* 77:706-718.

Cárdenas, G. 1976. "Illegal aliens in the Southwest: A case study." Pp. 66-69 in *Illegal Aliens: An Assessment of the Issues.* Washington, D.C.: National Council on Employment Policy.

Collins, R. 1975. *Conflict Sociology: Toward an Explanatory Science.* New York: Academic Press.

Cornelius, W.A. 1978. *Mexican Migration to the United States: Causes, Consequences, and U.S. Responses.* Cambridge, MA: Massachusetts Institute of Technology.

Dahrendorf, R. 1959. *Class and Class Conflict in Industrial Society.* Stanford: Stanford University Press.

Fagomen, A.T. 1973. *The Illegal Alien: Criminal or Economic Refugee?* Staten Island, NY: Center for Migration Studies.

Fernández, C. and L.R. Pedroza. 1983. "The Border Patrol and news media coverage of undocumented Mexican immigration during the 1970's: A quantitative content analysis in the sociology of knowledge." *California Sociologist.*

_____. Forthcoming. "Social and economic impacts of undocumented Mexican immigrants: A quantitative content analysis of newspaper coverage during the 1970s." Paper under review and available from the authors.

Gallup Organization. 1976. *The Gallup Study of Attitudes Toward Illegal Aliens.* Princeton: The Gallup Organization, Inc.

Gamio, M. 1930. *Mexican Immigration to the United States: A Study of Human Migration and Adjustment.* Chicago: University of Chicago Press.

Gans, H.J. 1979. *Deciding What's News: A Study of CBS Evening News, NBC Nightly News, Newsweek, and Time.* New York: Random House.

García, J.R. 1980. *Operation Wetback: The Mass Deportation of Mexican Undocumented Workers in 1954.* Westport, CT: Greenwood Press.

Glaser, B.G. and A.L. Strauss. 1967. *The Discovery of Grounded Theory: Strategies for Qualitative Research.* Chicago: Aldine.

Hoffman, A. 1974. *Unwanted Mexican Americans in the Great Depression.* Tucson: University of Arizona Press.

Human Resources Agency. 1975. *Illegal Aliens: Impact of Illegal Aliens on the County of San Diego, Part I.* San Diego: Human Resources Agency.

_____. 1977. *Illegal Aliens: Impact of Illegal Aliens on the County of San Diego, Part II.* San Diego: Human Resources Agency.

Katz, E., H. Adoni, and P. Parness. 1977. "Remembering the news: What the picture adds to recall." *Journalism Quarterly* (Summer), 231-239.

Lester, M. 1980. "Generating newsworthiness: The interpretive construction of public events." *American Sociological Review* 45:984-994.

Mills, C.W. 1956. *The Power Elite.* New York: Oxford University Press.

North, D.S. and M.F. Houstoun. 1976. *The Characteristics and Role of Illegal Aliens in the U.S. Labor Market: An Exploratory Study.* Washington, D.C.: Linton and Co., Inc.

Samora, J. 1971. *Los Mojados: The Wetback Story.* Notre Dame: University of Notre Dame Press.

POLICE CRIMES IN THE BARRIO

Larry Trujillo

> They can't do this and get away with it.
> I want to prevent somebody else's
> mother from suffering... I know that
> people are behind us because it affects
> everyone. Anyone could have been in
> Barlow's situation.
>
> —Mrs. Raquel Benavídez, June 1976,
>   on the shooting of her son by
>   Oakland police.
>
> ... the policeman has the power to
> remove you from the street and the
> power of legal execution.
>
> —Sgt. Art Ruditsky, LAPD.

Introduction

On May 17, 1980, the largest black rebellion since the "long hot summer" of 1967 erupted in the Black ghettos of Miami, Florida. The seemingly spontaneous rebellion ignited by the acquittal of four white police for the killing of a black insurance salesman, Arthur McDuffie, lasted four days. During this time over 7,000 police and military personnel were deployed, 18 people were killed, 400 people were injured, 1,300 were arrested, 150 buildings were destroyed, 2,000 jobs were eliminated, and economic losses were predicted at $400 million (Greenwood, 1980).

The rebellion was initially a reaction to the long-standing outrage concerning the police violence which continually occurs in the ghetto. Ghetto residents consistently view police crimes as happening with impunity.[1] The insurgency, however, soon became a forum for expressing black anger over the chronically escalating conditions of unemployment, lack of social services, inadequate schools, racist immigration policies, and generally oppressive social conditions of the urban ghetto. In short, the ghetto insurrection became a general attack against black oppression.

As in the black ghetto, the spiraling economic recession and deepening fiscal crisis continue to have a devastating impact on the Chicano community. Phenomenally high unemployment rates and severe cutbacks in social services affect every aspect of barrio life. During the current crisis, reliance on the police to maintain order in the barrio has intensified. Under these conditions, we find police brutality and police use of deadly force is also on the rise. And, as in the Miami ghettos, the police crimes are sparking growing unrest in the barrios.

Hence, as we enter the 1980s, the need for action around the issue of police crimes in the barrio is paramount. Action, however, without sound information, serious thought, and theoretical clarity is likely to be diffuse, ineffectual, and carries the potential of being repressive in practice. The goal of this paper is to probe the core dynamics of this question: raising key theoretical and political issues as they impinge upon the Chicano struggle for social justice. The central focus is on the dialectic between repression and resistance. The paper begins with a historical contour which points out that police crimes in the barrio are not a new phenomenon, but rather have long-standing historical roots. We then turn to a general discussion of the material conditions under which police crimes flourish. The current period has witnessed a rise in police crimes which we argue corresponds to the worsening urban fiscal crisis. The heart of the paper describes a concrete struggle against police crimes in the barrio—The Barlow Benavídez Committee Against Police Crimes (BBCAPC) in Oakland, California. Finally, we explore what suggestions the case study raises for future community organizing.

Gunpowder Justice: The Chicano Legacy[2]

> Ay mi Raza, we were born with oppression and resistance in our very bones! (From *450 Años del Pueblo Chicano.*)

The barrio is a product of over one hundred and fifty years of racism, legal and extra-legal repression, and active resistance. Police crimes (and vigilantism) are not new phenomena, but have been a mainstay of barrio life in the United States. To centrally locate the roots and comprehend the dynamics of the issue, we must analyze it within the broader context of the social development of the barrio and its relationship to the larger political economy. Although a comprehensive historical contour is beyond the scope of this paper, identification of several salient features of this social history will help deepen our understanding of the present and give direction to our future praxis.

By the 1870s, sparked by the wheels of capitalist accumulation and expansion, the Mexican people in the United States had lost political and economic control of their communities. Despite guarantees to the contrary clearly outlined in the Treaty of Guadalupe Hidalgo, Mexican civil and human rights were all but abolished as the process of barrioization (segmentation of Mexicans at the bottom of the class structure) unfolded (Camarillo, 1979; Barrera, 1979). The legal and the criminal justice systems, as well as vigilante mob action, played a crucial role in this process.

Lynch-law hangings, beatings, and other forms of violence were pervasive in the Mexican community, and police use of excessive and deadly force clearly seemed *beyond incrimination* (Bancroft, 1885; Hittell, 1885). Historian Leonard Pitt notes: "Every important lynch-law episode and most minor ones involved the Spanish-speaking" (1971: 154). A 1916 newspaper article in the *World's Work* further reports:

> The killing of Mexicans . . . throughout the border in these last four years is almost incredible . . . There is no penalty for killing, for no jury along the border would ever convict a white man for shooting a Mexican (as quoted in McWilliams, 1948: 115).

This early period was an extremely brutal and bloody period: it is estimated that between 1908 and 1925, 500 to 5,000 Mexicans were killed along the border by law enforcement personnel alone (Morales, 1980: 1). The fact that the police carried out these actions more or less with impunity set a dangerous historical precedent that carries over to the current period. In fact, until the 1977 conviction of Texas Marshall Frank Hayes for the killing of young Ricardo Morales, no police officer had ever been convicted for killing a Chicano.[3]

Chicanos rebelled against their oppression. This is demonstrated by the widespread Chicano social banditry *(bandidos chicanos)*[4] of this early period. Communities likewise resisted, as characterized by the Cart War,[5] the Salt War,[6] the Cortina War,[7] and *las Gorras Blancas* (white caps).[8] These Chicano resistance movements fought against the Anglo land companies, cattle barons, and railroad companies who were organizing to seize Mexican land and exploit Mexican labor (Castillo and Camarillo, 1973; Acuña, 1972). Chicano insurgents were viewed as "outlaws" and "criminals" by sensationalized newspaper cover stories which declared a "Mexican crime wave." As is often the case, this media propaganda became part of the general public consciousness and soon *all* Mexicans were perceived as criminals (Trujillo, 1974). Vigilante mob action and police violence escalated in the Chicano community (Hollen, 1974; Morales, 1972). Correspondingly, Mexican *mutualistas* (self-help, self-defense organizations) sprang up throughout the barrios to combat police and other forms of repression.

By the turn of the century, changes in the capitalist mode of production had transformed the central cities into the centers of capital accumulation. Likewise, the Mexican work forces became urban. The urban barrios, isolated and segregated from the Anglo community both residentially and institutionally, housed the segmented Mexican work force as well as the large Mexican surplus labor force. The poverty and unemployment so starkly visible in the current urban crisis became an enduring feature of barrio life during this period.

The police, responding to changes in the political economy, similarly transformed into a large-scale urban class control force (Berstein, et al., 1977; Chapter 2). Hence, we see the policing of the barrio change from protecting land and cattle barons to insuring urban stability for industrial capitalists. Thus, besides being victimized by racist police deployment and patrol practices (which often result in incidences of police abuse), Chicano workers faced police repression in labor disputes and labor organizing (Zamora, 1975; Cisneros, 1975). Further, Chicano political organizations developed to protect Mexican human and civil rights became increasingly penetrated by police spies and other intelligence-gathering agents.

Police repression in the barrio, although continual, has not always been highly visible. It appears to intensify during times of economic crisis. Perhaps this is because crisis creates scapegoats, and in a racist society, Third World people are the first to fill this role. For example, just as the Mexican undocumented worker today is blamed for the high unemployment rates, anti-Mexican sentiment swelled during the Great Depression. Signs appeared in cities stating "only white help employed," and white working class unions joined the campaign to "repatriate" Mexican workers. Police abuse became widespread as local police, the INS border patrol agents, and correctional officers provided the manpower for massive sweeps of the barrios. Mexicanos/Chicanos were rounded up and deported to Mexico—often regardless of their legal citizenship status (Hoffman, 1974).

Even in times of prosperity, however, police crimes in the barrio are commonplace. During the 1940s, for example, law enforcement agencies and military servicemen provoked an all-out attack on so-called Chicano "zoot suiters" and "pachucos" in major urban barrios like Los Angeles and Houston (McWilliams, 1943). Agitated by sensationalist propaganda from the Hearst and Chandler newspapers, a reign of police violence took place in the barrio (Citizen's Committee for the Defense of Mexican-American Youth, 1942). The servicemen's riots of 1943 epitomize this period (Gonzales, 1980). During this period *all* Chicano youth (like the *bandidos* of the 1850s and the *vatos locos* of the 1980s) were viewed as "criminals" and therefore were subjects of police repression.

The Current Situation

The historical examples above are not isolated incidents. Police crimes in the barrios occur daily and are mushrooming. Police use of deadly force is the most tragic consequence of this reality.[9] The death of José Barlow Benavídez, a young Chicano in East Oakland, is only one example of what barrio residents must face, a deplorable echo of the historical reality of "gunpowder justice."

The National Center for Health Statistics indicates a steady increase over the past five years in cases of police use of excessive force (U.S. Public Health Service, 1975-1980).[10] Statistical computations on police use of deadly force do not include a separate category for Chicano or Hispanic. Chicanos are reported as white. Consequently, police use of excessive and deadly force against Chicanos is extremely difficult to document statistically.[11] From newspaper reports collected from several clipping services, and careful documentation by Chicano community legal action groups, however, it is clear that police crimes in the barrio are on the rise (see Appendix 1).[12] For example, in Los Angeles County, police shootings have resulted in over thirty deaths per year, every year since 1975. Of these, 80 percent were members of racial minorities, with slightly less than 50 percent being Hispanic (Paz, 1980: 11). In 1975 alone, seventy-five people were killed by the LAPD—forty-seven blacks, eighteen Chicanos, and ten whites (Farrell, 1977: 72). Further, a recent report of police killings in Chicago shows Hispanic deaths to be 4.5 per 100,000 population. This data concludes that, between 1969 and 1970, Hispanics were killed by the police 13.2 times more often than whites (Harding and Fahey, 1973; also see Morales, 1979: 6). This is consistent with Takagi's findings on blacks on a national level (1974). Further evidence of an escalation of police crimes in the barrio is the fact that the Community Relations Service of the U.S. Justice Department received 142 percent more complaints in the first six months of 1980 than in the previous six months (Hudson, 1980). About half of these complaints were from Hispanics.[13] Community Service Director Gil Pompa suggests that there is "an undeclared war between Hispanics and the police."[14] In testimony before a congressional hearing on the issue of police use of deadly force, he states:

> No single issue will lead to serious community disruption as allegations or perceptions of the use of excessive force by police... one single charge of excessive use of force against a police department has the capability of snowballing into an avalanche of problems that may include a vicious cycle of police and citizen killings; a decrease in public confidence in not only the police, but the entire city and even state administrations... (U.S. Department of Justice, 1980: 2).

Police violence is alarming. It has become a key issue for most national Chicano organizations. For example, police brutality was the key issue at the 1979 LULAC (League of United Latin American Citizens) State Convention in Texas; MALDEF (Mexican American Legal Defense and Education Fund) recently sponsored a national conference on police brutality in Dallas where sixty cases were documented; and the National Council de la Raza recently held a conference on "Crimen y Justicia for Hispanics," in which police use of deadly force was a central topic. The issue is so pervasive that Chicano organizations like MALDEF, deploring the Attorney General's reluctance to deal with the issue, have recently asked the United Nations Commission on Human Rights to intervene in the "police reign of terror" in the barrio.[15]

The Material Conditions of Repression

Before turning to our case study, let us briefly outline the material conditions under which social problems in general and police crimes in particular flourish. This requires placing the issue of police crimes within the broader context of the crises and contradictions of monopoly capitalism. From this vantage point, three salient dynamics will be highlighted for discussion: 1) *the increased marginalization of Chicano youth,* which is generating a highly visible and alienated street youth; 2) *the urban fiscal crisis of the state* which is attempting to solve political problems with budgetary solutions on the one hand, while cutting back the very grassroot, community-based programs and services which have been dealing most effectively with community problems on the other hand; and 3) *the expansion of the police-industrial complex* which, interplaying with points (1) and (2), generates an explosive situation in the barrio.

The Marginalization of Chicano Youth

The majority of the victims of police crimes in the barrio are Chicano *youth.* The Chicano population is the fastest-growing population in the United States.[16] In fact, the high birth rate (the fertility rate of Chicanas is five times higher than that of Anglo women) and continued high rates of immigration from Mexico will make Chicanos the majority population in several states in the near future. The fact that over 50 percent of the entering kindergarten class in the Los Angeles City School District is Chicano reflects the reality of this projection (McLaughlin and Potter, 1980: 69). Thus, one of the most striking features of the Chicano population is its youthfulness. Forty-two percent of the Chicano population (compared to 29 percent of the Anglo population) is under 18 years of age (Martínez, 1979: 14). The Chicano youth population is dramatically increasing at the same time that the Anglo youth population is decreasing; Anglo youth are projected to decrease by 7.2 million in 1980 (SER, 1977).

Concentrated in urban neighborhoods with deteriorating social conditions, few options are available to this expanding Chicano youth population. Spiraling unemployment rates hover around 50 percent with another 20 percent who have given up prospects for a job and are no longer counted in the labor force (SER, 1977). Given the long-standing labor market segmentation in the barrio, the jobs Chicano youth are finding are dead-end, unstable, hazardous, low-paying and subject to mechanization (Moore, 1978; Bullock, 1973). Further, the current drop-out rate from high school among Chicanos is between 50 and 60 percent. Moreover, the few skills obtained in public schools rarely correspond to the needs of the job market (Rist, 1973; Bullock, 1973).

Clearly, then, we see an increasingly *marginalized*[17] Chicano youth population. Drug addiction, alcoholism, and street crime are high among this population, thus greatly affecting the individual and the community. There are larger numbers of Chicano youth living their lives on the streets. Likewise, a predominantly white police force (generally living outside the barrio) are also out in greater numbers. It is an explosive situation.

The Fiscal Crisis of the State

Further, we are in the midst of an urban fiscal crisis in both the public and private sectors. The realities of the urban crisis have had a devastating effect upon the barrio, again particularly its youth population. Symptoms of urban decay are highly visible in the barrio. The high infant mortality rates and tuberculosis rates, substandard housing and slumlord practices, urban renewal projects, and poor quality schooling are social indicators of the deteriorating social conditions in the barrio.

The Chicano working class is expanding. Concentrated in marginal occupational sectors of the economy, unemployment rates are swelling. The steady influx of undocumented workers, working for below-standard wages, fearing protest will bring deportation, compounds the situation. Moreover, as indicated by a recent Urban League study, industrial jobs are decreasing in the urban barrios and ghettos (Williams, 1979). Chicano workers are not being provided adequate training to assume the corporate/managerial and government jobs replacing the unskilled industrial jobs in the central cities. Thus, the barrios are losing jobs and tax revenues while the Chicano surplus labor force grows.

The fiscal crisis is also severely cutting back social services in the barrio at a time when they are needed most. Proposition 13 in California (the "tax revolt" initiative), for example, demanded a 57 percent cut in social spending. These cutbacks resulted in many human service delivery programs suffering substantial funding cuts. Grassroot youth programs felt the impact of this fiscal sword. In Oakland's Fruitvale District, for example, programs such as Centro Infantil, La Escuelita, The Emiliano Zapata Street Academy, Centro Legal de la Raza have all been cut back to the point of possible shutdown due to lack of funds. These grassroot community-based-and-operated institutions have been providing essential youth services and programs. The community trusts and utilizes these bilingual/bicultural grassroots institutions. They have provided solutions where the welfare state has failed.

The Expansion of the Police Apparatus

As the fiscal crisis escalates, first priorities in social spending go to the criminal justice system, particularly the police. The authors of *The Iron Fist and Velvet Glove* make the following point:

> During the current fiscal crisis, the reliance of the state on the police has intensified in order to back up with force the deteriorating economic situation of the working class and Third World

communities. As sources of public expenditure dwindle due to unemployment and inflation, the ruling class makes repression its spending priority, while urging working people to cut back their standard of living and to demand fewer social services (Bernstein, et al., 1977: 177).

In Oakland, for example, hard hit by poverty and unemployment, the City Council and City Manager make criminal justice spending their top priority. Approximately 30 percent of the City budget goes to the Oakland Police Department.

Consequently, the current period shows a dramatic growth and sophistication of the police apparatus. The Law Enforcement Assistance Administration (LEAA) has provided the organizational forum and fiscal support for standardizing, centralizing and coordinating police policies and programs.[18] Corporate technological and managerial expertise and innovation has accompanied the public sector focus on policing. Hence, the rise and expansion of the "police-industrial complex" (Bernstein, et al., 1977: 76-135). The police-industrial complex, for example, has fully penetrated Oakland Police Department operations. The OPD has also solicited numerous funds from the Law Enforcement Assistance Administration (LEAA), through the Alameda Regional Criminal Justice Planning Board. Some of the projects funded include: legal advisors for the police; hand-held, portable, two-way radios; minority recruitment; team policing; and a computer system to locate police cars and to sort out calls automatically by order of priority (BBCAPC, 1977). Hence, the Oakland Police Department is integrated into the expanding national criminal justice network. The OPD utilizes all the modern corporate-military managerial systems, sophisticated crime control technologies and weaponry and community pacification programs, i.e. the iron fist and velvet glove approach to policing (see Bernstein, et al., 1977).

The growth of police personnel is instructive. Takagi informs us that the police force in California "has been increasing at the rate of 5 to 6 percent compared to an annual population increase of less than two and one-half percent" (1974: 33). Takagi further predicts that if the current rate of increase continues, "California will have at the turn of the century an estimated 180,000 police officers, an equivalent of 10 military divisions" (1974: 33). In Los Angeles alone, the police have doubled over the past decade. These are salient facts for barrio residents. In Los Angeles, police deployment in the barrio is ten times greater than equally populated, predominantly white suburban areas (Morales, 1971: 54). Despite heavy police deployment, crime rates and victimization rates continue to rise (Paz, 1980; Mandel, 1979).

Further, police deployment in the barrio is largely carried out by white police officers (often carrying racial stereotypes to their workplace) who neither live in the barrio nor fully understand its culture. Barrio residents at once feel unprotected from "street crime" and "over-policed" by "racist cops." It is under this contradiction that police-community conflict increases. As this conflict grows, so does the potential for police crimes.

In summary, the material conditions for repression and resistance are intensifying in the barrio. The increased marginalization of the Chicano population, particularly the youth population, the urban fiscal crisis, and the expansion of policing the barrio have a direct relationship to the increase in police crimes. The political state (and its criminal justice institutions) are caught in a contradiction. They must demand that Chicano workers and residents continue to politically support the existing order (the legitimation process of capital), while paying *more* taxes for *fewer* community services. The state is asking for this allegiance in a period when Bakke, Weber, and intensified KKK activities demonstrate growing racist attacks against Chicanos. As organized and spontaneous community protest of these conditions ensues, the police are called upon to control discontent and maintain the social order. It is this environment of mistrust and contradiction that heightens the potential for police crimes in the barrio.

The Barlow Benavídez Case

Barrio residents desire and demand the elimination of police crimes in their communities. Currently, many grassroot community organizations are attempting to document daily police abuses of power towards barrio dwellers. These organizations are increasingly realizing the need to combat police crimes as part of the larger struggle for social justice and community self-reliance.[19] The Barlow Benavídez Committee Against Police Crimes in Oakland, California's, Fruitvale District is one example of an effort to educate and organize the community to stop police crimes. Reacting to police killing of a young Chicano, José Barlow Benavídez, the BBCAPC developed a broad-based coalition and actively organized around the issue for four years. A descriptive history of the BBCAPC should provide important lessons that may guide future social action.

Background of the Case

Around 1:45 p.m. on June 11, 1976, José Barlow Benavídez was leaving his parked car on the corner of 44th and East 14th Street, the heart of the heavily Chicano populated Fruitvale District of East Oakland. Responding to a robbery that had just occurred in the neighborhood, without any flashing red lights of warning, Officer Michael Cogley of the Oakland Police Department pulled up beside Benavídez and stopped him as a suspect. With a loaded and cocked shotgun in hand, Officer Cogley ordered Barlow to assume a search position (hands on top of the car and legs spread). Benavídez complied. Officer Cogley then transferred the shotgun to his right hand. With his finger on the trigger, and the gun aimed at Benavídez' left temple, Cogley conducted a pat down search. Cogley kicked Benavídez' legs farther apart and, simultaneously, the shotgun fired into Benavídez' left temple, killing him instantly.

Four days later (6/15/76), the *Oakland Tribune* reported that the Oakland Police Department had investigated the incident and found the shooting to be "accidental." Based on Officer Cogley's statement and those of three other witnesses, the investigation concluded that Benavídez had abruptly turned his head causing his body to strike the muzzle and discharge the shotgun. However, of the sixteen witnesses interviewed by staff members of the Centro Legal de la Raza (a local legal aid office specializing in services for the Spanish-speaking), who arrived on the scene ten minutes after the shooting, none confirmed the official police account that Benavídez made any movement towards Cogley. As one eyewitness recounts:

> I saw the officer come out, cock his shotgun, point it at someone. That someone came out of the car, hands raised in the air and placed his hands on the roof while the cop searched him. He searched him, he shot him for no reason at all... (*Black Panther*, 6/26/76; *Berkeley Barb*, 6/25/76).

The Coroner's Report showed that the bullet entered through the back of Benavídez' head and exited through his forehead, making it unlikely that he turned his head at the instant that the shotgun discharged (*Verdict of Coroner*, June 12, 1976). The *Tribune* article noted: "Since a felony had occurred, Cogley followed routine procedure by loading his shotgun and taking it with him to check the suspect" (6/15/76). According to the Oakland Police Department procedure, as outlined in training bulletin "One-Man Felony Car Stops III-b.2" (City of Oakland Police Services, April 2, 1976), however, Officer Cogley should have stayed behind the open door of his car until a back-up officer arrived before searching Benavídez. Then Cogley should have ordered Benavídez out of the car. After determining that the car was empty, Cogley should have frisked Benavídez unarmed, with the other officer providing armed backup.

Cogley clearly disregarded departmental procedure—procedures which were designed to prevent exactly what occurred.

The State Response[20]

The official public response, reflected by the Oakland City Council, the Oakland Police Chief, and the Alameda County District Attorney, was an attempt to politically play down the issue— accepting without question the Oakland Police Department internal investigation report findings of "accidental death." Even after it was clear that community pressure would not allow the case to disappear into the statistical column of an annual report, the tactics of local politicians and state agents were a mixture of police intimidation and government inaction.

The Oakland Police Department responded in a particularly callous manner. They never officially informed the Benavídez family of their son's death. Moreover, when the family met with Police Chief Hart, he offered no condolence to the family and criticized them for inserting human emotions and making the case a public issue. He also made it clear that the Oakland Police Department had no intentions of removing Cogley from the force (BBCAPC, 1977). The Oakland Police Department also harassed and intimidated potential witnesses.[21] These actions, documented by Centro Legal de la Raza, included illegal stop-and-frisk practices and arrests and threats of retaliation against those who threatened to testify against Cogley. These tactics persuaded several witnesses not to testify.

The Oakland City Council and the Alameda District Attorney and Grand Jury, on the other hand, continually attempted to abdicate their responsibilities of investigating the case fully. The Alameda County District Attorney Lowell Jensen undertook the investigation of Officer Cogley's possible criminal negligence. The District Attorney's Office, however, refused to investigate the case thoroughly. Instead it delegated the responsibility to the Alameda County Grand Jury. Yet, the District Attorney held influence in the selection of witnesses and permissible evidence and therefore had control over the Grand Jury. The Grand Jury, with no representation from the Fruitvale District, met in closed hearings, the proceedings being inaccessible to the public. On August 4th, after two days of deliberation, the Grand Jury found insufficient evidence to indict Officer Cogley.

The Benavídez family and BBCAPC faired no better in their attempts to achieve legal redress and social justice from the Oakland City Council. On June 29th, two hundred Benavídez supporters packed the Council meeting demanding prosecution of Cogley, greater police accountability to the community, establishment of a Police Civilian Review Board and an end to police harassment of eyewitnesses. The City Council yielded to community pressure by passing a series of motions, introduced by councilman Joe Coto, which:

1) Demanded a thorough investigation by the D.A.'s office;

2) Referred the policy request of suspension without pay to the Council's Public Safety Committee for study and recommendations;

3) Reinforced the policy of the Council that it does not condone police harassment of eyewitnesses to the slaying;

4) Asked the Public Safety Committee to explore methods to improve relations between the city's citizens and the police department;

5) Referred to staff a demand for an explanation of why the police department allows the use of shotguns by its officers (*Oakland Tribune,* 6/30/76; *El Mundo,* 7/7/76).

But none of the recommendations were implemented. While the Public Safety Committee did meet, the Benavídez case never appeared on the agenda.

Having exhausted local channels for addressing the serious issue of police crimes in the barrio, the BBCAPC campaigned for federal investigation of the case. With the support of politicians such as Congressman Dellums, Stark, and Roybal, church leaders like Father Oliver and Rev. York, local union leaders such as Edy Withington, president of OPEU (Office and Professional Employees Union), Local 29, and a variety of political and community organizations, the BBCAPC pressured the U.S. Attorney General's Office in San Francisco to submit the case to a Federal Grand Jury. The hopes were to prosecute under Federal Law 18 USC 242. This statute makes it a crime for any person acting under the color of the law (e.g., a police officer) to willfully deprive another of his/her constitutional rights or to subject that person to different punishments, pains, or penalties on account of his/her color or race. This law set the legal basis for the indictment of Sheriff Hayes for the death of Ricardo Morales in Texas.

In March 1977, the Benavídez family and the BBCAPC again returned to the Oakland City Council, this time requesting political support for the federal indictment. Oakland Mayor Lionel Reading denied the issue a place on the agenda. Reading argued that a pending family civil suit against the city prohibited Council comments on the case.[22] However, on a local TV news program that evening Mayor Reading stated that there had been a full investigation of the case by the Oakland Police Department, the District Attorney's Office, and the Alameda County Grand Jury. Reading stated that the Coucil was satisfied with the verdict—"accidental death."

The Community Reaction

> Wherever people gathered—in schools, on the street corners, at the market—people talked with anger and fear about Barlow's death and what it meant for themselves and their children's safety. (BBCAPC, 1976).

While local politicians and criminal justice managers reacted with insensitivity and apathy, the community responded to Barlow's death with indignation and social action. By no means were police crimes a new issue in Oakland. Police violence has a long history, particularly in Oaklands's black community. Further, the Oakland Police Department had killed five unarmed civilians the previous year in the city. Additionally, the Fruitvale barrio had recently mobilized around a case of police brutality against several well-respected Chicano mental health workers from Centro Salud Mental who were harassed for merely attempting to break up a fight between black and Chicano youth. Hence, the issue was a foremost concern in need of resolution. That Police Chief Hart, with the support of the City Council, absolved Officer Cogley outraged Fruitvale community leaders and residents. Where local officials declared the investigation comprehensive and the verdict of "accidental death" as conclusive, the BBCAPC and Benavídez family viewed it as a "whitewash." Official actions are reflected in a young Chicano resident's metaphoric statement:

> They called a firetruck to come and wash away the pieces of Barlow from the street. Right there you could tell the police were trying to wash it all away. Since then, there's been at least triple the amount of patrol cars watching everything and everybody. They're taking pictures of everyone. And they're stopping people on the streets and questioning them for no good reason. But they can do it legal-like. What's scary is that they're stopping everyone on suspicion of something. Probably no more than suspicion of looking suspicious. But that's how they blew Barlow away (BBCAPC, 1978).

Immediately following Barlow's death a community meeting was held to discuss the incident. Over one hundred concerned individuals and organization representatives attended. Another meeting the next day drew 150 people, who began concrete organizing for action. The following concerns emerged from these meetings:

1) The need to indict Cogley and seek justice for the Benavídez family;
2) The behavior of police who routinely abuse the legal and human rights of people in the Raza community; and
3) The absence of meaningful procedures to hold police accountable to the community (BBCAPC, 1976).

Understanding the need for a strong organizational base, activists formed the BBCAPC at this early meeting. The issue at hand was the death of a young Chicano, and Chicano community organizations initiated the mobilization for action. The BBCAPC, however, characterized the occurrence as not only a neighborhood issue but a denial of civil and human rights and it therefore attracted multi-racial support. The BBCAPC began meeting regularly and coordinating the strategies and tactics of the action. Frequent political-cultural-educational events increased the interest and participation of local residents and locally based political organizations. Political events included press conferences, marches, rallies, demonstrations, a community conference, and a radiothon.

On June 17, 1976, the BBCAPC began circulating petitions protesting the death of Benavídez and demanding that Officer Cogley be prosecuted. Over 2,000 signatures were collected from the neighborhood, local church gatherings, local campuses, and community agencies. The following day the Benavídez family and the BBCAPC held a rally and press conference in front of the Oakland Police station. Approximately 400 people participated. Rallies were also held at City Hall and the County Administration Building. In addition, a festive and spirited march through the city to a political rally at Sanborn Park drew over 1,000 supporters. Support messages were delivered from a wide variety of Bay Area organizations.

The BBCAPC understood the state and criminal justice system in its response to the failure of the Alameda County Grand Jury to indict Officer Cogley. The BBCAPC states:

> People in the East Oakland community question whether the Alameda County District Attorney conducted his investigation and presented this case as aggressively as he would in another criminal prosecution not involving a policeman. The District Attorney's motives are clear: every day he must work hand in hand with the Oakland Police Department. Usually when a person is murdered by another the suspect is forced to answer to the charge in an open court (BBCAPC, 1976).

Having raised the community's awareness of the issues through a series of marches, rallies, and demonstrations, the BBCAPC turned its organizing efforts towards a community-wide Conference Against

Police Crimes. A political leaflet states the purpose of the Conference as follows:

> This conference has the purpose of broadening Barlow Benavídez' murder and maintaining this issue in the eyes of the public. At the same time the Barlow Benavídez Committee wants to raise the community's consciousness with solid programs that will lead to the jailing of Michael Cogley, Barlow's murderer. Michael Cogley represents an entire system of injustice, an injustice that in this case is directed to Chicanos.
>
> The response with immediate demonstrations and demands for justice has taken the Barlow Benavídez committee through a tremendous amount of work and reaffirmation, and generally has given the community a viable vehicle for organization.
>
> When the committee formed, the members attended meetings coming from their work, school, and homes, maintaining a distinction between committee work and personal life. In the process of organizing ourselves we have been able to understand that these two aspects are not separated in reality.
>
> It is for these reasons that we proudly sponsor this community conference against police crimes. The work and organization must continue and the most essential elements for this work are people. With the massive support of the community we can spark a sphere of influence to other communities that are confronted with this same police repression and learn to resolve it.
>
> ¡Hasta La Victoria!

The leaflet is a substantial documentary comment on the energy and politics of the BBCAPC. It addresses the need for "solid programs" to fight injustices and the importance of a strong and viable organizational base for ideological and strategic work. Likewise, the leaflet emphasizes the false dichotomy between workplace and neighborhood organizing and between political life and personal life—each is interdependent and integration is necessary for successful praxis. And finally, they reaffirm the age-old axiom that "people make history."

The Conference was endorsed by over sixty individuals and organizations including the United East Oakland Clergy, the American Indian Center, several local MEChA chapters, the Peralta Federation of Teachers Local 1603, Congressmen Dellums, Assemblyman Tom Bates, Alameda Board of Supervisors member John George, the Puerto Rican Socialist Party, Community Service United, staff, students, and faculty from Chicano Studies UC Berkeley, OPEU Local 29, Bay Area Gay Liberation, and others. Local grassroot community organizations such as COMEXAS, Centro Legal de la Raza, Clínica de la Raza, Centro Salud Mental,

Centro Infantil, and Escuelita were prominent in the organization and success of the Conference. Also the multiracial Committee Against Police Abuse (CAPA) from Los Angeles participated— therefore springboarding a link between Northern and Southern California efforts.

The Conference Against Police Crimes was held November 20, 1977, drawing over 300 participants. Workshops organized by the BBCAPC included: 1) "The Oakland Power Structure"—showing the relationship between corporate control of peoples' lives, the police, and police crimes; 2) "Workers' Democratic Rights"— pointing out the use of policing in labor disputes and workers' legal rights (especially undocumented workers); 3) "The Police"— detailing the history of policing in general and the Oakland Police Department specifically; and 4) "Organizing Techniques"— discussing basic organizing principles and detailing various organizing techniques and methods.

The pamphlets were well written and researched by the BBCAPC. The police pamphlet, for example, clearly pointed out the contradictions of policing the barrio. It stated:

> We want to examine the contradiction that on the one hand an extensive police system serves the purpose of social control and law enforcement that discriminates against the poor and Third World people, while on the other hand an entire world of high crime by big business and government runs free and is in fact protected by the police establishment (BBCAPC, 1977).

The BBCAPC understood the police better than most criminologists. Take, for example, the following point:

> The police departments have developed from small substations into super departments staffed with hundreds of men, armed with the latest military equipment, and financed with budgets into the billions. Each budget or manpower increase in the police department has been rationalized by the rise in crime rates in big cities and the need for the police to decrease those crimes. Yet with all the millions of dollars pumped into the rapidly expanding police apparatus, crime has not decreased, but has increased along with unemployment, poverty, and police crimes (BBCAPC, 1976).

Searching for new avenues to communicate the issue and build the campaign, on April 22-23, 1977, a 48-hour radiothon on "Police Crimes in the Barrio" was sponsored by a local listener-sponsored radion station, KPFA. Produced jointly by KPFA and the BBCAPC, the program's purpose was twofold: to analyze and discuss the role of the police, and to raise money for the BBCAPC case. Through the radiothon, the BBCAPC informed a broad local audience and gained technical experience in media production. The monies raised were used to meet the expenses of the BBCAPC, to send BBCAPC representatives to Washington to lobby for a federal investigation, and to muster up national political support.

Participants in the radiothon included members of the BBCAPC; lawyers from the Lawyers Guild, the ACLU, and Centro de la Raza; the editors of *Crime and Social Justice;* representatives from the American Indian Movement, the Puerto Rican Socialist Party, the Texas Farmworkers Movement, and the United Farmworkers Union. Several discussants raised general theoretical, historical, and practical and legal points about the police while others discussed the interface and/or conflict their organizations had had with the police in community and labor organizing. Reforms such as civilian review boards, affirmative action policies, demilitarization, and community control initiatives were analyzed and critiqued in terms of their promise and failures. Although the need for greater community accountability and policy control were consistent themes of the discussion, equally pervasive was the notion that such reforms may be impossible under capitalism. In terms of the theme of the radiothon—police crimes in the barrio—the message was clear: at the root of police crimes is societal racism and class oppression.

During the time of preparation for the radiothon, the BBCAPC was continuing to build a case and to pressure for a federal indictment. The Centro Legal de la Raza, in a letter to the U.S. Attorney General, stated that police use of deadly force was not only an issue in Oakland's Chicano community but was a national pattern of police conduct. They also noted that the Benavídez Case represented a *growing* disregard for human rights in the United States (Centro Legal, 1977).

On March 15, 1977, the Benavídez family, the BBCAPC, and their supporters flooded the Oakland City Council Meeting. This time they came to get local political support for the federal investigation. We noted above the mayor's response. This official response points out the social contradictions of the "democrat" state. A lawyer from Centro Legal de la Raza further points out the legal contradiction. He states:

> ... most states, including California, have abolished the use of one-sided grand jury proceedings in favor of direct prosecution by the district attorney and in open preliminary hearing to determine whether prosecution should proceed. The district attorney's actions

in referring the prosecution of Michael Cogley to the Grand Jury
served only to remove the public issue from public scrutiny. Two
days after this Council resolved that there be a thorough
investigation by the district attorney, that investigation ceased and
the grand jury was convened. That action is inconsistent with both
the resolution of the City Council and with the duty of the district
attorney to pursue this case in the public interest.[23]

A community worker from Centro Infantil raised the political
contradictions of the city's response to the barrio:

> Time after time people have come here to denounce police violence
> and police crimes, and justly so. For too long we have seen the police
> department cover up for police officers who should be judged as
> firmly as any person who kills or commits a crime. But it's becoming
> clear to us in the community that this city council is covering up for
> the police by not taking action which would attempt to make them
> accountable. Why is it that issues concerning the economic
> development of Oakland are acted upon with lightning speed, yet, on
> the issues that deal with people, the Council becomes indifferent and
> even negligent... One cheap way is passing resolutions you never
> intend to act upon. It's like dangling a carrot in front of a horse, you
> keep us anticipating and waiting, hoping maybe we will forget
> ourselves what we are waiting for.[24]

In pushing for the federal investigation the BBCAPC made another
significant point:

> In our work to get justice for Barlow, and to begin to change racist
> and repressive police practices, we have learned from experience that
> only the organized and militant support of the community can force
> the authorities to act (Memo from BBCAPC, "The FBI is Now
> Investigating the Death of Barlow Benavídez," n.d.).

The BBCAPC, although hoping the Attorney General would use the
Morales case as a precedent and indict Cogley, maintained a realistic
vision of the limits of their legalistic approach. The BBCAPC
believed an unfavorable decision from the Justice Department would
both educate people as to the racist injustice of the legal system and
put the Benavídez case into national focus as one more case of the
denial of Chicano civil rights.

The Civil Rights Division of the Justice Department concluded
that evidence was insufficient to prosecute. The BBCAPC, which had
sent representatives to Washington, D.C., to lobby for the federal
indictment, began pursuing another avenue for seeking social justice.
They met with Congressmen Dellums, Stark, and Roybal to advocate
the establishment of congressional hearings on the issue of police

brutality and police use of deadly force in the United States. At the same time, the Committee started discussing plans for a commemoration of the second anniversary of Barlow's death.

Increasing political turmoil within the Committee, however, prevented either of these strategies from ever being carried out. First, a series of serious political splits depleted the BBCAPC of both membership and political energy. The negative decision on the federal indictment had put a serious wedge in further legal organizing, which had become a primary organizational weapon of the BBCAPC. This was compounded by the change in political and legal direction of the Benavídez family. The consequences of this political shift caused the withdrawal of the Benavídez family from participation in the BBCAPC and the dismissal of Centro Legal de la Raza as the legal representation. Since the family had a critical part in the final decision-making and the Centro Legal was a cornerstone of the BBCAPC leadership, the movement began to rapidly lose momentum. The Benavídez family ended up settling out of court and the future strategies of the BBCAPC were abandoned. The knowledge and expertise gained, however, live on in the experience of the community and will no doubt lead to a higher level of struggle when the next issue arises.

DEPARTMENT OF ETHNIC STUDIES
UNIVERSITY OF CALIFORNIA, BERKELEY

Notes

[1] The United States Justice Department is currently investigating 15 charges of police brutality and police use of deadly force involving Miami police officers.

[2] I borrow the term "gunpowder justice," which so aptly fits the historical experience of Chicano-police relations, from Professor Julián Samora. Dr. Samora, in turn, gives credit for the term to the Chicano scholar and labor organizer, Dr. Ernesto Galarza.

[3] In September 1975, in Castroville, Texas, Marshall Frank Hayes drove his prisoner Ricardo Morales to an isolated road, placed a sawed-off shotgun under Morales' armpit and pulled the trigger, killing him instantly. A local grand jury found Hayes guilty of aggravated assault. The case was appealed to the U.S. Attorney General, and Hayes was convicted under Federal Law 18 USC-242, i.e., depriving Morales of his civil right to live. Hayes was given a life sentence.

[4] One form of resistance to the growing vigilante mob actions and repressive state apparatus was Chicano social banditry (see Hobsbaum, 1969, for a theoretical discussion based on the European example). The "criminal" image of Chicano social

bandits, promoted by the popular press, however, found its way into the public consciousness and social science literature on Chicanos. This stereotype of the Chicano as "criminal," "bandit," and "outlaw" continues to be a theme in the literature of the current period (Trujillo, 1974; 1978).

[5] The Cart War of 1857 was a struggle between Mexican teamsters who transported goods between San Antonio and the Texas coast and Anglo teamsters who, with the support of the Texas Rangers, attempted to physically take over the Mexicans' business (Cortés, 1979:18).

[6] The El Paso Salt War of 1877 began when Charles Howard, an Anglo capitalist with government sanction, tried to take private control of the Guadalupe Salt beds which had been communally mined by the Mexican community for generations. The Mexican workers battled the hired guns of Howard, the Texas Rangers, and the U.S. Army (Acuña, 1972:50-52).

[7] Juan Nepomuceno Cortina became a folk hero, as handed down in *corridos* (Mexican ballads), along the Rio Grande for his organized resistance to the Texas Rangers' repression specifically and to Chicano oppression in general. More recently the Cortina Wars have re-emerged as a symbol of resistance in the contemporary Chicano movement (Moquin, 1971:206-209).

[8] *Las Gorras Blancas* of New Mexico was initially an organization of poor Mexicans who resisted the invasion of capitalist land speculators. They rode by night tearing down the fences and buildings these "invaders" had constructed around the Mexican communal grazing lands. They had a platform which explicitly stated that their purpose was the protection of the rights and interests of the Hispano community. Later *Las Gorras Blancas* became involved in electoral politics. The Mexican land elite seemed split in its position on this organization, some at least implicitly supporting *Las Gorras Blancas* while others denounced their activities (see Rosenbaum, 1980).

[9] For a review of the literature on police use of deadly force, see Law Enforcement Assistance Administration, *A Community Concern: Police Use of Deadly Force,* especially the article by Sultan and Cooper (1979).

[10] Dr. Lawrence Sherman of the Criminal Justice Research Center, Albany, New York, in comparing NCHS statistics with statistics from thirty-three city police departments, shows the police figures to be 100 percent higher than NCHS figures (1979).

[11] As a number of authors have pointed out, it is difficult in general to substantiate police killings of civilians with reliable statistics (Takagi, 1974; Kobler, 1975). Analyzing data on Chicanos is even more problematic. National categories are usually black and white, with Chicanos being classified either as white or "other." Even at the local level, statistics on police killings of Chicanos are not available. The Oakland Police Department, for example, does not keep records of police killings by race. They fail to do so even though they have been a focus of considerable national attention for their alleged violence towards blacks. To find out how many Chicanos have been killed by the OPD, one must look at the individual reports. Access to these reports is not available to the community.

[12] The author has been systematically cataloguing news clippings on Chicanos and the police, including files on police brutality and police killings, for the past five years. The news clipping services used are: Comité Mexicano de Aztlán (COMEXAS), which clips all materials on Chicanos from 12 major Southwest newspapers; North American congress on Latin America, which clips eight major U.S. newspapers on police issues daily; The Center for Research on Criminal Justice, which from 1976 to 1978 clipped seven major newspapers and maintained files on Chicanos and the police; and the

author's own collection of clippings from a variety of sources, including *Nuestro, El Tecolote, Guardián, Agenda, La Gente, El Grito,* etc. The major community legal action groups collecting this data include: Mexican American Legal Defense and Education Fund (MALDEF), League of United Latin-American Citizens (LULAC) and the National Council de La Raza (NCLR). The author realizes this is "soft" data. Newspapers, like the media in general, are racist; thus news on Chicanos and the police suffer from bias. Second, they filter the news, so if there is no public outcry over the issue or other more pressing "news" to report, the issue does not get covered. The advantage of newspaper clippings over quantitative data sets is that more information regarding the particular incident is received.

[13] Conversation with Gil Pompa, Director of Community Services, U.S. Department of Justice, Washington, D.C., July 1980.

[14] From speech delivered at the National Hispanic Conference on Law Enforcement and Criminal Justice, Washington, D.C., July 28-30, 1980.

[15] This is not the first time the issue of police crimes in the barrio has been taken to the United Nations as a violation of the Universal Declaration of Human Rights. See, for example, the 1959 report: *Our Badge of Infamy: A Petition to the United Nations on the Treatment of the Mexican Immigrant* (American Committee for the Protection of the Foreign Born, 1959; also see Morgan, 1954).

[16] According to the Bureau of Census figures, in 1977 there were approximately 7.3 million Chicanos in the United States (U.S. Bureau of Census, 1977). Current demographic estimates indicate the Chicano population to be as high as 15 million with about 2-5 million undocumented workers.

[17] Marginalization is used here to refer to the peripheral position of Chicano youth in relation to the labor market.

[18] LEAA is currently under political attack from both conservatives and liberals. Each group for its own ideological reasons feels LEAA has failed to solve the crime problem.

[19] The term *community* lacks analytical and political preciseness. The major weakness in using the term, as pointed out by the authors of *Community or Class Struggle,* is that is "conveys vague notions of harmonious social relations amongst 'the people' " (1975: 5). They further note, "no community exists; on the contrary one is confronted with a cluster of class positions, conflicts and interests, some of which are irreconcilable" (ibid., p. 5). With these critical limitations in mind, this paper uses the term *Chicano community* or *barrio* to stress the local and cultural dynamics of the issue. Although there are class differences in the barrio, barrio residents are overwhelmingly workers, with a significant percent of the population being unemployed. Thus, when we speak of Chicano community organizing we are speaking (albeit not always conscious) of class struggle.

[20] The *state* is defined as the public sector (government, police, courts, etc.) at the federal, state, and local level, which, although composed of autonomous bodies, essentially serves the capitalist needs of reproduction and accumulation, i.e., maintaining the system (see Edwards, et al., 1978: Chapter 6).

[21] The following incident recorded by the investigative staff of the Centro Legal de la Raza illustrates this point. "On June 13, 1976, six uniformed officers of the Oakland Police Department went to the home of one of the witnesses. This witness and his brother were ordered out of the house and told to assume the same search position Barlow was in when he was killed. One officer repeatedly attempted to kick the legs of the witness' brother out from under him. While both brothers were kept in this search position, several threats and taunting remarks about Barlow's death were made. They

were told, for example, "We killed your friend and you're next . . . " "Move an arm or a leg, motherfucker, so I can blow it off." No official justification was ever given for this conduct on the part of the six officers. (*Statement of Facts,* 1976).

[22] The Benavídez family filed a formal claim against the City of Oakland Police Department demanding 2 million dollars in damages for the death of José Barlow Benavídez.

[23] From interview for KPFA radio in Berkeley, April 1978.

[24] Ibid.

References

Acuña, Rodolfo. *Occupied America: The Chicano's Struggle Toward Liberation.* San Francisco: Canfield Press, 1972.

American Committee for the Protection of the Foreign Born. "Our Badge of Infamy: A Petition to the United Nations on the Treatment of the Mexican Immigrant." April, 1959.

Bancroft, Hubert Howe. *History of California.* San Francisco: History Company, Publishers, 1886-90. 7 vols.

Bancroft, Hubert. *Popular Tribunals.* San Francisco: History Company, Publishers, 1887. 2 vols.

Barlow Benavídez Committee Against Police Crimes (BBCAPC). "Statement of Facts." Oakland: BBCAPC, 1976.

Barlow Benavídez Committee Against Police Crimes. "Police Workshop Committee." Oakland, BBCAPC, 1977.

Barlow Benavídez Committee Against Police Crimes. "Who Polices the Police." *KPFA Folio.* Berkeley: April, 1978.

Barlow Benavídez Committee Against Police Crimes. "The FBI is Now Investigating the Death of Barlow Benavídez." Leaflet. Oakland: n.d.

Barrera, Mario. *Race and Class in the Southwest: A Theory of Racial Inequality.* Notre Dame: University of Notre Dame Press, 1979.

Berkeley Barb. "Eyewitness Contradicts Police Chief's Account." June 25, 1976.

Berstein, et al. *The Iron Fist and Velvet Glove: An Analysis of the U.S. Police.* Berkeley: Center for Research on Crime and Criminal Justice, 1977.

Black Panther. "Eyewitnesses Detail Account of Chicano Murder by Oakland Cop." June 26, 1976.

Bullock, Paul. *Aspirations vs. Opportunity: "Careers" in the Inner City.* Ann Arbor: Institute of Labor and Industrial Relations, University of Michigan, 1973.

Camarillo, Alberto. *Chicanos in a Changing Society: From Mexican Pueblos to American Barrios in Santa Barbara and Southern California, 1848-1930.* Cambridge: Harvard University Press, 1979.

Castillo, Pedro and Alberto Camarillo. *Furia y Muerte: Los Bandidos Chicanos.* UCLA: Aztlán Publications (Monograph No. 4), 1973.

Centro Legal. "Letter to U.S. Attorney General Griffin Bell." Oakland: Centro Legal, 1977.

Chicano Communication Center. *450 Años del Pueblo Chicano.* Albuquerque, New Mexico: Chicano Communication Center Publications, 1976.

City of Oakland Police Services. "One-Man Felony Car Stops." *Training Bulletin*, III, B.2, April 2, 1976.

Cortés, Carlos. "The Chicano—A Frontier People." *Agenda*, 1979.

Edwards, Richard, Michael Reich, and Thomas Weisshopf. *The Capitalist System.* Englewood Cliffs, N.J.: Prentice Hall, 1972.

Farrell, Barry. "The Deadly Sin of Police Panic." *New West,* September 26, 1977.

González, Alfredo. "The Police and Police Reaction to Mexicano/Chicano Youth: Some Historical Notes." Paper presented at the Academy of Criminal Justice Sciences Annual Meeting, Oklahoma City, Oklahoma, March 12-14, 1980.

Greenwood, Ray. "Miami Cop Acquitted in McDuffie Death." *Guardian,* December 31, 1980.

Hardin, Richard and Richard Fahey. "Killings by Chicago Police, 1969-1970: An Empirical Study." *Southern California Law Review* 46, no. 2 (March 1973).

Hittell, T.H. *History of California.* San Francisco: Pacific Publishing House, 1885.

Hoffman, Abraham. *Unwanted Mexican Americans in the Great Depression: Repatriation Pressures, 1929-1939.* Tucson: University of Arizona Press, 1974.

Hollen, Eugene. *Frontier Violence: Another Look.* London: Oxford University Press, 1974.

Hudson, Brian. "Police Abuse and National Unrest." *Guardian,* June 25, 1980.

Kobler, Arthur. "Figures (and Perhaps Some Facts) on Police Killings of Civilians in the United States, 1965-1969." *Journal of Social Issues* 31, no. 1 (Winter 1975).

Mandel, Jerry. "Hispanics in the Criminal Justice System: The 'Non-Existent Problem'." *Agenda*, May-June, 1979.

Martínez, Douglas. "Hispanic Youth Employment: Programs and Problems." *Agenda,* January-Februry 1979.

McWilliams, Carey. "Los Angeles' Pachuco Gangs." *New Republic* 108 (1943):1.

Moore, Joan. *Homeboys: Gangs, Drugs, and Prisons in the Barrios of Los Angeles.* Philadelphia: Temple University Press, 1978.

Moquin, Wayne. *A Documentary History of the Mexican American.* New York: Praeger Publishers, 1971.

Morales, Armando. *Ando Sangrando: A Study of Mexican American-Police Conflict.* La Puente, CA: Perspective Publications, 1972.

Morales, Armando. "Police Deadly Force: Government-Sanctioned Execution of Hispanics." National Council de la Raza Symposium, Crimen y Justicia: Crime and Justice for Hispanics, Racine, Wisconsin, June 28-30, 1979.

Morgan, Patricia. *Shame of a Nation: A Documented Story of Police-State Terror Against Mexican-Americans in the United States.* Los Angeles, Calif.: Los Angeles Committee for the Protection of the Foreign Born, 1954.

The Oakland Tribune. "Shooting Called 'Accidental'." June 15, 1976.

Paz, Samuel R. "Police Abuse and Political Spying: A Threat to Hispanic Liberty and Growth." National Hispanic Conference on Law Enforcement and Criminal Justice, Washington, D.C., July 28-30, 1980.

Pitt, Leonard. *The Decline of the Californios.* Berkeley: University of California Press, 1971.

Pompa, Gilbert G. "A Major and Most Pressing Concern." *e/sa forum-46* (1978).

Potter, Anthony and Bill McLaughlin. "We're Moving Up: The Hispanic Migration." NBC White Paper, National Broadcasting Company, New York.

Rist, Ray. *The Urban School: A Factory for Failure.* Cambridge, MA: MIT Press, 1973.

Rosenbaum, Robert. *Mexicano Resistance in the Southwest: The Sacred Right of Self-Preservation.* Austin: University of Texas Press, 1981.

SER National Digest. "Unemployment and the Spanish Speaking." Vol. 1, No. 2 (August 1977).

Sultan, Cynthia and Phillip Cooper. "Summary of Research on the Police Use of Deadly Force." In *A Community Concern: Police Use of Deadly Force.* LEAA, NILECJ, U.S. Justice Department, Washington, D.C., January, 1979.

Takagi, Paul. "A Garrison State in a 'Democratic Society'." *Crime and Social Justice* 1 (Spring-Summer 1974).

Trujillo, Larry. "Julián Samora, et al., *Gunpowder Justice:* A Reassessment of the Texas Rangers." *Crime and Social Justice* 13 (Summer 1980).

Trujillo, Larry. "La Evolución del 'Bandido' al 'Pachuco': A Critical Examination and Evaluation of Criminological Literature on Chicanos." *Issues in Criminology* 9 (Fall 1974).

U.S. Department of Justice. *Hearings on Police Use of Deadly Force.* Testimony by Gil Pompa, Director of Community Relations, U.S. Department of Justice, before the Subcommittee on Crime, Committee on the Judiciary, U.S. Congress, Los Angeles, 1980.

U.S. Public Service. *Vital Statistics.* National Center for Health Statistics, Division of Violent Statistics, Washington, D.C., 1975-1980.

"Verdict of the Coroner." Office of Charles R. Simmons, County of Alameda, California, June 12, 1976.

Williams, James, ed. *The State of Black America 1979.* New York: National Urban League, Inc., 1979.

(Appendix begins on next page.)

APPENDIX

Documented Cases of Police Crimes Against Spanish Speaking*

Case	Description of Incident	Legal Status
Sánchez, Guillermo Sánchez, Beltrán Fall, 1970 Los Angeles, CA	Cousins, Mexican nationals were shot and killed when police, allegedly looking for a murder suspect, opened fire on the skid-row room they and four other men occupied. They made no attempt to identify occupants of room, none of whom were the murder suspect.	Seven cops indicted on manslaughter and assault charges. Outcome uncertain.
Lucero, Richard Joseph July 22, 1972 Denver, CO	Responding to a report of a woman trapped in a restroom in Denver's Curtis Park, police arrived in full riot gear. Lucero, looking for his son in the confusion, asked an officer what was going on in the park. Two officers proceeded to strike Lucero, beating him with clubs and fists and kicking him.	Lucero filed a complaint with the police dept., which decided the actions did not require disciplinary proceedings. The case then went to the Colorado Civil Rights Commission which said it had no jurisdiction. The FBI investigated, but took no action. A damage suit in July 1974 also failed to implicate any city officials in wrongdoing or responsibility. However, a local judge fined one of the officers $750.

*Compiled from Mexican American Legal Defense and Education Fund (MALDEF), League of United Latin American Citizens (LULAC), National Council de la Raza (NCLR), Comité de México y Aztlán (COMEXAS), and the personal files of Dr. Larry Trujillo, U.C. Berkeley.

Rodríguez, Santos 1973 Dallas, TX	Rodríguez was picked up by officer Darrell Cain for questioning regarding a service station robbery. Cain handcuffed Rodríguez, who was twelve years old, in the back seat of a police car and in Russian roulette style put a gun to Rodríguez head and pulled the trigger, killing him.	Cain was convicted of criminally negligent homicide and sentenced to five years. The Justice Dept. declined to prosecute Cain on civil rights charges.
Montoya, Raymond February 28, 1974 Denver, CO	Montoya, joyriding in a stolen car, encountered a police cruiser in an alley. Although they were not looking for him, Montoya panicked, left the car, and ran. He claims police pursuing him clubbed him to the ground. He received numerous cuts and bruises to his body and head and required twenty-five stitches on his head.	Montoya filed a damage suit against the officers and the court upheld his charge that the officers had used excessive force, but awarded Montoya only $500 on a $175,000 complaint.
Gamboa, José Gamboa, Virginia Gamboa, Simón Trigueros, Raymond Trigueros, Ramona March 1, 1974 Columbus, NM	These persons were crossing the border and were detained by customs and border patrol agents. Once in custody, they were beaten by the agents.	The group has filed a damage suit seeking to receive $1 million, partly arising from assault charges filed against them that were later dismissed.
Terrones, Alberto April 19, 1974 Union City, CA	Terrones allegedly held up a store for some canned hams. Fleeing the scene on bicycle, Terrones was pursued by officer John Miner, who claimed that Terrones attacked him with a knife. In any event, Miner shot Terrones to death.	After Terrones' death, the community was in an uproar. The new police chief, William Cann, was slain by a sniper, but community members feel Cann's death was part of a cover-up by the city, since Cann was considered sympathetic to the city's Chicanos. Miner was exonerated and assigned to a desk job. No official investigation by the Justice Dept., although a representative visited twice.

Case	Description of Incident	Legal Status
López, Richard October 20, 1974 Albuquerque, NM	López, stopped for drunken driving, locked his car doors and refused to come out. When he did open the doors eventually, the officers proceeded to beat him. López received severe wounds to his face and head.	According to his attorney, Ronald Taylor, López' beating was never investigated by a grand jury or the federal government. A damage suit filed by López was settled out of court and one of the officers involved, Eduvigen Luera, was forced out of the department.
Gonzales, David Jackson, Lawrence November 1, 1974 Pueblo, CO	Gonzales was involved in an altercation in a bar. Hours later, he and his brother Lawrence returned to the establishment, arriving almost at the same time as the police. Without provocation, the officers attacked the pair, beat them with flashlights, and arrested them.	No district attorney's or grand jury investigation. Both men were sentenced to jail on charges of resisting arrest.
Semillón, Ester February 3, 1975 Oakland, CA	Ester was mentally ill. Family went to Oakland Police Dept. for help. When police arrived, Ester would not let them in or come out. Police attacked with tear gas, house caught fire. Ester leaped out window, killed in volley of shots.	Outcome not stated.
Costa, David February 8, 1975 Pima County Tucson, AZ	Shot three times in the back and permanently paralyzed by undercover drug agents. No marijuana found at the scene.	
Berelles, José February 18, 1975 Tucson, AZ	Was beaten by police during arrest for investigation of vandalism and larceny.	Police investigation showed officers acted properly.
Martínez, Manuel March 17, 1975 Oakland, CA	Martínez was stopped as suspect in a burglary. Was alleged to have gun. Shot in chest three times and killed.	Outcome not stated.

Espinosa, Edward Reyes May, 1975 Tempe, AZ	Police responded to a call reporting breaking and entering at a local school. Sheriff deputy Kelleher claimed that lights went out as he approached room. Espinosa emerged. According to Kelleher, Espinosa made a quick move, and Kelleher's 357 magnum discharged into Espinosa's head. He died later.	Outcome not stated.
Pérez, Paul June 2, 1975 Denver, CO	Shot and killed by police investigating drug trafficking in bar where Pérez sat with companion. Police claim Pérez had loaded gun and pointed it at them.	
Abeyta, Alfonso June 10, 1975 Santa Fe, NM	Mentally ill, Abeyta was jailed for forgery and protective custody. Officers should have known Abeyta was mentally ill. Instead he was beaten to death.	Wrongful death suit. Negligence.
Rodriguez, Israel June 13, 1975 New York, NY	Officers arrived at Rodriguez' home to investigate reports of a man with a gun. Officers allege that Rodriguez barricaded himself in a room and that he fired a shot through the door. Officers broke into the room, handcuffed Rodriguez, and Officer Thomas Ryan rammed Rodriguez' head into a stove and again into a sink. On the way to jail, and again at the South Bronx jail, Ryan beat Rodriguez, and Rodriguez died as a result of the beatings.	Ryan was indicted by the state grand jury and was found guilty of criminally negligent homicide. He was sentenced to up to four years in prison, the minimum sentence for that crime. No report of federal involvement.

Case	Description of Incident	Legal Status
Rodríguez, Modesto June 20, 1975 Frio County, TX	Rodríguez, active politically in the voting rights issue, met with other Chicanos to discuss information for Justice Department attorneys. Six officers from the Texas Alcoholic Beverage Control Agency (ABC), as well as state and local police officers, entered the bar where the meeting was being held and ordered the participants outside. Rick Dennis, of ABC, without provocation struck Rodríguez from behind, and then Dennis and the other officers beat and kicked Rodríguez.	Rodríguez was originally charged with three criminal counts which were dropped after his trial ended in a hung jury. The Civil Rights Division of the Justice Department has decided not to prosecute. MALDEF and San Antonio attorney Gerald Goldstein have filed a private action on Rodríguez' behalf.
Montoya, Alven August, 1975 Albuquerque, NM	Montoya and his son were working on their pick-up truck when officers investigating an auto burglary arrived. An altercation began, and Montoya suffered three broken ribs and a bruised lung as a result of the beating.	Montoya filed a $200,000 suit charging three officers with the beating. A federal jury ruled the officers were not liable, and Montoya has appealed.
Chávez, Roy October 22, 1975	Killed when fired upon by a Police Officer on the Santa Ana Freeway. According to witnesses there was no provocation. Police Officer Michael A. Lee claimed an object was thrown at him from car and that car tried to force him off road.	Outcome not stated.
Morales, Ricardo September 14, 1975 Castroville, TX	Castroville Marshall Frank Hayes picked up Morales on an arrest warrant in connection with a series of burglaries, took him to a deserted road, and killed him. Hayes' wife Dorothy and a friend, Alice Baldwin, took the body and buried it miles away.	Hayes was convicted of aggravated assault and given ten years. In Sept. 1977, Hayes was convicted of civil rights charges arising from the murder and given life imprisonment. Hayes' wife and Alice Baldwin were also convicted of accessory charges but their sentencing has not yet been set.

Abeyta, Richard Cruz, Barbel October 5, 1975 Central City, CO	Abeyta, Cruz, and Cruz' husband were drinking at a bar when a fight started among the group. Two city officers who were drinking at the bar escorted the trio out, but an altercation occurred outside and one of the windows of the trio's van was broken. The officers claim that they thought the group was shooting at them and the officers fired eleven shots, wounding Abeyta three times and Cruz once.	The Jefferson County authorities concluded that the officers committed no wrongdoing. Suit has been filed against the two, charging them with being intoxicated while on duty. No federal involvement reported.
Gonzales, Anselmo December, 1975 Rio Aruba, NM	Raza Unida Party chairman beaten by police while quelling a disturbance in a bar. Gonzales was a bystander. Subsequently arrested and beaten at the station with sticks and flashlights. Later hospitalized.	Outcome not stated.
Treviño, Daniel January 22, 1976 San Jose, CA	Police responded to a disturbing the peace complaint made by friends of Treviño and María Duarte (Treviño's girlfriend), who were involved in an argument. When police arrived they found the pair sitting quietly in a car but nevertheless ordered them out. As María opened her passenger door, shooting started, and Treviño was killed. No weapons were found in the car and Treviño, who did not die immediately, was left unattended in the car.	The officers were not charged. A lawsuit filed on behalf of Treviño's family is pending. The Justice Department ordered an FBI investigation in April 1976 but found no reason to carry out a full investigation.
Valverde, Mrs. Bertha Valverde, Pablo (son) February 7, 1976 El Paso, TX	Mrs. Valverde was beaten by police when she complained about police beating her son with flashlights. Son treated by doctor.	No action.

Case	Description of Incident	Legal Status
Blando, James February 20, 1976 Los Angeles, CA	Blando, fearful of gang reprisals for a previous incident, called for police protection. An hour elapsed, however, before police arrived, and during that time Blando purchased a knife for protection. When the police did arrive, they displayed aggressive behavior toward Blando, who ran. Officers fired more than a dozen shots at Blando and one officer actually fired a full clip of shots, reloaded, and fired off another full clip.	A formal complaint was filed with the Los Angeles Police Department, but investigation by the department concluded that the killing was justifiable homicide. A wrongful death suit has been filed by family. No knowledge of federal involvement.
Campos, Fernando February 29, 1976 El Paso, TX	A stakeout at a local pizza restaurant was in progress when customers Campos and Robert Domínguez heard an exchange of gunfire between a robber and the police. The two fled and as they were coming out the front door, police fired on them, killing Campos.	A wrongful death complaint has been filed against the city and the police department. No federal involvement reported.
Durán, Antonia March 5, 1976 San Antonio, TX	Pushed to ground after being dragged out of her car and handcuffed when she was stopped for speeding.	Durán booked for eluding arrest.
Rael, Fred March 11, 1976 Pueblo, CO	Rael, stopped at his home for allegedly driving without lights, claims he turned off his lights as he entered his driveway. An officer struck Rael, who then fled into his house. Two officers kicked open the door of Rael's house, entered, and beat Rael severely.	A suit filed against the officers and the chief of police resulted in the finding that they were not liable. No federal involvement has been reported.

Garza, Pablo
March 23, 1976
Bexar County, TX

Garza, arrested for drunken driving, was beaten by Bexar County jail guards Charles Harris, Robert Collins, and James Lovings. He was hospitalized only after his release from jail.

The guards were fired, but later reinstated with back pay by the county judge. Garza has begun civil suit proceedings but has had difficulty in obtaining help with his efforts, purportedly because he is an alcoholic. No federal inquiry into the matter.

Montoya, James
Montoya, Roger
Montoya, Robert
April 19, 1976
Denver, CO

A fight at a social club drew officers to the scene where Robert Montoya allegedly attacked Orlando Padilla, chief of detectives for the Bernalillo County Sheriff's Office. Padilla shot and killed Robert and James, and shot and wounded Roger.

Padilla was convicted of voluntary manslaughter and aggravated battery and sentenced to two to ten years. He is currently out on a $25,000 property bond pending appeal.

Lucero, Dennis
May 5, 1976
Denver, CO

Lucero was walking home and had a verbal exchange with James Connely, a private citizen. Connely brought a shotgun out of his house and shot and killed Lucero.

The shotgun used to kill Lucero was melted by the Denver Police Dept., so the charges against Connely were dropped since the shotgun was the main piece of evidence.

Muñiz, Stanley
May 5, 1976
Denver, CO

Brutalized by police while in custody on charges of driving under the influence. Beating resulted in head injuries and loss of teeth.

Benavidez, Barlow
June 11, 1976
Oakland, CA

Benavidez' car was stopped on a stolen car investigation by Officer Michael Cogley, who held a cocked shotgun to Benavidez' head while searching him. Cogley fired the shotgun, and Benavidez was killed. Cogley violated all Oakland Police Dept. rules in the search, and evidence exists of a police department coverup.

A civil suit by the Benavidez family has been filed for $3 million. Justice Department and FBI investigations have been made since June 1977, but no decision has been reached.

Case	Description of Incident	Legal Status
Herrera-Mata, Bernabé Garcia-Loya, Manuel Ruelas-Zavala, Eleazar August 18, 1976 Douglas, AZ	The Hanigans, a prominent Arizona ranching family consisting of a father and two sons, accosted three undocumented Mexican aliens at gunpoint, cattle-tied them at their four limbs, and tore off their clothes and hair with hunting knives. The aliens were then dragged naked through the sand. One of the aliens was branded with a piece of hot metal and two of them were shot in the back with shotgun pellets.	The Hanigans were acquitted on 22 felony counts after the trial judge denied the all-white jury's request to allow the panel to convict the ranchers on reduced charges carrying lesser penalties. An active national support committee for the aliens is pressing for federal civil rights charges against the Hanigans.
Corriz, Larry September, 1976 Rio Arriba County, NM	Corriz and friends were arrested on a heroin charge but, paradoxically, were told to leave. As they were driving away, officers opened fire, wounding Corriz.	Corriz initially was charged with trying to escape, but the charges were later dropped. He filed a civil suit of $350,000, and the suit is pending.
Devargas, Antonio September, 1976 Rio Arriba, NM	Devargas, a Raza Unida Party leader, was challenged with a gun by off-duty officer Anthony Griego. Devargas knocked Griego down and was subsequently sent to the state prison for safekeeping. After refusing an order from a prison guard to shave his moustache and sideburns, Devargas was beaten by eight guards.	Devargas was charged with aggravated battery against prison staff, but the Santa Fe Grand Jury dismissed the charges. A civil suit filed by Devargas is now pending. Devargas' attorney, Richard Rosenstock, claims the arrest and jailing are politically inspired because Devargas was very active in trying to oust Sheriff Emilio Naranjo and was also a candidate for Rio Arriba County Commissioner.
Rivera, Luis October 12, 1976 National City, CA	A city police officer, Craig Short, responding to a report of purse snatching at a local church, encountered Rivera more than a mile away from the scene. Rivera began to run at the sight of Short, and Short drew his .347 Magnum revolver, shot Rivera in the back and killed him. The purse was not found in Rivera's possession.	No charges were upheld in court against Short, who was initially charged with second degree murder. A wrongful death suit has been filed in the case but no official investigation is in progress.

Argüello, Oscar P. November 24, 1976 San Antonio, TX	An off-duty patrolman, Lorenzo Sánchez, claimed he saw four men arguing in the parking lot of a skating center (where he was a security officer) and told them to leave. Argüello allegedly scuffled with the officer, pulling on Sánchez' holster strap, and the two men wrestled for control of Sánchez gun. Sánchez finally took it away from Argüello, and shot and killed him.	Sánchez was cleared of any wrongdoing. The Bexar County Grand Jury is investigating. No knowledge of federal involvement.
Ochoa, Elfego Mendoza 1976 Tucson, AZ	Shot in the neck while pursued by border patrol agent Manypenny. Ochoa survived.	Unknown.
Cortez, Rubén January 19, 1977 Los Angeles, CA	Cortez, taken hostage at work, was forced to drive escape car with officers in pursuit. Officers were aware there was a hostage in the car, but fired nonetheless. The Cortez car crashed and police arriving on the scene continued to fire into the car, killing Cortez.	Investigations have been conducted by police and the district attorney. A coroner's inquest concluded that the officers were guilty of homicide. FBI has made inquiries.
Zepeda, Juan Februry 20, 1977 Bexar County, TX	Zepeda was arrested at a bar disturbance and subdued with blackjacks. Taken to jail, he was beaten there as well. He was later found dead in his cell.	Police, prison, and FBI investigations have occurred. FBI forwarded reports to the Justice Department. No decision yet.
Dominguez, David February 28, 1977 Los Angeles, CA	Dominguez was kidnapped by former Los Angeles Police Officer Billy Joe McIlvain, who had had run-ins with local Chicano youths. Holding Dominguez hostage, McIlvain called police and reported that Dominguez had kidnapped him. McIlvain killed Dominguez with nine shots from two different guns. He explained to police that he had killed Dominguez with a hidden gun.	McIlvain was found guilty of first degree murder and kidnapping and sentenced to life in prison by Los Angeles Superior Court Judge William B. Keene. No information on federal involvement.

Case	Description of Incident	Legal Status
Durán, Carlos March 18; August 17, 1977 El Paso, TX	Massive drug sweeps in the Chicano barrios of El Paso were the setting for the arrest of Durán, who was beaten in the street, taken to the City-County building, stripped, and beaten again. In another incident, Durán was beaten by one of the same officers at the scene of a community protest at a health clinic. The police reported that Durán did not stop protesting when police arrived, but the protest had been peaceful.	Durán filed complaints on the first incident and officers were suspended for ten days without pay. In the second matter, the officers were called to a hearing, but have not been suspended.
Hernández, Jesse Reyes, Adolfo March 20, 1977 San Fernando, CA	Victims were arrested for disturbing the peace and beaten by officer Eric Kahmann with Lt. William Trachsel, Acting Police Chief, looking on. The incident occurred at city jail.	Charges against Hernández were dropped but Reyes was convicted of carrying a loaded firearm. The officers were indicted on charges of assault and face felony counts. Trachsel has been fired and Kahmann is still under investigation. No federal inquiry.
Prieto, Eduardo April 3, 1977 El Paso, TX	Prieto was taken out of a bar on a disorderly conduct charge by officers, including Francisco González, who then proceeded to beat Prieto when he allegedly offered resistance.	Prieto filed a complaint with El Paso Police Department. González was fired. The attorney for Prieto, L. Taylor Zimmerman, is considering filing a civil suit or complaint with FBI.
Ramírez, Edward April 16, 1977 Los Angeles, CA	Undercover officers dressed as derelicts were beating a suspect when Ramírez approached. Unaware they were officers, Ramírez went to aid the suspect and was killed by officer Lony Hammond, who fired without identifying himself as a police officer.	The Coalition Against Police Abuse is pressing the case. A formal complaint has been filed with the Los Angeles Police Department, which has already dismissed the incident as justifiable homicide. No federal inquiry.

Montes, Armando May 5, 1977 Los Angeles, CA	An off-duty officer, Frank Long, claims he observed a robbery in progress while driving his private vehicle. Pursuing the alleged robbers on foot, Long grabbed Montes by the back of the shirt and spun him around. Montes pushed Long away and turned to run. Long shot him point blank in the back, killing him. Police reports do not indicate a robbery was in progress.	Montes' family has filed a formal complaint against the Los Angeles Police Dept. No knowledge of federal involvement.
Torres, J. Campos May 5, 1977 Houston, TX	Torres was arrested during a café disturbance and then beaten by six officers. When they arrived at the jail, the duty sergeant ordered Torres to the hospital. En route to the hospital, officer Terry Denson stopped at a downtown bayou, where he pushed Torres in. Torres drowned.	Three officers including Denson were convicted of civil rights violations leading to the death of Torres, but they each received suspended 10-year sentences. Federal Justice Dept. officials have ordered the sentence to be revised so that the three men are given prison time.
Zúñiga, Juan Veloz May 17, 1977 Hudspeth County, TX	Zúñiga was arrested for drunken driving and beaten by Sheriff Claymon McCutcheon with a sawed-off pool cue, allegedly to subdue him. Zúñiga died as a result of the beating.	FBI investigation showed possible violation of civil rights. Justice Department is considering filing federal charges.
Sánchez, Joe Roy June 2, 1977 San Luis, CO	Sánchez, who had been drinking, was waving a .22 caliber pistol he had in his possession. Officer Dave Marcus arrived, exchanged words with Sánchez, and struck Sánchez. Sánchez fell back, and his gun discharged. Marcus then fired six shots, killing Sánchez.	A petition for a civil suit has been filed by the Sánchez family. Marcus, initially placed on leave with pay, has been reinstated.

Case	Description of Incident	Legal Status
Osorio, Julio Cruz, Rafael June 4, 1977 Chicago, IL	Puerto Rican Day festivities at Humboldt Park in the Puerto Rican community were visited by police in riot gear after a minor incident. Police began to fire their guns and witnesses say Sergeant Thoms Walton took aim and shot Cruz in the back, killing him. At nearly the same time, Osorio was shot in the back of the neck by Walton and died of the wound.	The Justice Department and the FBI have investigated and a private suit for damages by the families of Osorio and Cruz has been made against the city, the police chief, the mayor, and the officers involved.
Reyes, José July, 1977 Philadelphia, PA	Officers claim that when they responded to a disturbing the peace complaint, Reyes came at them with an ax. Officer Gerard Salerno fired at Reyes through the front windshield of the van he was in, since both officers were still inside the moving vehicle. The shot missed and the officers followed Reyes into his house. According to the officers, Reyes tried to hit Salerno with a long metal bar, and Salerno fired twice, killing Reyes. However, eyewitnesses say Reyes did not provoke the police attacks.	Police department, district attorney, and grand jury investigations are all pending. The FBI and the U.S. Attorney's office are investigating.
Muñiz, Salvador July 2, 1977 Chicago, IL	Muñiz was standing on the corner drinking beer when officers arrived and ordered him to take the beer inside a club nearby. Muñiz said he had a personal problem with the bartender and poured the beer out on the street. The officers arrested him and at the jail slugged him in the stomach and beat him. Muñiz was released after processing and the next day, complaining of pains, went to the hospital where he	Charges against Muñiz were dropped. A civil rights brutality suit is pending. An FBI investigation was conducted, but community members feel it was not done in good faith.

Sinohui, José
July 2, 1977
South Tucson, AZ

underwent surgery for a ruptured liver and pancreas. He was in the hospital for two to three months, undergoing two operations.

A fight in a fast food restaurant drew an officer to the scene, but only after the participants in the fight had left. However, the officer's aggressive behavior prompted remarks by the youths present. The arrest of one of the youths prompted a loud protest and the officer panicked, sending in a general alarm call to which 50 officers responded. Sinohui, who had been in the restaurant, was leaving in his truck when officer Christopher Dean tried to run him down (although all eyewitnesses have disputed this) and proceeded to fire six shots at Sinohui, killing him.

Dean was indicted but acquitted on the charge of involuntary manslaughter by an all-white jury. Two civil suits have been filed and the Justice Department has been asked to investigate.

Moya, Robert Max
July 14, 1977
Albuquerque, NM

Officers stopped Moya's father for driving while intoxicated. Robert Moya went outside the house, where the events were occurring, to investigate. He was thereupon arrested by Officer James Babich for concealing his true identity, stemming from a previous incident with Babich. Fleeing the officers, Moya was struck repeatedly with a flashlight wielded by Babich.

Moya was convicted on a variety of charges, including misdemeanor assault on a police officer, and sentenced to a year in jail. Prior to sentencing, Babich killed Andrew Ramirez in a similar flashlight beating, but the judge in the case refused to reinterrogate Babich. No federal involvement reported.

Espinoza, Arthur
Hinojos, James
July 30, 1977
Denver, CO

Officers arrived at a park after reports of shootings and proceeded to fire at Espinoza and Hinojos, who were lying on the grass. Both men were killed.

A community uproar over the killings failed to prompt the firing or suspension of the officers. The Espinoza children have filed a $4 million wrongful death suit.

Case	Description of Incident	Legal Status
Zaragoza, Albert August 15, 1977 San Antonio, TX	Police officer Eloy González was shot and killed. Zaragoza had been trying to capture the suspect; he and the suspect were taken into custody and stripped nude. Zaragoza was beaten.	Zaragoza was eventually released and credited with assisting in the capture. The two officers involved, George Castañeda and Richard Domínquez, were suspended for brief periods of time.
Davis, José L. Hembree, Daniel P. August 20, 1977 Albuquerque, NM	Responding to a call about a loud party, officer James Babich beat both Davis and Hembree with a flashlight during an altercation.	Davis and Hembree were charged with misdemeanor counts of assault on a police officer. No charge filed against officer.
Fernández, Robert August 26, 1977 Pueblo, CO	Fernández' wife called police to enforce a restraining order she had obtained to keep her husband from abusing her. Officers arrived and placed Fernández under arrest. Fernández' wife says Fernández indicated he was going to put his beer down and in the process accidentaly touched the sleeve of one of the officers, who then began to beat Fernández with clubs, killing him.	Criminal charges have been filed against the officers. A $16.6 million suit has been filed, and there is no federal involvement to this point.
Flores, Ventura October 10, 1977 Brownsville, TX	A warrant for Flores' arrest was served by Detectives Robert Avitia and Chris Hess. An argument ensued and Hess shot and wounded Flores, who was drunk at the time.	There is evidence of a police cover-up because affidavits of the eyewitnesses were lost and never given to the grand jury. FBI is currently investigating.
Beltrán, Noé October 21, 1977 Brownsville, TX	Beltrán, an eyewitness to the shooting of Ventura Flores (see above), was handcuffed and kicked in the face by an officer.	Beltrán was taken to the police station to give a statement and wanted the abuse to be included. The officers refused to include the abuse in the statement but released Beltrán. The FBI is investigating.

Santomé, Tiburcio
November 10, 1977
Glasscock County, TX

Santomé was arrested for drunk and disorderly conduct but he reportedly pulled out a knife and lunged at Sheriff Royce Pruit, who was driving. Retired Deputy Sheriff G.B. Therwanger, a passenger in the back seat, shot and killed Santomé. Witnesses testified Santomé had not been searched and was not handcuffed, violating police arrest procedures.

Texas Rangers are investigating the shooting, and Ed Ibar, an attorney with the Texas State Attorney General's office, is investigating possible civil rights violations.

Ramírez, Andrew
November 10, 1977
Albuquerque, NM

Ramírez' mother called police to remove her son from the house because he was drunk and abusive. Officers began to beat Ramírez repeatedly over the head with a flashlight. They then dragged him out of the house, administered no first aid, and took him to the hospital, where he was pronounced dead on arrival.

The Internal Affairs Bureau of the Albuquerque Police Dept. is conducting an investigation. An autopsy shows that Ramírez died from a brain hemorrhage.

Barreras, Chris
November 19, 1977
Albuquerque, NM

Barreras was involved in a domestic dispute and was driving away when police arrived. A high-speed chase ensued and Barreras continued to flee on foot after his car broke down. Police surrounded him, striking him on the head and handcuffing him during the beating.

Felony charges were filed against Barreras but case has not yet come to court. An internal police department investigation has been completed, but decision has not been reached on any wrongdoing by officers.

Ramírez, Crescencio
November 29, 1977
Wasco, CA

A verbal argument resulted in the arrest of five youths, whose legal processing was conducted in secret, prompting Ramírez, a friend of one of the youth's fathers, to investigate. A couple of days later, Ramírez was accosted in his home by two police officers who entered without warrants. They beat Ramírez and his wife, and threw their children into rosebushes when they attempted to aid their parents.

Ramírez was never charged with any crime and the youths' charges were dismissed. Attorney Miguel Garcia has filed on behalf of Ramírez a petition with the State Supreme Court relating to violations by parole officers of one of the youths.

Case	Description of Incident	Legal Status
Galaviz, Juan December 1977 Big Spring, TX	Galaviz is alleged to have abducted a woman, robbed her, and led police on a chase. Trapped between two police cars, Galaviz reached for his coat pocket and was shot and killed by Sergeant Leroy Spires. Galaviz had only a pocket knife in his pocket.	District Attorney Rick Hamby and the Texas Rangers are investigating the shooting, but some witnesses are not testifying because they say they fear police reprisal. No federal involvement.
Lozano, Lorenzo Ortega January 22, 1978 Austin, TX	On January 10, 1978, Lozano's car slid off the road. When officers stopped, they beat Lozano with a flashlight when he tried to take out his license as they had asked. Handcuffed, Lozano was removed from an isolation cell. Complaining about poor jail conditions, he was taken to a hospital, sedated, and returned to a padded cell. That night Lozano was beaten by eight officers, including a state game warden, until he died.	The case has become a cause célèbre in Hispanic communities in Texas. U.S. Attorney Tony Canales has pressed an investigation, and strong evidence exists of possible cover-up.
Vásquez, Danny January 22, 1978 Moon City, TX	Vásquez attempted to aid a friend who was being frisked by officers, explaining that his friend had not been involved in the fight which had drawn the officers. Officer Sergio Guzmán, pointing his shotgun at Vásquez, stepped back and fired as Vásquez tried to push the shotgun barrel away. Vásquez was killed.	Guzmán was suspended with pay, pending a departmental investigation. A grand jury is preparing to investigate. No federal involvement at this point.

Garcia, Tony Amador, Bill April 4, 1978 San Bernardino, CA	The youths were driving in the Chicano barrio when they were stopped for allegedly driving without lights. Angel León, an off-duty officer in one of the cars, approached Amador and struck him in the face, challenging him to a fight. He then struck Garcia, apparently trying to start an altercation. Observers said León's son had been killed two weeks earlier and that León was on a vendetta against gang members.	No charges were made against the youths and the San Bernardino Police Dept. is investigating. The Community Relations Service of the Justice Dept. has been attempting to mediate the tension between police and community members over the incident. No action has been taken against León.
Ortiz, Edgardo June 18, 1978 Philadelphia, PA	A disturbance call brought officers to the Puerto Rican section of Philadelphia. Upon arrival, police said there was no disturbance in progress, but they claim Ortiz began to curse the officers and punched one of them. Eyewitnesses claim, however, that officers broke the front door of Ortiz' house, entered it, and then slammed Ortiz through a window and beat him with night sticks.	Ortiz was convicted of assaulting three police officers. Originally, the three officers were indicted for violating Ortiz' rights, but federal charges were later dropped. Then U.S. Attorney David Marston promised to investigate this alleged police cover-up, but when two of the eyewitnesses could not identify one of the indicted officers, who was not at the scene of the Ortiz incident, the investigation was dropped.
Griego, Fred Tórrez, Tony September 27, 1978 Albuquerque, NM	Plaintiffs claim police illegally shot at them, wounding both (no details given).	Civil suit charging brutality.
3 unnamed aliens July 3, July 4, and August 1, 1979 San Diego, CA	Four Border Patrol agents conspired to brutally beat at least three aliens who crossed into U.S. legally. They were later dumped on Mexican side of border.	All four indicted for conspiracy, assault and cover-up.
Loera, Thomas July 23, 1979 Los Angeles, CA	Police called about a domestic dispute chased Loera down and brutally beat him.	Loera charged with assault on police.

Case	Description of Incident	Legal Status
Juárez, Jerry January 7, 1980 Denver, CO	Shot in chest by police investigating disturbance involving knives. Police saw Juárez and put him in police car for questioning, then released him. Police allege Juárez drew a revolver and aimed at police. They fired. Juárez in critical condition.	Police suspended pending outcome of investigation.
Peña, Julián March 17, 1980 Albuquerque, NM	Arrested for disorderly conduct and beaten in jail by other prisoners.	Peña is charging city with failure to protect him.